France and Europe in 1848

France and Europe
in 1848

A STUDY OF
FRENCH FOREIGN AFFAIRS
IN TIME OF CRISIS

LAWRENCE C. JENNINGS

OXFORD
AT THE CLARENDON PRESS
1973

Oxford University Press, Ely House, London W. 1

GLASGOW   NEW YORK   TORONTO   MELBOURNE   WELLINGTON
CAPE TOWN   IBADAN   NAIROBI   DAR ES SALAAM   LUSAKA   ADDIS ABABA
DELHI   BOMBAY   CALCUTTA   MADRAS   KARACHI   LAHORE   DACCA
KUALA LUMPUR   SINGAPORE   HONG KONG   TOKYO

Printed in Great Britain
at the University Press, Oxford
by Vivian Ridler
Printer to the University

PREFACE

EIGHTEEN FORTY-EIGHT was a pivotal year in nineteenth-century French foreign policy. In that year of abortive European-wide revolutions the newly established Second French Republic refrained from imitating the First French Republic and failed to strike an aggressive pose to assist the spread of republicanism throughout Europe. The Second Republic's decision to pursue a peaceful foreign policy at this time has both fascinated and perplexed historians. They seldom fail to point out that the 1848 revolutionary movement, without receiving the assistance of France, the only major European country in which a republic was established as a result of the mid-century political upheavals, was inevitably crushed by the forces of reaction. A. J. P. Taylor has suggested, for example, that France's failure to act in 1848 'marked the decisive step on the path that led to Munich and to the French renunciation of her position as a Great Power'. Among French scholars, Émile Tersen has joined in the chorus of diplomatic historians castigating the 1848 French republicans for their cautious, unimaginative foreign policy. To many historians France's decision to pursue a non-revolutionary foreign policy in 1848 marked a great moment tragically missed.

Despite the general interest in the topic, no comprehensive study of French diplomacy in 1848 has ever been published. To be sure, various scholars have examined different aspects of the topic and have even attempted general syntheses. Probably the best general work on the subject was done by Charles Pouthas and issued as a mimeographed 'Cours de Sorbonne' in 1949. Unfortunately, this work on the foreign policy of the Second Republic and Second Empire devotes only 50 of its 252 pages to the year 1848; it was never widely read and is now almost impossible to find even in French libraries. An earlier work, Pierre Quentin-Bauchart's study of Lamartine's foreign policy, was published in 1907 and is now outdated. More recent works, by Tersen, Donald M. Greer, A. J. P. Taylor, and Ferdinand Boyer, have obvious limitations. Tersen's brief study covers only the period of the Provisional Government (25 February–12 May). Greer's work, which treats Anglo-French relations between 1846 and 1851, merely outlines the relations between these two nations in 1848, while Taylor's study is limited to a discussion of the diplomatic intricacies surrounding the Italian problem between 1847 and 1849. Boyer's recent book on Franco-Italian relations in 1848 is an unreliable apologia for France. In addition, numerous articles and theses touching upon different aspects of French foreign policy in 1848 have appeared within the last quarter-century, but neither individually nor collectively do they afford the reader a comprehensive analysis of France's relations with Europe in 1848. Moreover, almost all of them have been written from a rather limited selection of diplomatic documents and other primary sources.

The present study concentrates on French foreign policy from the February Revolution to Louis Napoleon Bonaparte's advent to power in December 1848. It does not purport to cover French relations with non-European Powers, or to narrate in minute detail the intricacies of France's day-to-day dealings with every European state. Rather, its dual purpose is to analyse the major lines of France's relations with Europe and to explain the reasons for France's pacific posture while much of the rest of Europe was in the throes of revolution. It takes into consideration all the published literature on the subject, but is based upon an extensive study of primary sources, much of it unpublished archival material. Every diplomatic document concerning Europe for the year 1848 in the *Correspondance politique, Correspondance politique des consuls*, and *Mémoires et Documents* series of the Quai d'Orsay has been examined. To supplement and verify these documents, the unpublished British, Sardinian, Austrian, and Danish diplomatic dispatches concerning France, as well as other published British, Italian, and Belgian documents, have been read. Finally, extensive use has been made of memoirs, historical works by contemporaries, French parliamentary debates, the French press, and the relatively unexploited Cavaignac archives in preparing this work.

Certain passages in chapters IV and VI of this work are drawn from my articles in *The Journal of Modern History* and *French Historical Studies* and reproduced with the kind permission of these journals. I wish to express my gratitude to the staff of several archives and libraries whose co-operation and assistance

made this work possible: the Archives du Ministère des Affaires
Étrangères in Paris, the Public Record Office in London, the
Rigsarkivet in Copenhagen, the Haus-, Hof-, und Staatsarchiv in
Vienna, the Archivio di Stato in Turin, the Archives départ-
mentales de la Sarthe in Le Mans, the Bibliothèque nationale
and the Archives nationales in Paris, the Library of Congress in
Washington, the New York Public Library, Columbia University Library, Wayne State University Library, the University of
Michigan Library, and the University of Ottawa Library. I am
deeply indebted to Messieurs Eugène and Godefroy Cavaignac
for granting me permission to consult the Cavaignac archives, and
to Professor Charles Pouthas of the Sorbonne and Professor Fritz
Stern of Columbia University for their encouragement and
advice during the early stages of my research. I am most grateful
to Professor John Weiss of Herbert Lehman College of the City
University of New York and Professor Richard Place of Wayne
State University under whose guidance this study first began to
take shape in a different and more limited form as a Ph.D. dissertation. I wish to thank my colleague, Professor Julian Gwyn
of the University of Ottawa, and my wife, Professor Chantal
Bertrand Jennings of the University of Toronto, for reading and
improving with their suggestions the nearly completed manu-
script of this work. Finally, I must acknowledge the generosity
of the Canada Council and the Social Science Research Council
of Canada in furnishing financial assistance which enabled me
to research, write, and publish this work. I extend my thanks
particularly to the Social Science Research Council of Canada,
which, using funds supplied by the Canada Council, provided a
grant to assist in the publication of this book.

LAWRENCE C. JENNINGS

Department of History
University of Ottawa

CONTENTS

I

REPUBLICAN FRANCE FACES EUROPE

THE courts of Europe were understandably taken aback by the three-day revolution in Paris that resulted in the establishment of the Second French Republic in late February 1848.[1] European statesmen had not forgotten the first French Revolution which had broken out less than sixty years earlier. In their minds the proclamation of a republican form of government in France was synonymous with a declaration of war on Europe. A republican France evoked images of the nation in arms, Jacobinism, the First and Second Propaganda Decrees, the war against kings, and French conquests. European statesmen undoubtedly believed war with the new French Republic to be even more likely because certain members of the new Provisional Government in Paris, among them Louis Blanc, Ledru-Rollin, and Marrast, were known to be strong critics of the July Monarchy's pacifism. It seemed that France and the French had not changed, that republican troops would again pour over the French borders into Belgium, Germany, and Italy as they had in the 1790s. The Austrian ambassador in Paris, for one, gave substance to these fears by reporting on the very day on which the Republic was proclaimed the false rumour that 50,000 French troops were about to descend upon Italy.[2] The European governments braced themselves for the attack and prepared once again to take up arms to ward off expansionist French Jacobinism.

Europe's anxiety can be measured by the intensity of the

---

[1] No existing work gives a detailed and thorough analysis of Europe's reaction to the February Revolution and to the new Republic's first foreign policy pronouncements. The best general accounts are by Charles Pouthas, 'La politique étrangère de la France sous la Seconde République et le Second Empire' (Cours de Sorbonne; Paris, 1949); Émile Tersen, *Le Gouvernement provisoire et l'Europe, 25 février–12 mai 1848* (Paris, 1948); Pierre Quentin-Bauchart, *Lamartine et la politique étrangère de la révolution de février, 24 janvier–24 juin 1848* (Paris, 1907).

[2] Austria, Haus-, Hof-, und Staatsarchiv (hereafter cited as Austria, HHS), Frankreich Korrespondenz Karton 337 (25 Feb., Apponyi to Metternich).

military and diplomatic activity with which the courts responded to the news from France. Throughout Germany troops were mobilized and moved towards the Rhine. On 4 March Prussia ordered her army corps on the Rhine to be placed on alert.[3] The Prince of Prussia was sent to take·charge of Prussian forces in the Rhineland. All fortified positions in Western Germany were armed and the garrison at Mayence was trebled. Hesse-Darmstadt recalled all ducal troops from leave. The government of Hanover took similar measures, while in Saxony the army was placed 'on a war footing'. Finally, the German Diet in Frankfurt took measures to strengthen the fortresses of Ulm, Rastadt, Luxembourg, and Landau.[4]

Mobilization, moreover, was not limited to Germany. Holland contemplated sending troops towards the Belgian border and Belgium herself took certain defensive moves along the French border.[5] Sardinia's army was enlarged by one-third.[6] Even Switzerland, believing a European conflict possible, considered raising an army of 60,000 men.[7] In the East, Russia, the very bastion of reaction, took energetic military measures. When word of the French Revolution reached St. Petersburg, it was rumoured that the Tsar broke the news to his officers by crying

[3] France, Archives des Affaires Étrangères (hereafter cited as FAAE), Correspondance politique, fonds Hambourg 149 (7 Mar., Tallenay to Lamartine). This dispatch, as well as most of the other French diplomatic dispatches dated from late February to the end of June 1848, can also be found, although in a somewhat abbreviated form, in the two volumes of diplomatic documents published by the Comité national du Centenaire de 1848, *Documents diplomatiques du Gouvernement provisoire et de la Commission du Pouvoir exécutif* (2 vols.; Paris, 1953).

[4] FAAE, Correspondance politique des consuls, Hesse-Darmstadt 1 (5 Mar., Engelhardt to Lamartine); Corr. pol., Hesse-Darmstadt 22 (2 Mar., Sercey to Lamartine); Corr. pol., Hanovre 68 (7 Mar., Béarn to Lamartine); Corr. pol., Saxe 108 (5 Mar., de Méneval to Lamartine); Corr. pol., Allemagne 805 (10 Mar., Billing to Lamartine).

[5] Ibid., Corr. pol., Pays-Bas 650 (10 Mar., Breteuil to Lamartine); Alfred de Ridder, *La Crise de la neutralité belge en 1848: le dossier diplomatique* (2 vols.; Brussels, 1928), i. 92–4 (4 Mar., Hoffschmidt to Ligne).

[6] Great Britain, *Parliamentary Papers*, vols. lvi–lix: *Correspondence Respecting the Affairs of Italy, 1846–1849*, lvii. 122; Federico Curato (ed.), *Le relazioni diplomatiche fra la Gran Bretagna e il Regno di Sardegna*, 3rd series, 1848–1860, Documenti per la storia delle relazioni diplomatiche fra le grandi potenze europee e gli stati italiani, 1814–1860, Fonti per la storia d'Italia (Rome, 1961), i. 91–2 (2 Mar., Abercrombie to Palmerston).

[7] FAAE, Corr. pol., Turin 321 (6 Mar., d'André to Lamartine); Corr. pol., Suisse 561 (10 Mar., Reinhard to Lamartine).

out: 'Saddle your horses, gentlemen, a republic has been proclaimed in France.'[8] For two days Nicholas I seriously contemplated immediately dispatching 300,000 men to the Rhine, a move which would have probably precipitated a European war. He finally decided simply to station imposing forces on his own borders. Throughout early March, though, the Tsar still thought war probable. On one occasion he told his youngest son: 'This summer you will continue your education on the field of battle.' As a final act of preparedness, on 11 March Nicholas placed his armies in a state of alert.[9]

European nations reacted to the events in France with a flurry of diplomatic activity which matched their military preparations. In Italy the Papal States and Tuscany undertook discussions to facilitate closer political co-operation between themselves and Sardinia.[10] Meanwhile, in Austria, Metternich, the aging self-appointed guardian of the established order, wrote notes to St. Petersburg, Berlin, and London in which he called for a united front by the three Great Powers in diplomatic relations with France; in dealing with France Metternich advocated holding out the olive branch of non-intervention and at the same time promising swift retribution with the sword if France broke existing treaties.[11] The Tsar, for his part, sent letters to Austria and Prussia to insist upon the necessity of maintaining the closest possible relations between the three Eastern Powers in face of the common danger.[12] The Russian minister in London also suggested that Belgium should discuss the state of her fortresses with the Eastern Powers.[13]

Holland and Belgium, fearing a French drive to the 'natural

[8] Edmond Bapst, *Les Origines de la guerre de Crimée: la France et la Russie de 1848 à 1854* (Paris, 1912), p. 2; *L'Empereur Nicolas Ier et la Deuxième République française* (Paris, 1898), p. 2.

[9] Id., *Les Origines de la guerre de Crimée*, pp. 4–5; *L'Empereur Nicolas Ier et la Deuxième République française*, pp. 3–4; FAAE, Corr. pol., Hambourg 149 (18 Mar., Tallenay to Lamartine).

[10] *Parliamentary Papers*, lvii. 147; Curato, *Le relazioni diplomatiche fra la Gran Bretagna e il Regno di Sardegna*, i. 99–100 (8 Mar., Abercrombie to Palmerston).

[11] First Clemens Lothar Wenzel von Metternich, *Mémoires, Documents et écrits divers laissés par le prince de Metternich, chancelier de cour et d'état* (8 vols.; Paris, 1880–4), vii. 598–9.

[12] Pouthas, 'La politique étrangère de la France sous la Seconde République et le Second Empire', p. 3.

[13] Ridder, i. 124–5 (6 Mar., Van der Weyer to Hoffschmidt).

boundaries' of the Rhine, consulted among themselves on means of common defence and also appealed to the Great Powers.[14] Holland spontaneously offered to 'support Belgian independence and neutrality'.[15] King Leopold I of Belgium requested his foreign minister to write and ask Prussia, Austria, and England for assistance in case of an eventual French attack.[16] The Belgian king seemed to be so shaken personally by the events in France that he contemplated stepping down from his throne. Upon hearing of the Paris revolution one of Leopold's first reactions was to begin to send his 'precious' goods off to England; and on 26 February he actually appeared before the Cabinet to offer his abdication.[17]

Prussia and Austria, two of the leading conservative Powers in Europe, undertook important consultations in Vienna. At the same time King Frederick William IV of Prussia, possibly at the instigation of his ally Austria, wrote a letter to King Charles Albert of Sardinia, informing him that the real danger to Italy lay across the Alps in France and not in Austria. He also offered the good offices of Prussia to bring about a defensive alliance between Austria and Sardinia.[18] The English government too suggested that Austria and Sardinia should forget their differences and form a defensive alliance as a contingency measure against an eventual French threat to the Peninsula.[19]

Austria herself made overtures toward Sardinia, attempting to profit from Italy's fear of France to keep the Peninsula docile under the suppressive but protective Austrian yoke. In a dispatch to Turin Metternich warned the Italians that 'we are returning to the most unhappy days of the First French Republic, and for the moment our common safety should be our only concern'. The Austrian chancellor then generously offered Italy a 'defen-

[14] Ridder, i. 34–5 (1 Mar., Baron Willmar to Hoffschmidt).

[15] Brison D. Gooch, *Belgium and the February Revolution* (The Hague, 1963), p. 32.

[16] Ridder, i. 14–15 (28 Feb., King Leopold I to Hoffschmidt).

[17] Arthur J. Vermeersch, 'L'opinion belge devant la révolution française de 1848', *Revue du Nord*, xlix (1967), 499; Gooch, p. 27.

[18] *Parliamentary Papers*, lvii. 123 (3 Mar., Ponsonby to Palmerston); Pouthas, 'La politique étrangère de la France sous la Seconde République et le Second Empire', p. 5.

[19] Curato, *Le relazioni diplomatiche fra la Gran Bretagna e il Regno di Sardegna*, i. 107–8 (13 Mar., Palmerston to Abercrombie, from Palmerston's private papers).

sive alliance'.[20] Sardinia, however, saw the wolf through the sheep's clothing and declined the Austrian proposition. Sardinia distrusted Austria at least as much as she feared France and therefore preferred to seek her salvation in the hands of a more distant and less self-seeking deliverer. On 2 March the British minister in Turin wrote to Lord Russell that 'it is to Great Britain, and to her alone that Sardinia appeals with perfect confidence in moments of difficulty and crisis'.[21] Instead of entrusting her defence to Austria, Sardinia asked for English support in case of French aggression.[22]

As the Sardinian example indicates, much of the frantic diplomatic activity of late February and early March centred around England, the nation which had held aloof from binding European alliances, but which was nevertheless indispensable in any system aimed at isolating or chastizing France. Belgium's first reaction upon hearing about the revolution in Paris was to ask Britain if Her Majesty's government would honour its treaty agreements to defend Belgian neutrality. When Britain replied in the affirmative, Belgium quickly withdrew her request to have the English fleet sent into the Scheldt, an action which demonstrated Belgian confidence that diplomatic measures by Great Britain would be even more efficacious than military demonstrations.[23] Holland joined Belgium in reminding Great Britain that 'we, of course, have a right to claim protection from England'.[24]

The Eastern European Powers also sounded out London on the diplomatic stand that England planned to take. The Tsar suggested that Great Britain should join the other Powers in

---

[20] Dispatch quoted by Quentin-Bauchart, *Lamartine et la politique étrangère de la révolution de février*, p. 221.

[21] Lord John Russell, *The Later Correspondence of Lord John Russell, 1840–1878*, ed. G. P. Gooch (2 vols.; London, 1925), i. 332.

[22] Curato, *Le relazioni diplomatiche fra il Regno di Sardegna e la Gran Bretagna*, 3rd series, 1848–1860, Documenti per la storia delle relazioni diplomatiche fra gli stati italiani e le grandi potenze europee, 1814–1860, part I, Documenti italiani, Fonti per la storia d'Italia (Rome, 1961), i. 68–9 (14 Mar., Revel to San Marsan).

[23] Ridder, i. 17–18 (28 Feb., Van der Weyer to Hoffschmidt); 32–4 (29 Feb., Van der Weyer to Hoffschmidt).

[24] Arthur Christopher Benson and Viscount Esher (eds.), *The Letters of Queen Victoria* (3 vols.; London, 1907), ii. 176 (26 Feb., King Leopold I to Queen Victoria).

concerted action if France upset the territorial *status quo* established at Vienna in 1815. The Prussian government also inquired
whether England would support her allies if France were to go
to war and break the existing treaties.[25] Frederick William IV
of Prussia wrote an impassioned letter to Queen Victoria, sup-
plicating God and Great Britain, and insisting that the 'power of
united speech' be used by all the European courts against France.
France, he said, should be warned that the Powers wished her
well, but that upon 'the first breach of peace . . . we should, with
all the power that God has given us, let France feel by sea and by
land, as in the years '13, '14, '15, what our union may mean'.[26]
The Quadruple Alliance, indeed the Holy Alliance, should be
resuscitated against the republican heirs to the Napoleonic
legions.

Not only the nations that felt threatened by possible French
aggression appealed to Great Britain. France herself, in the
person of her new Minister of Foreign Affairs, Alphonse de
Lamartine, turned to the nation across the Channel. Lamartine,
like other European statesmen, realized the value of acting in
concert with Great Britain. If the monarchies of Europe deemed
England to be the necessary link in any anti-French combination, Lamartine also 'knew that no serious coalition was possible
on the continent without English assistance and gold'.[27] Moreover, the French foreign minister recognized Great Britain to
be the only nation with which a liberal, republican France could
hope to have close relations. As Lamartine intimated to his
personal friend, Lord Normanby, the British ambassador in
Paris, he wished 'to reunite his country immediately with
England in bonds of the closest alliance'.[28] Accordingly, Lamartine's first diplomatic move was to undertake a campaign of
wooing Palmerston and the Whig Government.

Lamartine openly solicited Britain's favour in a series of communications in which he assured the Duke of Wellington that

---

[25] Pouthas, p. 4; Curato, *Le relazioni diplomatiche fra il Regno di Sardegna
e la Gran Bretagna*, i. 64–6 (6 Mar., Revel to San Marsan).

[26] Benson and Esher, i. 177–8 (27 Feb., King Frederick William IV to Queen
Victoria).

[27] Alphonse de Lamartine, *Œuvres complètes* (41 vols.; Paris, 1860–6),
vol. xxxix: *Mémoires politiques*, p. 148.

[28] Great Britain, Public Record Office (hereafter cited as Britain, PRO),
General Correspondence, France, F.O. 27/803 (2 Mar., Normanby to Palmerston).

France was peacefully disposed.[29] Then too, on 24 February, while street fighting was still going on in Paris, Lamartine had contacted Lord Normanby to ask him what stand Great Britain would take concerning the revolution in Paris.[30] Four days later Normanby and Lamartine had a long discussion in which the French foreign minister assured the British ambassador that his nation desired 'the complete development of the English alliance', that France had no desire to attack anyone, and that it was unfortunate that the Spanish marriages question under the July Monarchy had undermined relations between their two countries. Normanby replied that Britain would recognize the French Republic as soon as a regular government had been established in Paris. The English ambassador also praised Lamartine for the 'immense services he had rendered [France]'.

At the end of their conversation Normanby excused himself and prepared to leave, saying that he no longer wished to distract Lamartine from his many 'preoccupying affairs'; Lamartine, though, begged him to stay. The French foreign minister showed the importance which he attached to an English *entente* by the tenor of his oft-quoted words:

But you [England] are the only affair which preoccupies me! All now depends upon you. If England speedily puts in a shape which can be made public what you have expressed to me personally today, we are all saved here, and the foundation of the most lasting and sincere alliance is established between two great nations who ought always to be friends.[31]

Lamartine was hoping to persuade Normanby to make a public statement in which the ambassador would commit Britain to supporting and eventually recognizing the French Republic. But Normanby was most elusive whenever the question of official recognition was brought up. Despite other very determined efforts by Lamartine to get Normanby to commit his government definitely, the French foreign minister had to be satisfied with

---

[29] Spencer Walpole, *The Life of Lord John Russell* (2 vols.; London, 1889), ii. 31–7.
[30] Constantine Henry, Lord Normanby, *A Year of Revolution; from a Journal Kept in Paris in 1848* (2 vols.; London, 1857), i. 105–6.
[31] Ibid. i. 133–7; Britain, PRO, F.O. 27/803 (28 Feb., Normanby to Palmerston).

unofficial statements of friendship and understanding on the part of Great Britain.[32]

England was not yet ready to recognize officially the French government, but Lamartine was successful in winning over Lord Palmerston, the British Foreign Secretary, and gaining British support. To be sure, the English, like their continental counterparts, had at first shown some reserve about the course of the revolution in Paris. *The Times* of 26 February had expressed fear that the revolution might spread to all of Europe and become a general conflagration, auguring a 'very threatening future'.[33] Then too, Palmerston had originally displayed some antipathy toward the French Republic. Palmerston was understandably delighted to see his arch-enemy Guizot and Louis Philippe put to flight, but he thought that 'any successor would in his heart be just as hostile to England'. Moreover, Palmerston at first felt little sympathy for the revolutionary government in France, being revolted by the thought of 'a nation of thirty-three millions . . . despotically governed by eight or nine men who are the mere subordinates of 40,000 or 50,000 of the scum of the faubourgs of Paris'.[34] Nevertheless, Lamartine's assurances immediately calmed most British suspicions. The members of the House of Commons applauded when Lord Russell read them Normanby's dispatches from Paris.[35] And as soon as Palmerston realized that Lamartine was not continuing in the footsteps of Louis Philippe, he reassessed his entire policy toward France.

In late February Palmerston wrote to Lord Ponsonby, the English ambassador in Vienna, that support of Lamartine was the best guarantee of European peace. The British Foreign Secretary remarked that he still feared war, but he wrote '*vive* Lamartine!' in a dispatch to Normanby after he had received definite word that France would respect Belgian neutrality.[36] The latent

---

[32] Normanby, *A Year of Revolution*, i. 153–4. For a detailed discussion of the process which led to eventual recognition of the Second French Republic by Great Britain see the article by André Lefèvre, 'La reconnaissance de la Seconde République par l'Angleterre', *Revue d'histoire diplomatique*, lxxxii (1968), 213–31.

[33] Quoted in *Le Moniteur universel, journal officiel de la République française*, 28 Feb.

[34] Herbert C. F. Bell, *Lord Palmerston* (2 vols.; London, 1936), i. 424.

[35] Louis-Antoine Garnier-Pagès, *Histoire de la révolution de 1848* (10 vols.; Paris, 1861–72), ii. 4–5.

[36] Evelyn Ashley, *The Life of Henry John Temple, Lord Palmerston, 1846–*

hostility which Palmerston had previously felt toward France now turned into cautious but substantial diplomatic support for her new, peaceable government.

Lord Russell clarified his government's position toward the Republic when he informed Parliament that his ministry had no intention of interfering in the internal affairs of France.[37] Reassured of the Republic's peaceful dispositions, Palmerston also undertook to make certain that no other Power would in any way intervene in France. He instructed Normanby to inform Lamartine that:

We [Great Britain] will engage ourselves to prevent the rest of Europe from meddling with France, which indeed we are quite sure they have no intention of doing. The French rulers must engage to prevent France from assailing any part of the rest of Europe. Upon such a basis our relations with France may be placed on a footing more friendly than they have been or were likely to be with Louis Philippe or Guizot.[38]

The British Foreign Secretary also instructed his agents in St. Petersburg, Vienna, and Berlin to do everything possible to dissuade the governments to which they were accredited from taking up arms against the Republic. Bunsen, the Prussian minister in London, was convinced that Palmerston was advocating a policy based upon the idea that: 'Whatever happens, no offensive war against France, still less a war of principles [sic].'[39] Palmerston would do his utmost to preserve the peace by publicizing the restraint and moderation which Lamartine's statements contained. In the meantime Lamartine had himself taken measures to inform the European courts about the principles which were to govern France's foreign policy.

Lamartine tried to counteract the military preparations being made in Europe not only by throwing France into the arms of Great Britain, but also by directly allaying some of the fears haunting European statesmen. A new coalition of states which mistook the France of 1848 for the France of 1792 seemed to be in the making, and Lamartine felt obliged to make energetic

1865 (2 vols.; London, 1876), i. 80–2, 84 (28 Feb., Palmerston to Normanby; 29 Feb., Palmerston to Ponsonby).

[37] Cited in Ridder, i. 30–1.

[38] Ashley, i. 77–8 (26 Feb., Palmerston to Normanby).

[39] Britain, PRO, F.O. 27/797 (7 Mar., Palmerston to Normanby); Bell, i. 425–6

attempts to ward off this potential threat to the Republic. The
best method of doing so was to disabuse the European states as
to France's intentions. This was the aim of two important com-
muniqués that the French foreign minister issued in late February and early March.

Immediately upon assuming the portfolio of foreign affairs,
Lamartine dashed off a short but prophetic message to the
European Powers in the form of a note to the foreign diplomatic
corps residing in Paris. The communiqué announced that:

The republican form of the new government has changed neither
France's place in Europe nor her loyal and sincere dispositions to
maintain harmonious relations with the Powers which, like herself,
wish the independence of nations and the peace of the world.

It will be an honour for me . . . to remind Europe that the principle
of peace and the principle of liberty were born the same day in
France.[40]

The dual purpose of this circular was to assuage the overwhelming fears of the European courts and persuade the diplomatic corps to remain temporarily in Paris instead of returning
to their respective countries. Lamartine realized, though, that
this statement was not detailed enough to calm completely the
European capitals and convince them of the Republic's moderate
foreign policy. Moreover, France herself was anxiously awaiting
some indication as to the course French policy was to take;
within France many elements of the French public expected
Lamartine to denounce the pacific and inglorious foreign policy
of the defunct July Monarchy. These considerations determined
the French foreign minister to prepare a long and elaborate
diplomatic promulgation setting forth the Republic's diplomatic
aims. This was written in the form of a directive for the French
diplomatic corps, but it was also released to the press. More than
a simple diplomatic dispatch, it was a manifesto aimed at the
European people, their governments, and the French public as
well. Lamartine asserted that his purpose in writing the Manifesto was to tell Europeans to 'reassure yourselves if in error you
take the Republic of 1848 for the Republic of 1792! We are not a
revolutionary anachronism, we are not going against the stream

---

[40] FAAE, Mémoires et Documents, France 740 (27 Feb., Lamartine to the
diplomatic corps in Paris).

of civilization'.[41] There is no doubt, however, that many of the passages of the Manifesto which rejected the foreign policy of Louis Philippe and Guizot were meant for domestic as well as foreign consumption.

Lamartine's Manifesto, which was dated 2 March and which had been debated and approved in the governing council of the Provisional Government on that day, appeared in the official newspaper of the French Republic on 5 March. The pronouncement was ornate, verbose—and deliberately ambiguous. It was, nevertheless, of capital importance, for it was to serve as the purported guideline of French foreign policy for the early part of 1848.

Lamartine's first assertion in the Manifesto was: 'France is a republic: The French Republic does not need to be recognized in order to exist. She exists by natural and national right.'[42] The new French foreign minister realized that the new republic needed to affirm to the world her existence as a sovereign state. He was also aware that one of the most severe criticisms levelled against Louis Philippe's reign was that the July Monarchy had debased itself in the eyes of French opinion by too actively soliciting diplomatic recognition. The circular thus opened in a self-assertive and somewhat proud vein. Nevertheless, the passages which followed showed that Lamartine was not really uttering a challenge to Europe. He asserted that the Republic wished:

to enter into the family of established governments as an ordinary Power and not as the disturbing element of the European order. . . . The proclamation of the French Republic does not constitute an aggressive act against any form of existing government . . . Monarchism and Republicanism are not, in the eyes of true statesmen, enemies which must fight to the death. . . . Thus, war is not the essence of the French Republic as it was a fatal and glorious necessity in 1792. To go back, after half a century, to the principles of 1792 or to the Empire's desire for conquest, would be to regress and not to progress. Our revolution is a step forward, not a step backward. We want to walk with the world toward peace and fraternity.

[41] Alphonse de Lamartine, *Le Passé, le Présent et l'Avenir de la république* (Brussels, 1850), p. 56.
[42] This and the following references to the Manifesto are taken from the original copy of the document as it appeared in *Le Moniteur universel*, 5 Mar.

Further to assure the Powers of France's peaceful dispositions, Lamartine proceeded to stress the differences between the First and Second French Republics. He entered into a long discourse in which he strove to demonstrate that the Republic of 1848 was not divided within itself. In the Second Republic, he claimed, 'there are no class distinctions or inequalities', and war, therefore, would not have to be resorted to as a diversionary and unifying force as it had been in 1792. He added that war could also prove fatal to the new republic, for in a nation at war liberty is often the first victim: 'there is no doubt that the Second Republic wants glory, but she wants it for herself, and not for a Caesar— or a Napoleon.' Little did Lamartine realize that the Republic of 1848 would choose a Napoleon by election, even though she abstained from going to war.

Having reassured Europe as to France's intentions, Lamartine launched into what has been considered the most defiant part of his circular. He began by stating that, while France would declare war on nobody, she would 'happily' accept it if war were declared on her. This was understandably an assertion of self-respect and pride on the part of a new and threatened government. As Lamartine informs us elsewhere, when writing the Manifesto he felt that 'the Republic should not rush toward peace as a timid Power that fears war; she should declare peace possible, but not implore it as a necessity'.[43] Still, he then proceeded to refer to the existing treaties in a way which some of the Powers considered to be offensive:

The treaties of 1815 no longer exist as law in the eyes of the French Republic; nevertheless, the territorial delineations of these treaties are a fact which she does recognize as a basis and as a point of departure in her relations with other nations.

But if the treaties of 1815 now exist only as facts to be modified by common accord, and if the Republic declares her mission to be to arrive by regular and pacific means at a modification of them, the good sense, moderation, conscience, and prudence of the Republic do exist, and are for Europe a better and more noble guarantee than the letter of these treaties, which have already been so often violated or modified by Europe.

Although Lamartine had qualified his theoretical denunciation

[43] Alphonse de Lamartine, *Histoire de la révolution de 1848* (2 vols.; Paris, 1849), ii. 33.

of the 1815 treaties with assurances of his government's good intentions, other assertions on his part also sounded menacing to the established order. Lamartine proclaimed that:

if it seems to us that the hour of the reconstruction of some oppressed nationalities in Europe, or elsewhere, has come in the decrees of providence; if Switzerland, our faithful ally since the time of Francis I, were to be limited or menaced in the movement of growth which is now in effect there, a movement which is adding [Switzerland as] another element in the cluster of democratic governments; if the independent states of Italy were invaded; if limits or obstacles were imposed on their internal transformation; or if their right to ally themselves together to consolidate their Italian homeland were challenged by armed might, the French Republic would feel she would have the right to arm herself to protect these legitimate movements for the growth of peoples' nationalities.

The Republic . . . proclaims herself the cordial and intellectual ally of all the rights, progress, and legitimate institutional developments of nations which want to live by the same principle as herself. She will not make underhand or incendiary propaganda in neighbouring countries. . . . But she will exercise, by the glow of her ideas, by the spectacle of order and peace which she hopes to give the world, the only honest kind of proselytism, proselytism of the mind and spirit. This is not war, this is only natural. This is not agitation against Europe, this is a part of life. This means not setting the world aflame, but shining on the horizon of peoples in order to act as their guide.

For the sake of humanity, we wish peace to be preserved. We even hope that it will be.

Lamartine then added that it was not the Republic but the July Monarchy which had threatened the peace by its quarrel with Great Britain over the Spanish marriages; the Republic sponsored no claimant to the throne of Spain, and desired only that the Spanish should govern themselves. The Manifesto ended by stating that French foreign policy would be marked by both 'strength and moderation' and that the words 'liberty, equality, and fraternity', when applied to France's foreign policy, meant:

the freeing of France from the chains which weighed upon her principles and dignity; the recuperation of the position she must occupy among the great European Powers; finally, the declaration of friendship and alliance of all peoples. If France is conscious of her part in the civilizing and liberal mission of the times, not one of her words signifies *war*. If Europe is prudent and just, not one of her words does not signify *peace*. [Italics in the original.]

While the latter part of Lamartine's Manifesto was to prove disquieting to some Powers, it is easy to determine the real sense of this major policy pronouncement. With almost rhythmical regularity the tone of Lamartine's phrases alternated from the peaceful to the menacing. The new French foreign minister was fully aware that the treaties of 1815 'weighed upon France's memory'.[44] As Louis Blanc remarked in explaining the general attitude of Frenchmen toward these treaties prior to 1848, 'one can say without exaggeration that at the thought of these treaties, not a fibre of France fails to quiver'.[45] Lamartine professed to Normanby 'that it was impossible, situated as the Provisional Government were [*sic*], not to give an expression as to the Treaties consistent with what had long been the unanimous sentiments of France'.[46] One of the opposition party's main criticisms of French foreign policy between 1830 and 1848 had been directed toward the monarchy's recognition of these treaties. Now that Lamartine and other members of the opposition had been elevated to power by the February Revolution, the French Republic was obliged theoretically to renounce these loathsome treaties. The treaties' territorial provisions had already been altered by the establishment of Belgium and by the Austrian seizure of Cracow in 1846. Now France too publicly rejected their inviolability, although still recognizing their *de facto* existence. In fact, the Manifesto did not constitute any real threat to the peace of Europe, for the Republic pledged itself both to abide by the treaties and to preserve the peace. The French Provisional Government simply believed that the diplomatic humiliations suffered during the Restoration and countenanced during the July Monarchy should disappear along with the remnants of those regimes.

Lamartine felt compelled to denounce the treaties of 1815 because of the pressures of public opinion. In a similar manner, the Republic determined that it must proclaim itself the protector of certain oppressed nationalities. Under the July Monarchy the republican opposition was the most vocal of those

[44] Alphonse de Lamartine, *Histoire de la révolution de 1848*, ii. 18.
[45] Louis Blanc, *Histoire de la révolution de 1848* (2 vols.; Paris, 1870), i. 234.
[46] Britain, PRO, F.O. 27/804 (9 Mar., Normanby to Palmerston).

elements of the French political scene which had demonstrated on behalf of suppressed peoples, such as the Poles. Furthermore, since the rupture of the *entente cordiale* with England in 1846, Louis Philippe and Guizot had moved toward an understanding with Austria and had seemingly worked with Metternich against the interests of aspiring nationalities. In 1847 Guizot had supported Metternich's efforts to intimidate the liberal Swiss Confederation; and in the same year he had acquiesced in Austria's occupation of Ferrara, Parma, and Modena. A republican government could not tolerate the continuation of this anti-liberal, Eastern orientation in French foreign affairs. It is interesting to note that the Manifesto made specific reference to the 'oppressed nationalities' of the very nations, Switzerland and Italy, whose fate had seemed to be compromised by Guizot's diplomatic machinations. To proclaim support for these peoples served to challenge Metternich and the Austrians, rebuke the July Monarchy's adoption of an anti-liberal foreign policy between 1846 and 1848, and placate French public opinion favourable to suppressed nations.

Lamartine's Manifesto also served to reassert France's traditional interest in the Italian peninsula. The French Republic could hope to bring about a *rapprochement* with a liberal Italy and Switzerland which might serve as a basis for an alliance of liberal states. Such an alliance, its axis being an Anglo-French *entente*, could offset any combination by the reactionary Eastern Powers (Russia, Austria, and Prussia) and liberate France from the diplomatic isolation and impotence which she had experienced during much of the July Monarchy.[47] England played an important role in any such alliance, and the reference made in the Manifesto to the Spanish question was another attempt to cement an *entente* with Great Britain by burying the bone of contention which had previously divided the two countries.

The Manifesto, therefore, was inspired by questions of traditional diplomacy as well as by internal policy considerations. It was written in such a way as to assert French pride and announce France's reappearance on the European diplomatic scene, but it in no way foreshadowed war with Europe. Its language alternated between vaguely implied threats to the established order and outspoken assurances of France's pacifism: all in all, the pacific

[47] Lamartine, *Œuvres complètes*, xxxix, 143.

tone far outweighed any veiled threats. Lamartine had repeatedly emphasized the words 'peace' and 'moderation', and had specifically proscribed war and 'incendiary propaganda'; even the alliances which he envisaged were of a decidedly defensive nature. Lamartine had demonstrated his extreme caution by severely qualifying French support to suppressed nationalities, by insisting that France would only be their 'intellectual ally'. It is interesting to note that, while he had referred to Switzerland and Italy, he had not even mentioned Poland, for he realized that active support for the Polish cause might entail complications with Germany, Austria, and Russia. At the end of the Manifesto, he had stated bluntly that the Republic meant peace, not war. The established Powers should have realized that Lamartine's circular was bombastic, but not bellicose.

Nevertheless, the ambiguous nature of the Manifesto, and especially the official denunciation of existing treaties, lent itself to varied interpretations of France's real intentions. Within France herself the Manifesto was received with mixed reactions.[48] The conservative Parisian daily, the *Journal des débats*, correctly interpreted Lamartine's pronouncement. The circular should disabuse European statesmen of their fears that the word 'republic' meant war with all of Europe.[49] The *National* and the *Réforme*, two newspapers which had been the organs of the republicans under the July Monarchy and which were now considered to be in many ways unofficial spokesmen for the Provisional Government, concurred in the belief that the Manifesto meant peace. However, both papers insisted that France should have the right to protect 'other peoples who wished to imitate our glorious example'. The *Réforme* went so far as to say that the guarantees of peace contained in the Manifesto applied only to peoples, not to kings. France could maintain formal, but not cordial relations with monarchies; and the Republic should always feel free to propagandize her principles peaceably among

---

[48] Previous historians of French foreign policy in 1848 have largely failed to exploit the French press as a means of assessing French attitudes toward foreign policy. Although the press not always necessarily reflects public opinion, it seems that in the period immediately following the Revolution of February, a period when all restraints had been removed from the French press and when over 300 different sheets sprang up in Paris alone, an examination of the press does afford some insight into public sentiment toward important foreign policy questions.   [49] *Le Journal des débats*, 6 Mar.

other peoples.[50] The revolutionary *Père Duchêne* decried Lamartine's circular as too moderate. France did not want war, but if war came, so much the better, for France desired revenge for 1815.[51] The monarchist sheet, *L'Assemblée nationale*, disagreed with the liberal newspapers and considered the Manifesto to be an actual provocation to Europe. No reference whatsoever should have been made to either the existing treaties or the oppressed nationalities.[52] The conservative *Constitutionnel*, foreseeing how many European statesmen would react, remarked that Lamartine's communiqué could be taken as 'either a serious motive for peace, or a pretext for war'.[53]

The Manifesto evoked varied interpretations from the European Powers just as it had from the Parisian press. With his typical boastfulness, Lamartine later claimed that 'the Manifesto was received with applause by all of France, and with respect by Europe'.[54] But Europe was still not completely convinced of France's pacifism, and the circular had not reassured many courts any more than it had the editors of certain Parisian newspapers. The Sardinian ambassador in Paris, like *Le Constitutionnel*, perceived the duality of Lamartine's pronouncement, noting that while it called for peace it did not exclude the possibility of war.[55] The ambiguity of the pronouncement led Switzerland to express concern that France's denunciation of the treaties of 1815 might precipitate war.[56] The Danish minister in Paris took note of the moderation of Lamartine's policy statement, but the Danish cabinet was disquieted by those clauses of the Manifesto which denied the validity of the treaties of 1815 and which expressed France's sympathy for those suppressed European nationalities who wished to reconstitute themselves.[57]

---

[50] *Le National*, 6 Mar.; *La Réforme*, 6 Mar.

[51] *Le Père Duchêne, ancien fabricant*, 12 Mar.

[52] *L'Assemblée nationale*, 9 Mar.

[53] *Le Constitutionnel*, 6 Mar.

[54] Lamartine, *Histoire de la révolution de 1848*, ii. 42.

[55] Sardinia, Archivio di Stato (hereafter cited as Sardinia, AST), Lettere Ministri Francia (5 Mar., Brignole to Saint Marsan).

[56] FAAE, Corr. pol., Suisse 561 (10 Mar., Reinhard to Lamartine).

[57] Ibid., Corr. pol., Danemark 211 (20 Mar., Dotézac to Lamartine); Denmark, Rigsarkivet, Udenrigsministeriet, Frankrig II (5 Mar., E. C. L. Moltke to Reventlow). E. C. L. Moltke, the Danish minister in Paris, should not be confused with A. W. Moltke, who acted as Danish prime minister throughout much of 1848 and assumed the post of Danish Minister of Foreign Affairs in November 1848.

Dutch diplomats in London avowed that they felt war with France to be inevitable because of what they believed to be France's revived interest in the Rhine boundaries. The Austrian ambassador in London, Count Dietrichstein, was even more disconcerted by the circular, believing it to be an actual declaration of war on Austria; Palmerston tried to allay his fears, but the ambassador correctly observed that the Manifesto was a direct challenge to Austria.[58] The Austrian ambassador in Paris, Apponyi, agreed in substance with his colleague in London. In analysing the circular Apponyi admitted that its tenor was 'essentially peaceable' and conceded that the republicans of 1848 need not necessarily follow in the bellicose footsteps of the 'republicans of 1792', that a 'peaceful and conservative republic could exist, living side by side with the monarchies' of Europe. Still, he was distressed by passages of Lamartine's communiqué dealing with Italy and Switzerland. He believed that they augured 'an inevitable general war'.[59]

Ancona, the Legations, and other parts of Italy recently threatened by Austrian troop movements were understandably delighted with Lamartine's policy statement. They saw it as presaging union among themselves and the liberation of Northern Italy from Austrian influence.[60] Germany as a whole seemed to approve of the Manifesto's moderation, but the French agent in Frankfurt was informed that the German Diet viewed with 'deep regret' the renunciation of the treaties of 1815. Moreover, troop movements continued throughout Germany, and Prussia demonstrated its continual distrust of France by suggesting to England a 'common *entente*' of all the Powers to insist that France must respect existing treaties.[61]

Perhaps the most favourable and accurate analyses of the Manifesto came from the Foreign Secretary of Great Britain. In a letter to Lord Clarendon dated 9 March Palmerston stated:

Any government which wishes to pick a quarrel with France might find ample materials in this circular. But it seems to me that the true

[58] Ridder, i. 102, 143–4, 161 (5, 7 Mar., Van der Weyer to Hoffschmidt).
[59] Austria, HHS, Frankreich Korr. Kart. 337 (5 Mar., Apponyi to Metternich).
[60] FAAE, Corr. pol. des consuls, Rome 3, Ancône (14 Mar., Duault to Lamartine).
[61] Ibid., Corr. pol., Allemagne 805 (10 Mar., Billing to Lamartine); Ridder, i. 106–7, 210–14 (5 Mar., Briey to Hoffschmidt; 16 Mar., Van der Weyer to Hoffschmidt).

policy of Europe at present is, to say as little and do as little as possible, so as not to stir matters in France beyond their natural turbulence. . . . The circular is evidently a piece of patchwork put together by opposite parties in the Government, the one warlike and disturbing, the other peaceful and conciliatory. I should say that if you were to put the whole of it into a crucible, and evaporate the gaseous parts, and scum off the dross, you would find the remains to be peace and good-fellowship with other Governments.[62]

As Palmerston remarked to Normanby, the tone of Lamartine's pronouncement revealed 'the Peace Party' in France 'to be in the ascendant'.[63]

In his interpretation of the Manifesto, Palmerston had under-lined the internal policy considerations which he believed explained much of the circular's ambiguity. His insight came, no doubt, partly from his own astute analysis of the document. A close examination of the Manifesto shows that many of its more caustic passages were designed to mollify public opinion. Never-theless, it is clear that he was relying also on evidence from cer-tain confidential reports which had come out of Paris. True to his word, Lamartine had kept no secrets from the British ambassador in Paris. On 3 March he informed Normanby that the Manifesto was soon to appear and remarked that Normanby was certainly aware of 'the feeling which had existed for the last thirty years in France upon the subject of the treaties of 1815, the humiliation of which had been considered as the constant record [sic]'. Lamar-tine confided that 'he should have wished to have said nothing whatever about them [the treaties], but this seemed impossible'. Therefore, 'he should be obliged to allude to the manner in which they had been violated by others and therefore to deny that France would be any more bound, as of right, to observe them'. He assured Normanby, nevertheless, that this allusion to the treaties 'was accompanied by earnest and most serious protestations of desire to maintain peace'.[64] Normanby informed Palmerston that his own conviction was that: 'both for the style and form of this production, I take it Lamartine's extremely difficult position is more answerable than his character. So many absurd expectations

[62] Quoted in Ashley, i. 86-7.
[63] Britain, PRO, F.O. 27/797 (7 Mar., Palmerston to Normanby).
[64] Ibid., F.O. 27/803; Normanby, *A Year of Revolution*, i. 165-6 (3 Mar., Normanby to Palmerston).

have already been inevitably checked, that it may be necessary that public impatience should be fed by high-sounding phrases.'[65]

Lamartine had also informed the Duke of Wellington that in order to establish a really durable republic in France:

it has been necessary to have recourse to the people and the masses; they will require, no doubt, concessions in exchange. The Provisional Government plans to make some concessions; but with these concessions it intends in no way to sacrifice the English alliance. [The Provisional Government] wishes to defend free peoples against the aggressions of the Northern courts, and hopes to find support in England. It will make an energetic declaration [the Manifesto] to the nations of Europe, but the Duke of Wellington will understand its real sense. The Republic cannot afford to seem frightened when she is not afraid and when all of the masses are ready for war: there is a superabundance of population.[66]

With the aid of these confidential assurances, the English Foreign Secretary could understand the 'real sense' of Lamartine's Manifesto. The Republic meant peace, and any bellicose intonations in its pronouncements were mere 'gaseous parts' meant for internal and not external consumption.

In formulating his foreign policy statement Lamartine displayed a marked concern about developments within France. During the period immediately following the February Revolution the Parisian-based Provisional Government was in fact experiencing enormous difficulties in simply establishing and maintaining itself in power.[67] The actual overthrow of the July Monarchy had been largely the handiwork of the Parisian

---

[65] Britain, PRO, F.O. 27/804; Normanby, *A Year of Revolution*, i. 171 (6 Mar., Normanby to Palmerston).   [66] Walpole, ii. 33–4.

[67] For a detailed and reliable discussion of French internal developments during the spring of 1848 see the classic studies by Garnier-Pagès and Stern (Daniel Stern [pseud. for the Comtesse d'Agoult], *Histoire de la révolution de 1848* [2 vols.; Paris, 1862]). See also the histories by Louis Blanc, Quentin-Bauchart, Chérest, de la Gorce, and McKay (Pierre Quentin-Bauchart, *Lamartine, homme politique: la politique intérieure* [Paris, 1903]; Aimé Chérest, *La Vie et les Œuvres de A.-T. Marie* [Paris, 1873]; Pierre de la Gorce, *Histoire de la Seconde République française* [2 vols.; Paris, 1914]; and Donald Cope McKay, *The National Workshops: A Study in the French Revolution of 1848* [Cambridge, Mass., 1933]). The best recent secondary studies treating French internal policy in the spring of 1848 are Charles Pouthas, 'La Révolution de 1848 en France et la Seconde République' (Les Cours de Sorbonne; Paris, 1952); Jean Dautry, *1848 et la IIe République* (Paris, 1957); Louis Girard, *La IIe République* (Paris, 1968).

artisans and workers, aided and abetted by the students and National Guard. These revolutionary elements were deeply suspicious of the newly appointed Provisional Government, whose members had been chosen in the offices of the republican newspapers *Le National* and *La Réforme*, but which was dominated by moderate republicans, like Dupont de l'Eure, Arago, Marie, Marrast, and Garnier-Pagès, and liberal monarchists, like Lamartine and Crémieux. The Parisian populace, after all, had made the Revolution of 1830, only to see that revolution aborted by the establishment of the July Monarchy. Fearful that once again the revolution might be usurped by moderate, anti-revolutionary elements, the Parisian populace continued to agitate, demonstrate, and generally exert pressure upon the Provisional Government throughout the remainder of February and during the first days of March. Crowds pressed around the governmental seat at the Hôtel de Ville, urging the government to accept as members the radical 'social republicans', Louis Blanc, Flocon, and Albert, calling for the immediate establishment of the Republic, and making other more radical demands: the declaration of 'the right to work', the adoption of the red flag, the creation of a Ministry of Progress. The government agreed to the immediate declaration of the Republic and, somewhat more grudgingly, accepted within its midst the aforementioned 'social republicans'. But it adamantly refused to adopt the red flag and establish a Ministry of Progress. Instead, to placate the radical populace, the government decreed the creation of the so-called National Workshops and of a 'Government Commission for the Workers'.

During the days immediately following the February Revolution the members of the Provisional Government felt themselves buffeted by radical and socialistic currents which, they believed, threatened them personally and menaced established society and the social order in general. Under these circumstances Lamartine and his hard-pressed colleagues must truly have felt that there was a 'superabundance of population' in the French capital. Quite understandably, these internal developments had a profound effect upon the foreign policy which the new French republican government was formulating at this time.

By early March the Provisional Government's position had improved to the point where on 5 March Lamartine could write to his friend Circourt, French chargé d'affaires in Berlin, that 'we have been fortunate enough to interpose ourselves between anarchy and order, and we have succeeded with God's assistance'.[68] Nevertheless, the Provisional Government still possessed little power of its own and was threatened by revolutionary elements that would continue to exert pressure upon it during the following months. Moreover, throughout much of the early spring French finances were in complete disarray and the army was demoralized. The revolution had brought a republic to France, but it had left her so weak and divided internally that it would have been practically impossible for her to carry out 'a campaign against kings'. The members of the moderate majority in the Provisional Government had all they could do to keep control of the revolution at home. The fact that Lamartine did not even find time to go to the Ministry of Foreign Affairs until the evening of 29 February, while all other ministries had been occupied as of 24 February, is symbolic of the fact that in the eyes of the Provisional Government internal affairs took precedence over foreign affairs. As Lamartine himself said: 'Foreign affairs could wait without inconvenience until France was calmed. The presence of the [foreign] minister in constant contact with the people had been more necessary in the centre of the revolution [the Hôtel de Ville] than in the office of his ministry.'[69]

By the end of February, then, the young French Republic would have found it difficult to carry out an energetic foreign policy, even if its members had wished to do so. But in fact the majority of the government was inclined to do no such thing. The moderates were content with the fact that they had been able to save society by averting the proclamation of a Jacobin or socialistic republic. They could not be expected to enhance their adversaries' position by implementing a Jacobin foreign policy. It is possible that if the Parisian artisans, workers, and students who fought on the barricades had retained control of the revolution they might have taken moves which would have shattered the peace of Europe, for these elements were to display bellicose tendencies throughout much of the spring. Already in late February, for example, a press report indicated that some ·20,000 Parisians who had signed up for the National Guard

[68] Alphonse de Circourt, *Souvenirs d'une mission à Berlin en 1848*, ed. by Georges Bourgin (2 vols.; Paris, 1908), i. 80.
[69] Lamartine, *Histoire de la révolution de 1848*, ii. 9.

shouted 'to the frontiers!' while queuing up to receive their arms.[70] Still, by the end of February these elements had already lost control of their revolution; and their frequent attempts throughout much of the spring to regain what they had lost would not in the least encourage the moderate-dominated governing council to become emmeshed in foreign adventures. Europe had no need to worry about the aggressiveness of a radical French Republic, for the leadership of the Second Republic was not radical.

[70] *La Sentinelle du peuple*, 28 Feb.

II

FORMULATING THE REPUBLIC'S FOREIGN POLICY

WHEN Lamartine finally found time to occupy his ministry, he applied himself to writing the Manifesto, reorganizing his ministry, and determining a foreign policy. Lamartine, with extensive diplomatic experience both as a critic of the July Monarchy's foreign policy and as a diplomat under the Restoration, knew that the institution of a new political regime necessitated important changes among the personnel of the foreign ministry. Accordingly, one of his first moves was to appoint Jules Bastide Under-Secretary of State for Foreign Affairs. Bastide had had no previous experience in diplomacy, but he was an important former member of the secret societies under the July Monarchy and a well-known republican of the *National* school. This irreproachable republican background seems to have been Bastide's outstanding qualification, for Lamartine admits that:

The people knew M. Bastide . . . [Lamartine] had thought that this man would be a precious auxiliary in a revolution that was going to be an every day struggle for several months against demogogy . . . [Lamartine] had also calculated that the name of Bastide, a long time republican, would cover by its fame within the [republican] party the name of Lamartine, whose republicanism, purely philosophical until this time, would be promptly suspected by the multitude. Under Bastide's guidance, no treason to the republic could be feared. The minister could moderate the revolution in its relations with Europe, hold back war, save the blood of France and humanity, without being accused of betraying the revolution.[1]

Internal policy considerations were important enough to dictate the selection of Lamartine's major assistant within the foreign ministry.

Once his chief assistant had been chosen, Lamartine turned to

---

[1] Lamartine, *Histoire de la révolution de 1848*, ii. 7–8; *Œuvres complètes*, xxxix. 9.

the task of appointing diplomatic agents who could aid him in implementing his foreign policy. He retained many of the functionaries within the ministry itself, but promptly recalled all French ambassadors from their respective capitals. Lamartine stated that he wished to remove diplomats whom he felt to be too committed to the cause of the defunct monarchy.[2] As a result, many Orleanist ambassadors were retired and put on pensions.[3] Nevertheless, the turnover in diplomatic personnel was not nearly as profound as might be expected from a republican government.

After recalling ambassadors and other important diplomats in early March, Lamartine dealt for a time in personal diplomacy. He made contacts with members of the foreign diplomatic corps in Paris, such as Normanby of England and Apponyi of Austria, and also sent out special agents on specific missions to foreign states.[4] Lamartine began making permanent diplomatic appointments only after he had become familiar with the diplomatic personnel at his disposal, sending out agents with the title of chargé d'affaires or minister plenipotentiary to head the embassies because as a gesture of republican equality the title of ambassador had been abolished.[5]

Some of Lamartine's new appointees were republicans, such as Sain de Boislecomte and Bixio, both of whom were sent to Italian capitals. However, agents who were rabid republicans could prove unacceptable to the foreign courts to which they were assigned; the special agents who had been sent to Belgium early in March were recalled upon the request of the Belgian government because of the contacts that they made with Belgian secret societies.[6] In reality, the vast majority of the important diplomatic appointments which the new republican government made tended to be given to career diplomats who had served under the former monarchies. A common procedure was to replace ambassadors with the men who were second in command in the embassy under the previous regime.[7] The result was that

---

[2] Lamartine, *Histoire de la révolution de 1848*, ii. 28–9.
[3] Comité national du Centenaire de 1848, *Documents diplomatiques du Gouvernement provisoire et de la Commission du Pouvoir exécutif*, i, pp. vii, x.
[4] Ibid., i. pp. vii–viii.   [5] *Le Moniteur universel*, 16 Mar.
[6] Ridder, i. 235–7 (21 Mar., Hoffschmidt to Ligne).
[7] Comité national du Centenaire de 1848, *Documents diplomatiques . . .*, i. p. x.

diplomatic ranks were not really republicanized or greatly altered; and certain contemporaries could justly charge that the majority of Lamartine's diplomatic appointees were monarchists.[8] It seems that diplomats in general were chosen on grounds of their suitability for a certain post rather than their revolutionary credentials. It is interesting to note that Lamartine himself seems to have become foreign minister because it was felt that he would prove to be the most acceptable of all the members of the Provisional Government to the established Powers.[9] Everything points to the fact that the French republican government was not interested in antagonizing but in carrying on cordial relations with the European courts.

Once Lamartine had taken the reins of his ministry he began to formulate the major lines of the foreign policy which the Republic was to follow during the first three months of its existence. With enormous problems of reorganization facing the new government, each minister had considerable autonomy and decision-making powers. Lamartine, like the other ministers, made periodic reports to the governing council and also brought up important matters for discussion before the entire government. Still, he had great independence in formulating and implementing foreign policy.[10] One can notice the personal imprint of the great poet's hand not only upon the original directive which he sent out, the Manifesto, but also upon the entire evolution of French foreign policy during the first three months of the Republic. It could be said, in fact, that Lamartine almost single-handedly conducted French foreign policy between late February and early May 1848.

In the early part of March Lamartine seemed to be glowingly confident about France's diplomatic situation. In a letter to a close friend on 5 March, he stated: 'Except for the treasury . . . everything is going wonderfully. God has his hand in this. [France's] foreign affairs were not more assured after Austerlitz. We shall have a French system in place of isolation.'[11] Such a statement is an exaggeration and probably reflects Lamartine's

[8] Charles Robin, *Histoire de la révolution française de 1848* (2 vols.; Paris, 1849–50), ii. 58–9.   [9] Stern, i. 320.

[10] Lamartine, *Histoire de la révolution de 1848*, ii. 145; *Œuvres complètes*, xxxix. 243.

[11] Alphonse de Lamartine, *Correspondance de Lamartine* (6 vols.; Paris, 1873–5), v. 454.

sentiments concerning his success in riding out the initial revolutionary storm during the first few days of his period in office. Lamartine always flattered himself about his powers of persuasion, but he could not truthfully claim that all of Europe had been won over by the new French government as easily as the English had been. Still, the Manifesto was somewhat effective in reassuring Europe, and during the early part of March Lamartine was undoubtedly quite content with the generally favourable reception which the circular received throughout Europe.

By early March reports indicating that Europe would at least passively accept the revolutionary regime in France began trickling into Paris. This development, which tended to preclude the possibility of war, must have been looked upon as a tacit success by Lamartine. The Belgian government was among the first to reply to the French diplomatic pronouncement, offering to recognize unofficially the new republic if the French in turn would acknowledge Belgian neutrality.[12] The French agent in Frankfurt astutely observed that all of Germany was maintaining a strictly defensive posture and would not think of attacking France. The attitude of the German states became still clearer when the Diet at Frankfurt, as soon as it was presented with Lamartine's circular, declared that it would not intervene in French internal affairs.[13] Prussia too, under pressure from England, expressed her intention not to interfere; she made it known that French internal affairs did not concern her as long as France respected the territorial integrity of Europe, especially of Germany and Italy.[14] No European country followed the example of the American minister in Paris, Rush, in immediately officially recognizing the French Republic, but it was becoming apparent that European states were willing to live at peace with France as long as she did not disturb the established territorial order of the continent.

While France's relations were becoming regularized with some states, French relations with Austria were quite precarious, for the Manifesto was universally recognized as a direct challenge to that Power. That Lamartine was quite aware of the effect

12 Ridder, i. 53 (2 Mar., Hoffschmidt to Lamartine).

13 FAAE, Corr. pol., Allemagne 805 (6, 10 Mar., Billing to Lamartine).

14 Ibid., Corr. pol. des consuls, Hambourg 149 (14 Mar., Tallenay to Lamartine); Corr. pol., Allemagne 805 (7 Mar., Billing to Lamartine).

which his policy statement would have upon Franco-Austrian relations is apparent from his discussion of the issue in his historical writings. Lamartine avowed that:

The first disagreements between the French Republic and the continent would probably begin over Italy or Switzerland. A war of principle thus existed between Vienna and Paris, even though not declared, or rather, it was neither war nor peace but a mixed attitude which partook of both elements. The [French] government did not endeavour to conceal this situation . . . [Lamartine] wanted neither to deceive M. Metternich by insincere subterfuge nor to deceive himself. He frankly admitted this disposition of the Republic to M. Apponyi, Austrian Ambassador to Paris.[15]

Austrian diplomatic documents corroborate this statement, showing that in early March Lamartine calmly informed the Austrian ambassador that war between France and Austria would be inevitable if hostilities of any kind were to break out in the Italian peninsula. The Austrian ambassador was astonished to hear from Lamartine that French public opinion would almost certainly oblige the Republic to support the Italians in any conflict with Austria, even if the Italians were to initiate hostilities. After listening to Lamartine, Apponyi was of the opinion that, although the Provisional Government wished to maintain the peace, the Republic would be 'entirely powerless' to avoid becoming involved if war erupted in the Peninsula. Lamartine had followed up his pronouncements concerning Italy in the Manifesto by giving notice to Vienna that his government was honouring France's 'long-standing commitment to Italy' and could not acquiesce in Austria extending her sphere of interest in that area.[16]

---

[15] Lamartine, *Histoire de la révolution de 1848*, ii. 172–3; *Œuvres complètes*, xxxix. 155.

[16] Austria, HHS, Frankreich Korr. Kart. 337 (8 Mar., Apponyi to Metternich). It has been the practice for historians of the French Revolution of 1848 to stress the unreliability of Lamartine's personal writings as source material. Peter Amann, for example, has characterized Lamartine's *Histoire de la révolution de 1848* as a 'completely unreliable apologia' ('Writings on the Second French Republic', *The Journal of Modern History*, xxxiv [1962], 409). There is no doubt that historians should approach Lamartine's historical works with particular caution, for the great poet was pompous, proud, and deceitful, and his evaluation of his own role in history is often exaggerated and misleading. Nevertheless, an intensive analysis of Lamartine's personal writings in light of the diplomatic record and other primary sources indicates that these writings are more trust-

Austria, for her part, was greatly concerned about the possibility of France becoming involved in the Peninsula if the revolutionary spark struck in Paris were to spread south of the Alps to Austria's Northern Italian provinces of Lombardy and Venetia. As a gesture of compromise toward France, Metternich informed the Provisional Government that Austria had no desire to become involved in the internal affairs of France as long as France did not violate the existing treaties.[17] Lamartine's government reciprocated by informing Austria that the Republic was the friend of Italy, but that she 'recognized, in fact, what the treaties of 1815 had established and would take that loyally into account in her international relations'.[18] Neither France nor Austria wanted war, but both realized that if war were to break out in Italy they could find themselves on opposing sides in the conflict. As of the middle of March, the two rival Powers at least understood each other.

After Metternich had proclaimed Austria's intention not to become involved in French internal affairs, Russia remained the only great Power which had not declared itself concerning the February Revolution. That Russia's attitude toward the new republican regime in France was not one of friendship and camaraderie is shown by the fact that on 13 March the *Abeille du Nord* of St. Petersburg, the personal organ of the Tsar, had referred to the February Revolution as the work of 'the most vile riff-raff' and to the leaders of the Second Republic as 'stupid, bragging buffoons' who had been 'drawn up from the gutter'.[19] Still, in due course the Tsar, who was primarily concerned about developments nearer to Russia, and especially about a possible uprising in Poland, made his own pronouncement of non-interference in French internal affairs.[20] In the month of March Lamartine could be satisfied with his diplomacy, for the possibility of an offensive war waged by a European coalition against France now seemed precluded. France would not have to be concerned with the possibility of facing a hostile coalition as

worthy than has hitherto been allowed, at least as far as those sections on foreign affairs are concerned. On numerous occasions his statements and evaluations are corroborated by the diplomatic record or by the testimony of other historical figures.   [17] Metternich, vii. 601–2.
[18] FAAE, Corr. pol., Autriche 435 (12 Mar., Lamartine to Delacour).
[19] Quoted in *Le National*, 29 Mar.
[20] FAAE, Corr. pol., Russie 202 (16 Mar., Mercier to Lamartine).

long as she herself did not take up the sword. With the French Republic's immediate existence no longer endangered, the French foreign minister could begin to formulate some long-range diplomatic projects.

In his letter of 5 March Lamartine had mentioned the 'French system' which he optimistically believed to be coming into existence. The idea of a 'French system' which would end France's diplomatic isolation was not new to Lamartine. As an independent opposition member in the Chamber under the July Monarchy and a virulent critic of many aspects of its foreign policy, one of Lamartine's foremost demands had been that France should play the important diplomatic role on the European scene worthy of her. In 1846 he had accused the July Monarchy of having 'abnegated national dignity' during the Egyptian crisis of 1840, of having risked war in Spain because of the Spanish marriage question, and of having become an accomplice of Austria.[21] In reflecting upon France's diplomatic stance since 1815, Lamartine felt convinced that under the Constitutional Monarchies his country should have broken out of its isolation and created a 'French system' by making an alliance with either Germany or Russia, thus possibly obtaining for France either 'developments in Savoy, in Switzerland, in the Prussian Rhineland' or in 'Belgium and on the borders of the Rhine'.[22] Shortly before the February Revolution Lamartine had made a speech in the Chamber severely rebuking the July Monarchy for its foreign policy and at the same time putting forward his own diplomatic programme. In the Chamber on 29 January 1848 Lamartine conjured up the possible threat of the 'Northern Powers' [Russia, Prussia, and Austria] and went on to question Guizot's government concerning its foreign policy objectives:

Have you never thought of the situation which the Alps will create for you against [the North], serving as a citadel to Italy and to France combined, having Switzerland as a bastion, the Rhine and the two seas as frontiers? Have you never felt that . . . with the twenty-six million men of the regenerated Italy as allies, despite the injustice that you do them, you would be inaccessible to all storms, and to the assaults of the North? . . . I wondered why there had

---

[21] Quentin-Bauchart, *Lamartine, homme politique: la politique intérieure*, p. 130.   [22] Lamartine, *Histoire de la révolution de 1848*, ii. 13–14.

been such a deviation . . . from all the traditions of our policy in the world, from Marignan to Marengo. . . . Why are you forced into alliances that are akin neither to your constitutional and liberal nature in the world, nor to your geographical situation next to Switzerland and Italy. . . . It is because your policy is committed in Madrid through the Spanish marriages. . . . The day when you committed your policy in Spain, all of your acts went in the wrong direction. . . . From that day on, it was necessary that France, going against her nature, going against time and her tradition, should become Ghibilline in Rome, sacerdotal in Bern, Austrian in Piedmont, Russian in Cracow, Prussian in Poland, French nowhere, counter-revolutionary everywhere.[23]

This criticism of the July Monarchy's 'unnatural' and 'counter-revolutionary' foreign policy indicates Lamartine's ideas on foreign policy even before the February Revolution and presages the sort of alliance system which Lamartine tried to develop when he came to power less than one month later.

The instructions which Lamartine gave to most diplomatic appointees consisted primarily of the Manifesto, a document which itself contained many ideas similar to those he had expressed in his January speech in the Chamber. He also gave more detailed instructions to members of the diplomatic corps who were being assigned to certain nations which he hoped might take part in the rather elaborate diplomatic system that he envisaged. From an examination of these instructions and of Lamartine's personal writings it becomes evident that the new French foreign minister, despite his courting of Great Britain, realized the disadvantages of over-reliance on any one Power. Lamartine had, after all, severely criticized Guizot for having subscribed to an 'English peace'. He had decried the fact that 'England alone' had responded favourably to the July Monarchy's overtures for an alliance, accepting them only with 'conditions' which 'subordinated' France to Great Britain.[24] Now that France's position vis-à-vis the other Powers was somewhat more stabilized, Lamartine sought to broaden France's diplomatic commitments so that she would no longer be entirely dependent upon Great Britain, although Britain would still play

[23] Alphonse de Lamartine, *La France parlementaire: 1834–1851, œuvres, oratoires et écrits politiques* (6 vols.; Paris, 1865), v. 120–50.

[24] Quentin-Bauchart, *Lamartine, homme politique: la politique intérieure*, p. 113; Lamartine, *Histoire de la révolution de 1848*, ii. 15.

an important role in the French alliance system that Lamartine hoped to be able to put into effect.

Lamartine hoped to achieve 'a triple alliance of republican France, constitutional Italy, and federal Switzerland to off-set, if necessary, the weight of the North'.[25] This 'triple alliance' would be one element in an even larger alliance system, a system directed primarily against Austria, France's natural enemy, as well as against reactionary Russia. As part of this system the French foreign minister decided to win over Austria's greatest rival in Germany, Prussia, a nation which could also serve as a barrier against Russia. Lamartine had told Circourt, when he departed for Berlin, to reassure Frederick William IV of Prussia concerning France's peaceful intentions and to strive to:

form or prepare between the three great Powers that are essentially pacific, Prussia, England, and France, the basis of a system of equilibrium and peace from the Rhine to the Alps; to bring into accord with this system, slowly and at the rate of events themselves, Belgium, Spain, Switzerland, and the independent Powers of Italy; to allow each people entering into this system their own special form of government, the expression of its customs and its needs; to constitute, thus, union instead of isolation, peace instead of a truce, that is our idea.[26]

The French foreign minister optimistically felt that Prussia would welcome an opportunity for an alliance with liberal France because of Prussia's own innate liberalism and her desire to dominate Germany. Lamartine was convinced that 'the inquietude that Prussia might have felt concerning the Rhine provinces would not prevail over her joys of national ambition'.[27] He was correct about Prussia's desire to dominate Germany, although, tragically, in the spring of 1848 he did not foresee how this could ultimately affect France.

Lamartine's elaborate diplomatic plans were thus being laid. He aptly summarized them when he remarked that he had instructed French diplomatic agents to pursue a policy whose purpose was 'to wait with dignity for England, to search out Prussia, to observe Russia, to calm Poland, to caress Germany,

[25] Lamartine, Œuvres complètes, xxxix. 143.
[26] Circourt, i. 79.
[27] Lamartine, Histoire de la révolution de 1848, ii. 17.

to avoid Austria, to smile at Italy without exciting her, to re-assure Turkey, to abandon Spain to herself'.[28] Lamartine visual-ized a most ambitious alliance system which, if realized, would have greatly enhanced France's position in Europe.

One of the cornerstones of the Republic's diplomacy consisted of re-establishing good relations with Spain. In his Manifesto Lamartine had deplored the effect that French involvement in Spanish politics had had upon Orleanist foreign policy, an utterance undoubtedly meant to appeal to Great Britain. The French foreign minister was convinced that the July Monarchy had condemned itself to diplomatic impotence because of its dynastic ambitions in Spain at the time of the Spanish marriages crisis. Lamartine believed that France had incurred the wrath of England and contributed to Spanish suspicions of her northern neighbour because of a trivial matter in which the French should never have become involved.

Spain had sent troops to the Pyrenees when the Revolution broke out in France. However, when Lamartine came to power he took measures to regain Spanish confidence. He withdrew his country from the intrigues which France and England had been carrying on in the Peninsula. This seems to have brought about a marked improvement in Franco-Spanish relations.[29] Perhaps Lamartine exaggerated the effect of his policy when he exclaimed that 'the Pyrenees were better guarded by reciprocal loyalty than by force', but the new French policy did guarantee the Republic's southern border at the same time as it served to gratify Great Britain.[30] France's entire European position was enhanced by her withdrawal from a dispute which had in many ways restricted her diplomatic activity.

Switzerland was even more vital to French diplomatic plans than Spain, but an *entente* with Switzerland proved extremely difficult to achieve. When word reached Switzerland on 27 Feb-ruary that a revolution had occurred in France, the Swiss liberal faction rejoiced. Banquets were given and speeches were made in honour of the French revolution; the city of Bern even ordered

---

[28] Lamartine, *Œuvres complètes*, xxxix. 28–9.

[29] Ibid. 153–4.

[30] Lamartine, *Histoire de la révolution de 1848*, ii. 171; Ferdinand de Lesseps, *Recollections of Forty Years* (New York, 1888), p. 122. de Lesseps was French chargé d'affaires and minister in Madrid during 1848.

the firing of a 101 gun salute to the Republic.[31] The French agent in Bern reported that 'the large majority of cantons' reacted with 'striking manifestations of public satisfaction' upon hearing of the revolution in France; but he then added that some fear of an invasion by France was also evident, even among liberal circles. It seems that many influential Swiss were beginning to wonder whether the French denunciation of the treaties of 1815 had negated the clause assuring Swiss neutrality.[32] Members of a Helvetian workers' club in Paris might exclaim that they would aid France in republicanizing Europe, but many of their compatriots in Switzerland showed considerable apprehension about the establishment of the French Republic.[33]

Lamartine's Manifesto had proclaimed to all Europe that France would guarantee the territorial integrity of Switzerland. Marrast, Lamartine's colleague in the Provisional Government, re-emphasized this policy by declaring in a speech to a delegation of Swiss workers in Paris that if Switzerland were threatened in any way, 'today you would have not only the heart of France [with you], but if necessary you would also have her force, her arms'.[34] Switzerland was still most concerned with the possibility of intervention by Austria against the liberal cantons or by Prussia against the canton of Neuchâtel, which had just broken its final ties with the Prussian crown. Therefore, the Swiss government did not openly reject the French guarantee. The government of the canton of Fribourg acknowledged its indebtedness to the 'providential revolution' in France which, it asserted, had saved Switzerland from 'intervention and dismemberment'.[35] The Swiss Diet itself intimated that it might request 'French mediation in Berlin' concerning the Neuchâtel problem, but it refrained from mentioning any need for overt French assistance. The March revolutions in Vienna and Berlin soon removed any threat to Switzerland by Austria or Prussia.[36] The Swiss un-

---

[31] Hans Bessler, *La France et la Suisse de 1848 à 1852* (Paris, 1930), pp. 27–8. This work and the recent study by Roger Bullen ('Guizot and the "Sonderbund" crisis, 1846–1848', *The English Historical Review*, lxxxvi [1971], 497–526) offer insights into Franco-Swiss relations during this period.

[32] FAAE, Corr. pol., Suisse 561 (2, 17 Mar., Reinhard to Lamartine).

[33] Longepied and Laugier, *Comité révolutionnaire, club des clubs et de la commission* (Paris, 1850), pp. 73–6.

[34] *Le Moniteur universel*, 13 Mar.   [35] Garnier-Pagès, ii. 29.

[36] FAAE, Corr. pol., Suisse 561 (13, 20 Mar., Reinhard to Lamartine); Allemagne 805 (3 Mar., Billing to Lamartine).

doubtedly uttered a sigh of relief when it became evident that French armed intervention on Switzerland's behalf would not be necessary.

Switzerland played an important role in French diplomatic projects, being an indispensable link in Lamartine's 'triple alliance' system. The French, accordingly, presented the Swiss with alliance proposals. In one of the most detailed letters of instruction which Lamartine sent to any of his diplomatic agents he admonished his representative in Bern to 'show the greatest possible consideration toward Switzerland'.[37] Lamartine instructed his minister to inform the Swiss government that the Republic's policy was diametrically opposed to that of the defunct monarchy, that the new French government aspired to 'an intimate union between the two republics'. Switzerland should realize that neutrality 'is no longer a sufficient guarantee either for her or for France. It is an alliance that is now necessary between the French Republic and the Republic of Switzerland, not an offensive alliance hostile to other states, but a pacific alliance, founded upon an identity of principles and interests.'[38]

Switzerland failed to respond to Lamartine's efforts to draw her into a French alliance. She refused any combination which might infringe upon her neutrality, although she 'expressed her sympathy for France' and as an act of friendship recognized the French Republic in the spring.[39] Only in the autumn of 1848, when Austria presented the Swiss canton of Ticino with an ultimatum and massed Imperial troops on the Swiss frontier following border incidents involving Italian irregulars operating from Swiss soil, did the Swiss government express its willingness to arrive at a mutual defensive agreement with France. But by this time Lamartine had fallen from power and French diplomacy was restricted by an Anglo-French mediation agreement.[40]

Lamartine was quite conscious of France's failure to establish a 'triple alliance' in the spring with Switzerland as its cornerstone. He avowed that he was 'bitterly deceived' by the 'attitude of Switzerland', admitting that his system was 'adjourned by the coolness of Switzerland and impaired by the battles of Goito and Novare [in the war between Sardinia and Austria that was soon

[37] Lamartine, Œuvres complètes, xxxix. 150.
[38] FAAE, Corr. pol., Suisse 561 (18 Mar., Lamartine to Thiard).
[39] Ibid. (21 Apr., Thiard to Lamartine).   [40] Bessler, pp. 56–63.

to alienate Italy from France]'.[41] Lamartine was not nearly as successful in winning over Switzerland as he had been in implementing his less ambitious Spanish policy. Switzerland, like Spain, was willing to establish friendly relations with the new French Republic, but she was not as yet willing to go any further than this and compromise her traditional neutral foreign policy.

On the one hand, Lamartine's projected 'triple alliance' was failing to get off the ground. On the other hand, developments elsewhere in Europe in the month of March gave Lamartine some reason to rejoice. In mid-March revolutions swept across Europe like wildfire. Uprisings broke out in Vienna on 13 March and in Berlin on 15–21 March, bringing the two great conservative Powers to their knees. The 'five days' revolt in Milan, 18–22 March, and the proclamation of a republic in Venice on 22 March had the effect of liberating much of Northern Italy from Austrian control, while developments in Hungary and Bohemia in late March and early April seemed to indicate that Hapsburg rule was crumbling everywhere. Metternich fled ignominiously from Vienna, revolutions spread over much of Germany, and Frederick William IV of Prussia promised to re-establish Poland. To French republicans these developments seemed God-sent. Much of Europe seemed to be adopting liberal, constitutional, or even republican regimes.

The more devoted French revolutionaries had hoped that the rest of Europe would follow France on the revolutionary path. In early March the *Réforme* assured its readers that European kings were in a state of fear, that they were 'burning' on their thrones. Shortly thereafter Bakunin, writing for the same paper, predicted that soon all of Europe would be republican, even his native Russia.[42] When revolutions did sweep Europe in mid-March, French republican circles reacted with marked enthusiasm and optimism. Daniel Stern reports that when the 'magnificent news' of the European revolutions reached France, 'it caused an extraordinary sensation in Paris. It was viewed, not without reason, as the certain indication of an entirely new situation in Europe.'[43] Radical newspapers echoed this sentiment, proclaiming that 'the alliance of despots' was being replaced by

[41] Lamartine, *Œuvres complètes*, xxxix, 143, 150.
[42] *La Réforme*, 3, 13 Mar.
[43] Stern, ii. 145.

an 'alliance of people'.[44] Even the moderate *Siècle* announced that kings were in flight and called for a 'salute' to the 'triumph of peoples'.[45] The French press exulted that, to borrow Napoleon's words, Europe was to be 'republican, not Cossack'.[46] Europe was in flux, and France was elated.

After the revolutions had taken place, many French liberals were convinced that their recent example in establishing a republic in France had set the stage for the transformation that Europe was undergoing. The *Réforme* proclaimed 'the holy, three times holy, alliance of peoples to be forming', and asserted that Europe had followed the French example.[47] 'By a sort of electric telegraph of revolutions, the idea of Paris has become the idea of Germany and Italy', the *National* reported. In a similar vein *La Sentinelle du peuple* extolled the efficacy of 'that sublime' revolutionary 'cry' that had originated in France and had touched off revolutions everywhere in Europe, while *La Patrie* declared that the Republic was 'a bright beacon which shows all peoples the path to liberty'.[48] Even such conservative dailies as the *Journal des débats* and the *Constitutionnel* credited the French 'idea' with revolutionizing the world.[49] Lamartine himself made a similar assertion when he remarked that the Revolution of February, as he saw it, was a revolution of ideas and not of territory.[50]

It was quite natural for the French to believe that these earth-shaking developments throughout Europe would weaken the great conservative Powers and enhance France's position throughout Europe. Moreover, the French felt that these universal uprisings guaranteed peace by removing the possibility of a coalition forming against France.[51] Lamartine proudly remarked that in the latter part of March every time he reported to the council on matters concerning foreign affairs it was to inform them that another revolution had occurred. Furthermore, he attested to the fact that when reporting this news to the government, 'his colleagues rejoiced with him. The sad preoccupations of the

[44] *L'Alliance des peuples*, n.d.; *L'Atelier*, 26 Mar.   [45] *Le Siècle*, 22 Mar.
[46] *La Liberté*, 23 Mar.; *Le National*, 26 Mar.; *Le Courrier français*, 22 Mar.
[47] *La Réforme*, 23 Mar.
[48] *Le National*, 1 Apr.; *Le Sentinelle du peuple*, 24–5 Mar.; *La Patrie*, 26 Mar.
[49] *Le Constitutionnel*, 20 Mar.; *Le Journal des débats*, 13 Mar.
[50] Lamartine, *Histoire de la révolution de 1848*, ii. 25–6.
[51] *Le Siècle*, 26 Mar.; *Le Peuple constituant*, 21 Mar.

interior were dissipated for a few moments in their hearts by reassuring exterior developments.'[52] Each revolution was interpreted as a peaceful victory for France. As Lamartine remarked, 'the name, attitude, and reserve of the Republic fought peacefully for her'.[53] Throughout the spring the French government defended its decision not to take up the sword by arguing that Europe was successfully republicanizing herself without armed French assistance.

The French had wistfully exaggerated both the importance and the profundity of the March revolutions. Nevertheless, these revolutions did have the effect of considerably altering France's relations with several countries, such as the Italian states, which had been severely shaken by the revolutionary quakes. Italy as a whole played an important role in Lamartine's diplomatic programme. In the Manifesto Lamartine had announced that he was spreading France's protective veil over the Peninsula, shielding her against Austria. He undoubtedly hoped that the Italians would recognize their dependence upon France and slowly slide into the French sphere, joining the French and Swiss in his projected 'triple alliance'. However, the March revolutions had the effect of temporarily removing the Austrian menace and greatly enhancing Italy's relative power, as well as her confidence. To Lamartine's consternation, the Italians took the initiative in mid-March and rose in revolt against the Austrians in both Lombardy (Milan) and Venetia (Venice), making it quite clear that they did not rely upon France for assistance. Italy's determination to pursue a policy independent of France became evident by late March. In addressing an Italian delegation headed by Giuseppe Mazzini in Paris on 27 March, Lamartine proclaimed that 'your cause is ours' and swore that if Italy were threatened 'the sword of France' would be at her disposition. Upon hearing these words a spokesman for the delegation immediately retorted that Italy could liberate herself.[54] Moreover, Charles Albert, the King of Sardinia who was assuming the ascendency in the movement for Italian liberation and unity, made it clear that he wished to create a strong Kingdom of North

[52] Lamartine, *Histoire de la révolution de 1848*, ii. 277; *Œuvres complètes*, xxxix. 243–4.
[53] Alphonse de Lamartine, *Lettre aux dix départments* (Paris, 1848), p. 4.
[54] *Le Moniteur universel*, 28 Mar.; *Le National*, 29 Mar.

Italy which might threaten France. Republican France had hoped that the movement for Italian consolidation would be federative rather than unitary, that it would be led by constitutionalist forces friendly to France rather than by the Sardinian monarchy.

Lamartine had desired close ties with Italy, but the kind of alliance he envisaged with Italy was of a defensive rather than an offensive nature. Lamartine, it seems, considered Italy a second-rate Power and was reluctant to allow such a Power to endanger French interests by drawing France into a disadvantageous war.[55] War fever, coupled with hatred of Austria, was, nevertheless, increasing in Italy. By the middle of March the French foreign minister foresaw the approaching storm in Italy and began to fear that his proposed diplomatic combinations might be shattered by an Austro-Italian war, a war in which France might become involved against her wishes. Fearing a general war and realizing the complications which war in Italy might bring to French relations with Europe, Lamartine made energetic diplomatic moves in an attempt to preserve the peace in Italy, sending a special envoy, Bixio, to carry 'words of peace and moderation' to Sardinia in an effort to persuade that country not to declare war against Austria.[56] He also tried to dissuade Austria from taking any moves toward war by informing Vienna that he had advised the Sardinians to use moderation.[57] Furthermore, Lamartine admonished Austria to respect the Italian states' 'incontestable right to modify their internal institutions',[58] and, using a different tactic, also informed the Austrians that if war did break out the French would find it hard to refuse to enter the conflict on the Italian side because of the pressure of French public opinion.[59]

When Sardinia did commence war operations against Austrian troops in Lombardy on 25 March, the French government assumed an aloof and disinterested attitude. Upon going to war the Sardinian government had requested France to make public her 'sympathy' for Sardinia and the Italian cause, but Lamartine

---

[55] Alphonse de Lamartine, *Le Piémont et la France en 1848: lettre de M. de Lamartine à M. Sinéo, député piémontais* (Paris, 1859), pp. 3–4.

[56] Sardinia, AST, Lettere Ministri Francia (15 Mar., Brignole to Saint Marsan).

[57] Austria, HHS, Frankreich Korr. Kart. 337 (8 Mar., Apponyi to Metternich).

[58] Sardinia, AST, Lettere Ministri Francia (15 Mar., Brignole to Saint Marsan).

[59] See above, p. 28.

refrained from making any 'manifestation of sympathy' in Sardinia's favour.[60] Lamartine later remarked that France did not mistake Sardinia for the representative of all Italy; France respected the Sardinian people, but she would not hitch her destiny to Charles Albert's star.[61] When Brignole, the Sardinian ambassador in Paris, informed Lamartine that Sardinia had declared war on Austria, Lamartine claims to have remained impassive, refusing to show either his approval or disapproval:

Approve it? This was to make a tacit engagement to follow the eventualities and carry on indirect war with Austria. Disapprove of it? This was to discourage the effort for Italian independence by the Italians themselves. [Lamartine] remained silent and limited himself to pushing the formation of the Army of the Alps, for if it was either a success or failure, Piedmont's war on Austria would bring the French army across the Alps, either to act, or to carry on armed negotiations.[62]

'Armed mediation' in Italy was another concept which Lamartine had formulated already by 1847.[63] Now as French foreign minister Lamartine conceived of a policy of 'armed mediation' on Italy's behalf if Austria were to invade Sardinia, for he was aware that 'France for her personal security could not permit Austria, a military Power of the first order, to substitute herself in Piedmont and Savoy in place of a second-rate Power [Sardinia] that poses no danger for us'. But 'armed mediation' could also mean something quite different. In a letter which Lamartine wrote to an Italian patriot after his fall from power in June 1848 he defended France's Italian policy and asserted that he had made it clear to Charles Albert that France would assist Sardinia if she were invaded by Austria. At the same time, though, he claimed to have warned the Sardinian monarch that:

If on the contrary you are victorious, if you are accepted as king of Italy, if you become a power of twenty-six million people, instead of being a harmless power of a few million subjects . . . we will ourselves decide to strengthen against you our too thin and too

---

[60] Sardinia, AST, Lettere Ministri Francia (24 Mar., Pareto to Brignole; 30 Mar., Brignole to Pareto).

[61] Lamartine, *Le Piémont et la France en 1848*, pp. 4–5.

[62] Lamartine, *Histoire de la révolution de 1848*, ii. 278–9; *Œuvres complètes*, xxxix. 244–5.

[63] Bauchart, *Lamartine et la politique étrangère de la révolution de février*, p. 80.

exposed border of the Alps from Lyons to Toulon. This border, sufficient today, would not be strong enough to carry the weight of a nation of twenty-six million people . . . which could eventually ally itself in turn to Austria against us . . . Savoy and Nice will be remade in a French way. Any French government, be it monarchy or republic, which would let the House of Savoy [Charles Albert] conquer and govern twenty-six million close-knit and brave people without occupying the Alps would be a traitor to France.[64]

Although an examination of the Sardinian archives does not substantiate Lamartine's claim that he had actually addressed the Sardinian government in this manner, everything suggests that in this letter Lamartine was revealing a basic concept of his Italian strategy. It is interesting to note, for example, that in the summer of 1848 Lamartine shocked his colleagues in the Constituent Assembly's Committee of Foreign Affairs by openly admitting that 'in forming the Army of the Alps he had some view to finding a compensation for France for any changes on the other side of the Alps, in the possession of Nice and Savoy'.[65] There is little doubt that in the spring of 1848 Lamartine had France's traditional strategic interests foremost in mind.[66] 'Armed mediation' meant offering aid to a defeated Sardinia, or applying pressure upon a victorious Sardinia and requesting territorial compensation. Either way Lamartine hoped to be able to acquire Nice and Savoy.[67]

The Sardinians as yet were unaware of Lamartine's Italian designs, but they had their own reasons for being apprehensive about French intervention in Italy. The British government had done its best to discourage Sardinia from going to war and requesting French military assistance; Palmerston had warned that such 'assistance would not be received without some considerable sacrifice on the part of the King of Sardinia as its

---

[64] Lamartine, *Le Piémont et la France en 1848*, pp. 11–12.

[65] Britain, PRO, F.O. 27/810 (25 July, Normanby to Palmerston). The minutes of the Committee of Foreign Affairs, preserved in the French Archives nationales, C 926, 3, afford no detail as to what occurred within the Committee. Bastide, then French foreign minister, reported this statement confidentially to Normanby, who was concerned about the proceedings of the Committee.

[66] For an analysis of Lamartine's policy toward Italy see Lawrence C. Jennings, 'Lamartine's Italian Policy in 1848: A Reexamination', *The Journal of Modern History*, xlii (1970), 331–41.

[67] Lamartine, *Le passé, le présent et l'avenir de la République*, pp. 62–3.

price'.[68] Charles Albert's government was already fearful about France trying to republicanize Italy. Now Great Britain's warning undoubtedly made the Sardinian government suspicious of France's territorial designs beyond the Alps as well. The Sardinian government demonstrated its apprehensions by officially querying France as to her intentions in forming a 100,000 man Army of the Alps.[69] Unassured by French statements that the Army of the Alps was being formed merely as a matter of military contingency, the Sardinian government requested France to remove her troops from stations near the border to less advanced positions. Moreover, Charles Albert's cabinet asked the Republic to cancel a proposed visit of the French fleet to the port of Genoa, for it feared that the presence of the French fleet might cause a republican revolution within that city.[70] Sardinia's opposition to the spread of republicanism in Italy is also witnessed by a note which the foreign office in Turin sent to all the Powers, France excepted, stating that Charles Albert was rendering a service to the European monarchies by entering Lombardy before a revolution might establish a republic in Milan.[71] As Bixio, who had just become the French envoy in Turin, reported, Charles Albert's government seemed to fear 'the contagion of republican ideas' more than it feared 'Austrian arms'.[72]

Fearful of the consequences of French intervention south of the Alps, at the very time that the Sardinian government informed France of its intention to invade Lombardy it had

---

[68] Curato, *Le relazioni diplomatiche fra la Gran Bretagna e il Regno di Sardegna*, i. 133–4 (27 Mar., Palmerston to Abercrombie).

[69] Sardinia, AST, Lettere Ministri Francia (29 Mar., Pareto to Brignole; 30 Mar., Brignole to Pareto); Britain, PRO, F.O. 27/806 (3 Apr., Normanby to Palmerston). On 11 Mar. the Provisional Government had instructed the Minister of War to send to Dijon the first contingent of troops destined for what was to be called the Army of the Alps (Comité national du Centenaire de 1848, *Procès-Verbaux du Gouvernement provisoire et de la Commission du Pouvoir exécutif, 24 février–22 juin 1848* [Paris, 1950], p. 59). By early April the headquarters of the Army of the Alps had been established at Grenoble. For a detailed study of the structure and role of this army see the article by Ferdinand Boyer, 'L'Armée de Alpes en 1848', *Revue historique*, ccxxxiii (1965), 71–100.

[70] Sardinia, AST, Lettere Ministri Francia (29 Mar., 5 Apr., Pareto to Ricci; 2, 9 Apr., Brignole to Pareto).

[71] FAAE, Corr. pol., Turin 321 (29 Mar., Bixio to Lamartine).

[72] Ibid. (31 Mar., Bixio to Lamartine).

requested that France should not become involved in the Austro-Italian war.[73] Throughout the spring the Sardinian government continued to assure the Republic that its intervention in Italy was neither required nor desired. Charles Albert himself summed up the Sardinian position when he announced to all of Europe that *Italia farà da se* (Italy will do it herself). France and Sardinia were moving progressively further apart. Already in late March and early April the Sardinians were in many ways as distrustful of the French as the French were suspicious of the Sardinians.

There is little doubt that the Italian revolutions, and the war between Italy and Austria which they occasioned, had an adverse effect on France's relations with the Italian states. Lamartine had been optimistic when he declared that the war in Italy had 'impaired' his proposed 'triple alliance'. It had, in fact, nearly destroyed the possibility of such an alliance.

[73] Sardinia, AST, Lettere Ministri Francia (29 Mar., Brignole to Pareto).

III

INTERNAL PROBLEMS RESTRICTING
FRENCH DIPLOMACY

WHILE the events of March brought about a deterioration of French relations with Italy, the March Revolutions had a much more salutary effect upon France's relations with Germany. Immediately following the Berlin Revolution Lamartine appears to have had some reservations about the possibility of a radical revolution in Prussia forcing Frederick William IV into the arms of the Tsar.[1] However, one of the first concessions that the Prussian king granted, when faced with a capital city in revolution, was to promise to reconstruct a new Polish state out of Prussia's portion of Poland, the area around Poznań [Posen]. This move negated the possibility of Prussian co-operation with Russia and was immediately regarded as the realization of one of France's fondest diplomatic goals. An astute Belgian diplomatic observer in Germany remarked that not only had Frederick William IV's espousal of the Polish cause broken the alliance of the Northern Powers, but that 'Germany was nearer to war with Russia than with France' because of Russia's innate hostility to a resuscitated Poland.[2] Then, too, France had every reason to hope that a regenerated Poland, sponsored by Prussia, would form a new barrier against Russia. The French press rejoiced at a move which seemed to presage the creation of an independent Poland and to constitute a definite setback to Russia.[3] A Germany which supported Poland was a Germany breaking with the East and turning toward France. A Franco-German *rapprochement* appeared to be even more likely when the French chargé d'affaires in Frankfurt reported that all of Germany wished to establish friendly relations with the Republic.[4]

---

[1] Lamartine, *Œuvres complètes*, xxxix. 159–60.

[2] Ridder, i. 240–1 (23 Mar., Northomb to Hoffschmidt).

[3] *Le Peuple constituant*, 23 Mar.; *Le Journal des débats*, 6 Apr.

[4] FAAE, Corr. pol., Allemagne 805 (6 Apr., Salignac-Fénelon to Lamartine). Although German unification had not been achieved by 1848, mid nineteenth-

It seemed that France had at least one important ally besides Great Britain, that at least part of Lamartine's alliance scheme might be successful.

The Berlin Cabinet was rightly concerned about the possibility of Prussia's Polish policy involving her in a conflict with Russia at the very time when Prussia's internal weaknesses rendered her vulnerable to the attack of such a formidable foe. Therefore, in late March and early April Frederick William's government inquired whether France would come to Prussia's assistance if the latter were attacked by Russia. Berlin sounded out the French government about the possibility of a French squadron being sent to the Baltic as a diversionary move and also asked France to make a 'declaration of alliance and solidarity' with Prussia if war were to break out with Russia. In reply to Prussia's inquiries, Paris unofficially assured the Prussians that 'if Russia attacks Prussia and invades her territory in seizing Posen, France will give armed support to Prussia'.[5] Recognizing the possibility of war between Prussia and Russia over Poland, the French foreign minister took measures to create an army on the Rhine to 'cover Germany' and assist her if necessary.[6] Poland seemed to have cemented the alliance between Paris and Berlin.

From the time of the partitions of Poland and the Great French Revolution, Poland and the Poles had been especially close to the heart of the French, who saw in them revolutionary brothers suppressed by the Great Powers.[7] After the Polish rebellion of 1830 the French had adopted a policy of offering a haven to refugees from Poland who came westward in considerable numbers. Even under the July Monarchy, Frenchmen had faithfully expressed their hopes that Poland would some day regain her independence. Now it seemed that France's dreams of a regenerated Poland would become a reality.

Lamartine had not mentioned Poland in the Manifesto.

century European diplomats continually used the term 'Germany' to designate an area comprising those states which were an integral part of the German Confederation, Austria often excepted. In this work the term 'Germany' is used in this same sense.

[5] Circourt, i. 307–8, 325–6, 329–30.

[6] Lamartine, *Histoire de la révolution de 1848*, ii. 279; *Œuvres complètes*, xxxix. 246.

[7] For a detailed discussion of France's policy toward Poland in 1848 see the article by Paul Henry, 'Le Gouvernement provisoire et la question polonaise en 1848', *Revue historique*. clxxviii (1936), 198–240.

Nevertheless, even before the March Revolutions had obliged Berlin to promise the re-establishment of Poland, the French foreign minister had issued a long diplomatic directive to French agents in Eastern European capitals in which he committed the Republic to using all of its influence and energies to advancing the Polish cause. In this dispatch he had announced that:

The cause of the re-establishment of a Polish nationality . . . is one of the causes of France herself, one of the causes that she will neither ever desert nor forget, a cause for which she offers her diplomatic assistance first of all, and finally her active aid for that day and that hour when events will reasonably permit her, with sensible [diplomatic] arrangements prepared in advance, to intervene with her natural auxiliaries in the cause of Polish independence.[8]

Lamartine was quite aware of French sympathy for Poland. From its very outset the Second Republic was obliged, it seems, to express its sympathy for the Polish cause because of France's traditional support for that much-suffering nation.[9]

The Polish refugees in France, transported with revolutionary glee, took the Republic's assurances of sympathy and assistance for Poland in the most literal sense. They immediately began organizing themselves both politically and militarily, forming delegations to petition the French government for assistance in their efforts to liberate the fatherland. They inserted advertisements in newspapers eliciting 'patriotic gifts' and public support.[10] Partisans of Poland also distributed pamphlets and plastered walls with posters—several of which have been preserved—which went further and asked for arms as well as funds.[11] In a rather unusual approach *Le Tribun du peuple*, the self-styled 'organ of the workers', even printed an appeal in song for arms and assistance for the Poles.[12]

In an effort to oversee in some manner the Poles' activity within France, the French government proclaimed on 11 March the

[8] Garnier-Pagès, viii. 378; Comité national du Centenaire de 1848, *Documents diplomatiques du Gouvernement provisoire et de la Commission du Pouvoir exécutif*, i. 145 (11 Mar., Lamartine to diplomatic agents).

[9] This, at least, was the opinion of the English ambassador in Paris (Normanby, *A Year of Revolution*, i. 271–2; Britain, PRO, F.O. 27/805 [27 Mar., Normanby to Palmerston]).

[10] *La Réforme*, 26 Mar.; *La Commune de Paris, moniteur des clubs*, 31 Mar.

[11] Paris, Bibliothèque nationale, Lb 53. 1649; Lb 53. 1650; Alphonse Lucas, *Les Clubs et les clubistes* (Paris, 1851), p. 131; *La Réforme*, 30 Mar.

[12] *Le Tribun du peuple*, 26 Mar.

creation of a Polish legion under the jurisdiction of the War Ministry.[13] Then, on 24 March, the beleaguered Frederick William IV announced that Polish refugees from France could cross Germany to go and join the ranks of an independent Poland if these refugees presented themselves in small unarmed groups at the border.[14] The Poles prepared to depart; and many began the long trek, leaving under the auspices of the French government which offered them food, transportation, and support for their families in France, but in turn controlled them so that they would not depart armed.[15]

Though many Poles left, others remained behind in France, where they strove to influence the French government to assist the Polish cause. The Club polonnais, for example, published an announcement admonishing Frenchmen and Poles to join in applying pressure on the Provisional Government.[16] Some of the Poles, not satisfied with Lamartine's programme of working through Germany for Poland, demanded that France offer armed support to the Polish cause. Lamartine, for his part, was quite aware that granting the Poles their request for armed assistance would have the effect of alienating the European Powers. Still, he could not ignore the Poles, for he knew that they had the backing and sympathy of most of the revolutionary elements within the French capital. Analysing his position toward Poland, Lamartine stated:

France, no doubt, owed a great deal to this brave nation in ruin, but she did not owe her [the control of France's] policies and the rupture of world peace. The Poles demanded no less than this. Not being able to obtain it from the government, they tried to get it from the people. . . The Poles are the ferment of Europe. . . . They agitated Paris and menaced the government. . . . But to declare war on Prussia, Austria, and Russia for them was a crusade to conquer a sepulcre.[17]

France would do her utmost to advance the Polish cause, but, as Lamartine had suggested in his directive of 11 March, in so doing she would limit herself strictly to diplomatic means.

[13] Comité national du Centenaire de 1848, *Procès-verbaux du Gouvernement provisoire et de la Commission du Pouvoir exécutif, 24 février–22 juin 1848*, p. 75; *Le Moniteur universel*, 12 Mar.   [14] Circourt, i. 126.
[15] Garnier-Pagès, vii. 275.   [16] *La-Voix des clubs*, 26 Mar.
[17] Lamartine, *Histoire de la révolution de 1848*, ii. 156, 256.

The Provisional Government, therefore, proceeded cautiously in its Polish policy; and Lamartine seized the first opportunity to rebuke the over-anxious Polish refugees residing in Paris. The occasion presented itself when a delegation of Poles to whom Lamartine was speaking became over-enthusiastic and suggested that they had more influence in Paris than the French government, that if Lamartine did not abide by their wishes they could have his government overthrown. In reply to these threats Lamartine made a discourse in which he appealed to French patriotism and declared that France wanted to remain at peace with all of Europe, that:

the Provisional Government could not let its policy be changed by the hand of a foreign nation [Poland], no matter how close she might be to our hearts. We love Poland, we love Italy, we love all oppressed peoples, but we love France above all, and we have the responsibility of her destiny, and perhaps that of all of Europe at this moment. . . . The day when it will appear to us that the providential hour will have sounded for the resurrection of a nation [which has been] unjustly erased from the map, we will fly to [Poland's] aid. But we justly reserve for ourselves what belongs to France alone, the appreciation of the hour, the moment of justice, the cause and the means by which it suits us to intervene. . . . In thirty-one days the natural and pacific results of this system of peace and fraternity, declared to peoples and governments, have been worth more to the cause of France, to the cause of liberty and Poland herself, than ten battles and floods of human blood.[18]

Lamartine had reiterated his government's determination to proceed slowly and peaceably in approaching the outstanding diplomatic problems facing Europe. With his speech Lamartine succeeded in quieting the more vociferous Poles for the moment, although he still had to deal with other refugee groups that were making demands similar to those of the Poles.

Refugees and workers from almost every European country resided in Paris. In the course of the first two months following the February Revolution almost all of them seem to have appointed delegations to go to the Hôtel de Ville to salute the French Republic, and also at times to request either direct or indirect French assistance for their respective causes. The usual tactic on the part of the French government was to have some

---

[18] *Le Moniteur universel*, 27 Mar.

important official address these deputations in an attempt to satisfy them by extolling 'the pastoral virtues' of the Hungarians or the 'example of liberty' which the Norwegians had given to the world.[19] However, these speeches, which were often delivered extemporaneously and with an air of excitement, could lead to complications in France's relations with other nations. Great Britain, for one, was especially susceptible to some of the sentiments uttered by members of the Provisional Government in addressing deputations of foreign refugees within the French capital.

Lamartine had continued to cultivate the English *entente* even though he hoped to broaden France's diplomatic ties to include other nations as well. Throughout March relations as a whole between the two Powers were quite good, except for a few isolated incidents. The English, it seems, were somewhat sceptical for a time about France's intentions toward Italy and Belgium, but this did not seem to affect adversely Anglo-French relations. The French, for their part, began displaying certain traits of traditional Anglophobia. One French newspaper stated bluntly that the French did not like England, while another subtly asked why France's avowed friend, Palmerston, had supported an increase in the Royal Navy's budget.[20] However, the incidents which did threaten to impair gravely Anglo-French relations in the spring of 1848 arose out of two ambiguous speeches made by members of the Provisional Government to English and Irish delegations in Paris.

On 5 March Garnier-Pagès delivered an address to a group of Chartists in which he insinuated that the English government did not possess the complete confidence of its people. Normanby immediately protested to Lamartine, who disclaimed any intention of encouraging English dissidents and suggested that Garnier-Pagès might have been misinterpreted.[21] Then, on 17 March Lamartine himself delivered an address to an Irish group in which he referred to Ireland's 'religious' and 'soon-hoped-for constitutional independence'.[22] Everything points to the fact that Lamartine had become carried away when haranguing

[19] Ibid. 16 Mar.
[20] *Le Père Duchêne, ancien fabricant*, 12 Mar.; *Le National*, 25 Mar.
[21] *Le Moniteur universel*, 6 Mar.; Normanby, *A Year of Revolution*, i. 225.
[22] *Le Moniteur universel*, 18 Mar.

the deputation; but the English took it as a clear case of interference in their internal affairs. Palmerston, deeply disturbed by both Garnier-Pagès's and Lamartine's statements, suggested that France should 'abstain' from 'interfering or meddling in any manner whatsoever with the Internal Affairs of the United Kingdom', just as England had promised not to interfere in French internal affairs.[23] In a series of discussions with Lamartine, Normanby censured his speech and criticized the Provisional Government's practice of consenting to address foreign delegations. The British ambassador persuaded Lamartine to atone for his speech by being stern with the Irish at his next opportunity.[24] Lamartine duly complied in his speech of 3 April when he told the Irish:

When one does not have a blood relationship with a people, one is not permitted to intervene [in their affairs]. . . . We are at peace and we wish to remain in good relations of equality, not with such or such part of Great Britain, but with Great Britain as a whole. . . . We will commit no act, we will say no word, we will make no insinuation in contradiction with the principles of reciprocal inviolability of peoples, which we have proclaimed, and whose fruit the continent is now reaping.[25]

Upon receiving Lamartine's assurances, Palmerston told Normanby: 'Pray tell M. Lamartine how very much obliged we feel for his handsome and friendly conduct about the Irish deputation. His answer was most honourable and gentlemanlike, and just what might have been expected from a high-minded man like him.'[26] The British government was obviously pleased with Lamartine's reply to the Irish, and Lamartine's conciliatory gesture had served to preserve the Anglo-French *entente*.

Although the Irish problem was now resolved, Lamartine's difficulties with foreign refugees were far from being ended. At the very time that Lamartine was addressing the second Irish delegation, refugee groups in France were planning and carrying out armed attacks upon their native countries without the French making any visible concerted effort to contain them. These invasion attempts by Savoyard, German, and Belgian workers and

---

[23] Britain, PRO, F.O. 27/797 (22 Mar., Palmerston to Normanby).
[24] Normanby, *A Year of Revolution*, i. 244–6, 250–5, 259–60.
[25] *Le Moniteur universel*, 4 Apr.
[26] Britain, PRO, F.O. 27/798 (7 Apr., Palmerston to Normanby).

refugees were to compromise severely French foreign relations. They rendered suspect France's good intentions toward her neighbours and seriously blemished the peaceful image which Lamartine was arduously striving to create for France.

The Savoyards, like the Poles, began organizing themselves and looking forward to the day when they could help revolutionize their own country, in this case an area which had close cultural and historical ties with France. They were possibly encouraged in their exploits by a speech which Lamartine delivered to a Savoyard delegation on 19 March. On this occasion the French foreign minister remarked that when speaking to Savoyards he felt as though he were addressing 'a part of France herself'. Then Lamartine went on to assure the delegation that:

We will not break the peace of the world. But if, independently of us, the peace of the world happened to be broken by an attack on the independence of Italy, we will fly to your assistance, we will deliver Italy, we will join our flag to yours, and then if the map of Europe comes to be torn up without us and against us, rest assured, citizens of Savoy, that a fragment of that map will remain in your and in our hands.[27]

Moreover, Savoy itself was shaken by internal agitation that was both republican and Francophile in nature and which seemed to indicate that Savoy might soon secede from Sardinia. The English minister in Turin, for instance, reported that republican agitation was widespread in 'the Duchy of Savoy, which if not already gone from the crown of Sardinia [would] go in a few days'. Lamartine himself predicted in a meeting of the Provisional Government at this time that 'within six weeks Savoy will request to be reunited to France'.[28]

The Savoyards in France, many of whom were now unemployed, decided to try to accelerate the process of revolution by going to the aid of their brethren in Savoy. The Savoyard contingent in Paris left for Lyons, where they were joined by more of their countrymen and several revolutionary clubs in requesting arms and munitions from Emmanuel Arago, the government's commissary in Lyons and the son of François Arago, a member of the Provisional Government.[29] Emmanuel Arago

[27] *Le Moniteur universel*, 20 Mar.
[28] Russell, i. 334–5 (4 Apr., Abercrombie to Russell); Garnier-Pagès, vii. 297–9.
[29] Garnier-Pagès, vii. 299–300.

treated the Savoyards with all possible circumspection, for he realized that they had the solid support of the Lyonnais revolutionary clubs. He tried to persuade them not to carry out their attempt on Savoy, but to no avail. He finally ended up by giving them the provisions and travelling funds which it was now the government's policy to distribute to emigrating workers. Still, Arago abided by Lamartine's orders and steadfastly refused to supply them with the arms for which they clamoured. The Savoyards were, nevertheless, given some arms, and a great deal of encouragement, by the clubs. Scantily armed but extremely optimistic, a group of around 1,500 Savoyards, and a few French volunteers from the clubs in Lyons, set off to liberate their homeland. The French army was given the order not to allow any armed men to cross the border. But somehow the order arrived too late, and the motley band of invaders, armed mostly with clubs and farm instruments, crossed the border and entered Savoy on 2 April.[30]

The Savoyard legion was amazingly successful at first. The Sardinian authorities in Chambéry fled upon their approach, but the invaders received a cool reception from the inhabitants who looked upon them as brigands and conquerors. The indomitable refugees, nevertheless, began laying the groundwork for a republic. There is considerable evidence to indicate that the Savoyards eventually planned to request annexation by France. However, they never received the opportunity to do so. On the morning following the invasion church bells rang and the peasants, led by their priests, swarmed into town to drive out the invaders. The battle was an unequal one: a few refugees were killed, some 800 were captured, and the rest were put to flight.[31] The short-lived invasion attempt had collapsed even before Sardinian troops arrived in Chambéry.

After the debacle Lamartine assured the Sardinians that the French government had not been implicated in the invasion attempt and that he had done everything within his power to prevent the refugees from leaving in armed bands.[32] French officials had notified the Sardinian authorities in advance about the possibility of an attempt on Chambéry; and, when the in-

---

[30] Justin Godart, *À Lyon en 1848, 'les Voraces'* (Paris, 1948), pp. 45–6; Garnier-Pagès, vii. 302–3.   [31] Godart, p. 47; Garnier-Pagès, vii. 304–5.
[32] FAAE, Corr. pol., Turin 321 (8 Apr., Lamartine to Bixio).

vasion was in progress, Lamartine had offered Sardinia the use of a French army to reconquer the city, something which the Italians undoubtedly saw as a pretext to put the French Army of the Alps in motion.[33] In the end the Sardinians accepted the French government's assurances that if the French 'had wanted to intervene, even indirectly, the struggle would have been much more difficult than it had been'.[34] Still, the invasion attempt on Savoy could not have endeared the French to Charles Albert, the Sardinian king who already deeply suspected that his neighbour to the north wanted to annex part of his kingdom. Moreover, in spite of the official reconciliation between the two countries, the Sardinians had good reason to doubt that the French, and especially Emmanuel Arago, had done all that they could have done to prevent the invasion attempt.[35]

A similar incident on the Belgian border was to have even more serious implications for France's foreign policy. The Belgian government had continued to be suspicious about France's ultimate intentions towards Belgium, despite Lamartine's guarantee that France did not want to export revolution to her neighbours. These fears were enhanced when Belgian authorities in the French capital saw a legion of Belgian refugees, which was being formed in Paris, openly advertising in a French newspaper for volunteers to carry the revolution to Belgium. The French government seemed to disregard these happenings, procrastinating when the Belgians asked it to take measures against these legions. With her suspicions confirmed by the Provisional Government's attitude, the natural move for Belgium was to turn once again to England; and the English replied by offering to intercede in Paris on Belgium's behalf.[36] England's sponsorship of the Belgian cause made it quite probable that any incident on the Belgian border could estrange England from France and destroy the good relations that were the very basis of Lamartine's diplomacy. The French foreign minister was quite aware of the repercussions which an attack by Belgian refugees upon their

[33] Sardinia, AST, Lettere Ministri Francia (30 Mar., French commissar in Grenoble to Governor-General of Savoy); Lamartine, *Histoire de la révolution de 1848*, ii. 255–6; *Œuvres complètes*, xxxix. 224.

[34] FAAE, Corr. pol., Turin 321 (7 Apr., Bixio to Lamartine).

[35] Sardinia, AST, Lettere Ministri Francia (5 Apr., Pareto to Ricci).

[36] *La République française*, 27 Feb.; Ridder, i. 109–11, 182–3 (5, 11 Mar., Ligne to Hoffschmidt; 27 Mar., Van der Weyer to Hoffschmidt).

homeland could have on Anglo-French relations. Lamartine acknowledged the fact that the annexation of Belgium 'at this time' would have constituted 'an inopportune declaration of war against Great Britain'.[37] Still, Lamartine was as unsuccessful in restraining the Belgian refugees as he had been in deterring the Savoyards.

The Belgians, among the most active of the refugee groups within Paris, were obviously preparing themselves for a triumphant return to their homeland. They had marched openly in the streets of Paris, cheering the 'Belgian republic' that they hoped to establish. Their aims were so evident that the Belgian ambassador in Paris could keep his government fully abreast of their activities. Belgium, therefore, had plenty of time to prepare her border defences before the legions left for the north in two separate groups in the latter part of March.[38]

The Belgian refugees had at least the moral support of certain men within the French government, including Ledru-Rollin, a member of the Provisional Government and Minister of the Interior, Delescluze, the commissary in the Département du Nord, and Caussidière, the Paris Prefect of Police in the spring of 1848. All of these men sympathized with the refugees and hoped that continual agitation within Belgium would lead to the establishment of a republic. Delescluze, for example, revealed his sentiments toward Belgium in early April, when he proclaimed, while officiating at the planting of a 'liberty tree' in Lille, that he hoped the roots of liberty would spread across the border to overthrow the Belgian monarchy.[39] In fact, Ledru-Rollin and Delescluze might have colluded in planning actively to encourage the legions to attack Belgium at some future time when an internal uprising within Belgium would enhance the chances of the refugees' success.[40] Nevertheless, this opportune moment never came, and the entire episode of the invasion of Belgium by the legions was marked by ineptitude on the part of both the refugees

---

[37] Lamartine, *Histoire de la révolution de 1848*, ii. 164–5; *Œuvres complètes*, xxxix. 148–9.

[38] Ridder, i. 250–3 (25 Mar., Ligne to Hoffschmidt; 25 Mar., Hoffschmidt to Ligne).

[39] Marcel Dessal, *Un révolutionnaire jacobin, Charles Delescluze, 1809–1871* (Paris, 1952), p. 64.

[40] Marcel Dessal, 'Les incidents franco-belges en 1848', *Actes du congrès historique du centenaire de la révolution de 1848* (Paris, 1948), p. 112.

themselves and those members of the French government who supported them.

The first convoy of Belgians left Paris by train at very short notice on the evening of 24 March. Delescluze, who had not been informed that Belgian legionnaires were aboard the train, thought that this was only a contingent of unemployed Belgian workers returning peacefully home. He did not want the responsibility of quartering this refugee group in his *département*, so he made arrangements with Belgian authorities to have the train pass through into Belgium without stopping at the border.[41] This ruined the refugees' plans, for they had hoped to regroup and acquire arms before entering Belgium. Instead, they saw the train speed across the border and deliver them into the waiting hands of the Belgian authorities. Cries of 'treason' were uttered by some of the refugees who threw themselves from the speeding train at the border. These cries were echoed by radical elements in Paris which consequently accused Ledru-Rollin and Delescluze of having betrayed the revolutionary cause, much to the dismay of Delescluze.[42]

The invasion attempt by the second and more numerous convoy of Belgians also resembled a mock-heroic episode. This group of 1,200 men left Paris shortly after the first contingent and was briefly quartered along the border by Delescluze, who seemed to be awaiting an opportune moment to unleash them against Belgium. However, his orders concerning just what should be done with the *émigrés* were ambiguous. In an attempt to clarify his orders before yielding to the pressures of the refugees, who wanted to depart immediately, Delescluze asked Ledru-Rollin for instructions by telegraph. Ledru-Rollin's reply, a very definite refusal to allow the refugees to enter Belgium, arrived too late, for Delescluze had already allowed them to cross the frontier, armed with guns which had been earmarked for the French national guard in the Département du Nord.[43]

The armed refugees who crossed the border cut a sorry figure in battle with the contingent of the Belgian army that awaited them.

[41] Ibid., pp. 110–12.

[42] Alvin Calman, 'Delescluze, Ledru-Rollin et l'échauffourée de Risquons-tout', *La Révolution de 1848*, xvi (1920–1), 46–8; *La Sentinelle des clubs*, 2 Apr.

[43] Dessal, 'Les incidents franco-belges en 1848', pp. 112–13; Adolphe Chenu, *Les Conspirateurs: les sociétés secrètes, la préfecture de police sous Caussidière, les corps francs* (Paris, 1850), pp. 165–70.

After a brief skirmish at a village just inside Belgium, which was appropriately named Risquons-tout, the invaders were routed, a large part of them fleeing back to France.[44] The 'invasion' of Belgium had failed as dismally as the 'invasion' attempt on Savoy.

The Risquons-tout incident, nevertheless, was more compromising for the French government than the Savoyard affair had been. This time it was difficult to deny the fact that a French minister had played a role in the episode and that the invaders had been supplied with French arms. Still, in an article published in *Le Moniteur* Lamartine did attempt officially to disavow both facts by claiming that the French government was not implicated in the affair. Belgian authorities realized quite well what had actually happened. But, like the Sardinians, they did not wish further to embitter their relations with France and they feigned to be satisfied with Lamartine's assurances.[45]

There is no doubt that Lamartine was personally opposed to the attempt on Belgium, having actually ordered Ledru-Rollin not to become involved.[46] As for the Savoy affair, Lamartine might have wished to see Savoy united with France, but he did assure Normanby that 'he had sent positive orders that this expedition should be prevented, and by force if necessary'.[47] Moreover, Lamartine's assertions seem to be substantiated by the fact that a subaltern figure in the French administrative system, who was favourable to an armed foray against Savoy, bemoaned the fact that the French foreign minister opposed such a measure.[48] Lamartine could later boast that not one of the nations threatened by refugees from France ever charged France 'with complicity or even negligence in repressing these attempts'.[49] Nevertheless, all Europe realized that the French government had not done all it could to curtail the refugees who openly broadcast their intention of invading their homelands. Furthermore, in the Risquons-tout affair at least, certain members of the French government had very evidently been implicated both morally and materially in the attempt.

[44] Garnier-Pagès, vii. 292–4.
[45] *Le Moniteur universel*, 2 Apr.; Ridder, i, p. xiii.
[46] Lamartine, *Lettre aux dix départements*, p. 4.
[47] Britain, PRO, F.O. 27/805 (31 Mar., Normanby to Palmerston).
[48] FAAE, Corr. pol., Turin 321 (6 Apr., Petetin to Lamartine). Petetin was the Provisional Government's commissioner in the Ain and Jura departments.
[49] Lamartine, *Œuvres complètes*, xxxix. 223.

The *émigré* invasion attempts staged from French territory in the spring of 1848 had definitely compromised the fledgling Republic's foreign policy. Lamartine himself was well aware of this fact. Still, he had made no really concerted effort to curtail or interdict these armed forays against France's neighbours. In fact, the French government not only failed to suppress refugee activities, but even supplied them with transportation to the border and provisions for their journeys. Part of the explanation for this course of action by the Republic seems to be that unemployment was rampant in France and that the French government, accordingly, decided to do all that it could to encourage foreign workers to emigrate.[50] One of the long-range causes of the revolution was undoubtedly the economic recession which had set in after 1845, a recession which in turn became more chronic as a result of the February Revolution. In the spring of 1848 unemployment was so high in France that it led to several attacks by unemployed Frenchmen on foreign workers. A considerable number of the Savoyards who invaded Savoy, for example, had been ejected from their jobs in Paris.[51] The Provisional Government as well as several newspapers made appeals for Frenchmen to treat foreigners fraternally, but to little avail.[52] Realizing that France was having enough difficulty finding employment for her own workers, in the month of March the Provisional Government adopted a programme of encouraging foreign workers to leave France. A decree to this effect actually appeared in the official newspaper on 20 March.[53]

Pressures caused by unemployment and economic stagnation obviously played a role in the Provisional Government's decision to encourage the emigration of foreign workers. An examination of the internal situation within France at the time, though, reveals other more pressing motives which determined the French government to encourage the expatriation of foreign workers living in France, even at the risk of complicating and compromising French foreign policy objectives. Throughout all

---

[50] This is the thesis persuasively argued by Paul Guichonnet, 'L'affaire des "Voraces" en avril 1848', *Istituto per le storia del Risorgimento italiano, Comitato di Torino*, Ser. 1, no. 4 (1949), 1–52.

[51] *Le Constitutionnel*, 9 Apr.; Britain, PRO, F.O. 27/806 (6 Apr., Normanby to Palmerston).

[52] *Le Moniteur universel*, 9 Apr.; *La Réforme*, 7 Apr.; *Le Siècle*, 26 Mar.

[53] Garnier-Pagès, vii. 271; *Le Moniteur universel*, 20 Mar.

of March and much of April the Provisional Government felt its hold upon the reins of France to be almost as tenuous as it had been immediately after the February Revolution. The major threat still came from the radicals; and, because the foreign refugees within France were the close allies of the Parisian radicals, the French government welcomed every opportunity to rid itself of these foreigners. Moreover, the Provisional Government was still powerless to guarantee order within France, especially within Paris. Lamartine and his colleagues could probably not have physically prevented the legions of foreign refugees from agitating even if they had wanted to do so. Normanby reported that 'Monsieur Lamartine seemed most deeply to feel how powerless he was to prevent' the march on Savoy, for he feared that French troops might join the Savoyard legion if the army were sent to the border in an attempt to block the departing workers.[54] British diplomats felt that Lamartine was 'pacific, but he [had] no power to continue so, and he [would] have either to quit office or allow himself to swim with the stream'.[55] Lamartine, it seems, had decided to 'swim with the stream' and not expose France to certain internal disorders by interfering with the refugee groups.

There were between 15,000 and 20,000 foreigners in Paris, many of whom, Lamartine asserted, 'caused the government most serious worries'.[56] Lamartine's concern about this situation can be seen by the fact that he asked Ligne, the Belgian ambassador in Paris, to allow some Belgian refugees to return peacefully to their homeland after the Risquons-tout affair. When Ligne seemed to hesitate, Lamartine exclaimed: 'In the name of God, take them off our hands!'[57] In a similar manner, Lamartine confided to Apponyi that he would be 'delighted' to see the German refugees depart from Paris because they were 'always recalcitrant'.[58] The Danish minister in Paris also noted that the French government would be most pleased to see all of the

---

[54] Britain, PRO, F.O. 27/806 (8 Apr., Normanby to Palmerston).
[55] Russell, i. 334–5 (4 Apr., Abercrombie to Russell).
[56] Lamartine, *Histoire de la révolution de 1848*, ii. 154.
[57] Ridder, i. 356–8 (8 Apr., Ligne to Hoffschmidt).
[58] Austria, HHS, Frankreich Korr. Kart. 337 (25 Mar., Apponyi to the Austrian Chancellor of State). For a discussion of the episode which saw German refugees from France invade the Rhineland states of Germany in late April, see below, pp. 66–70.

different groups of refugees which were 'troublesome' with their 'noisy demonstrations' leave Paris.[59]

If France were to attempt to contain the refugees within Paris or prevent the invasion attempts it would have been necessary to use the army. But, as Lamartine explained to Normanby when the British ambassador asked him why he did not use the army to protect English workers who were being expelled from the Le Havre area, the Provisional Government believed that it was impossible to use troops, the recent enemy of the people during the February Revolution, against the people, 'at least for some time'.[60] Lamartine told the Belgian ambassador in Paris that he was entirely powerless to protect the Belgian embassy or to interfere with the Belgian legions, but that Belgium had the right to 'receive the legion with gunshot' once it had invaded Belgian territory; his argument was that he had no power other than words, that other nations should realize that France's 'position was still a special one', because of rampant internal disorder. When reprimanded about his foreign policy, Lamartine replied by arguing that if he were criticized too much by foreign Powers and this led to his resignation, 'then you would see bands, and much larger ones, rush toward neighbouring countries'.[61] As Lamartine remarked when trying to justify to Normanby his friendly reception to the first Irish delegation, he was convinced that 'we are on a volcano'.[62] This 'volcano' had erupted on 17 March when French workers once again asserted their authority within the French capital.

On 16 March conservative elements of the National Guard solemnly paraded in front of the Hôtel de Ville to protest against the dissolution of certain élite companies, distinguished by their bearskin hats (bonnets à poil), by the Provisional Government. The radical populace and the clubbists interpreted this demonstration as a reactionary challenge to the government; to counter it they planned a massive counter-demonstration for the following day. On 17 March between 100,000 and 150,000 people, most of them workers and artisans, assembled on the square in front of the Hôtel de Ville in support of the Provisional

[59] Denmark, Rigsarkivet, Frankrig II (29 Mar., E. C. L. Moltke to Knuth).
[60] Normanby, A Year of Revolution, i. 179.
[61] Ridder, i. 261–2, 296–300, 356–8 (27 Mar., 1, 8 Apr., Ligne to Hoffschmidt).
[62] Normanby, A Year of Revolution, i. 246.

Government.[63] The radicals once again displayed their strength, inspiring awe and fear in an impotent government. The day of 17 March clearly indicated that the radicals were still capable of toppling the moderate Republic, that in the month of March they still controlled the streets of Paris. In the face of this 'volcano' of radical agitation, the Provisional Government preferred to compromise its diplomatic position over the refugee question rather than face the possibility of civil war in the French capital.

The internal instability which plagued the Republic immediately after the Revolution continued to cause France embarrassment on the diplomatic scene during April. In late April another group of foreign workers would flock to the French borders and attempt to carry out an expedition to republicanize their native land. And once again the Provisional Government would give in to the refugees rather than incur the certain wrath of the Parisian radicals who wholeheartedly supported the refugees' efforts. The multitude of internal problems facing the French government still excluded the possibility of a confrontation with the radicals at this time. These same difficulties also made it virtually impossible for the Provisional Government to contemplate embarking upon an adventurous foreign policy.

The Austrian ambassador in Paris, Apponyi, remarked that the Revolution had left French finances in utter confusion and had completely demoralized the French army.[64] Both of these problems still plagued France in April and were of primary concern to the Provisional Government. Financially, the Revolution added to the economic ills resulting from two years of European-wide recession. Following the February Revolution the French economy ground to a practical stop and the French treasury suffered from lack of funds. Throughout the spring the members of the Provisional Government devoted considerable energy to struggling with the financial problems which faced them. In March and April the Danish minister in Paris, an astute observer of the French internal scene, attested to the fact that the state of the French economy was the major problem

---

[63] Stern, ii. 61–75; Garnier-Pagès, vi. 393–432.

[64] Rudolphe Apponyi, *Vingt-cinq Ans à Paris, 1826–1852: journal du comte Rudolphe Apponyi, attaché de l'ambassade d'Autriche à Paris* (4 vols.; Paris, 1913–26), iv. 166–7.

facing the French government.[65] Lamartine himself asserted
that 'the men of the Provisional Government preoccupied themselves above all with the financial question'. Lamartine, for one,
insisted that financial problems had definitely affected the conduct of foreign affairs, for French 'finances were engaged to the
point where all liberty of action was removed. . . . Everything
was engaged for a period of long peace.'[66]

The depressed financial situation was one of the gravest problems facing the French government in the spring of 1848. Still,
there is every indication that throughout this period the Provisional Government was equally concerned about the state of
the French army. The French military establishment was
weakened as a result of the Revolution, and for reasons of both
internal and external policy the Provisional Government felt it
imperative to restore and increase France's military might.

A recent historian of the army, basing his conclusions upon a
thorough examination of army archives, has pointed out that
the disorganization and demoralization of the army after the
Revolution of February was not nearly as great as that which had
occurred after the Revolution of 1830. Mutinies and acts of insub-
ordination during the spring of 1848 were limited to 32 of the
180 regiments in metropolitan France, and the wave of desertion
concomitant with the February uprising seems to have ebbed by
early March.[67] Still, it seems that the troubles which the army
experienced as a result of the February Revolution were serious
enough greatly to reduce its reliability as an effective fighting
force from late February well into April.

During the street fighting in February a dissolution of military
discipline occurred in numerous units; often troops tended to
mix in with the crowds or even leave their units to return to
their homes.[68] Army units had been humiliated by their loss of
arms and their general inability to cope with the revolutionary
crowds. Immediately after the Revolution indiscipline increased

[65] Denmark, Rigsarkivet, Frankrig II (22 Mar., E. C. L. Moltke to Reventlow;
5, 15 Apr., E. C. L. Moltke to Knuth).

[66] Lamartine, *Histoire de la révolution de 1848*, ii. 54–5, 95–6. The mono-
graph by Alfred Antony (*La politique financière du Gouvernement provisoire,
février–mai 1848* [Paris 1910]) affords a detailed analysis of the French financial
and economic situation in the spring of 1848.

[67] Witold Zaniewicki, 'L'armée au lendemain de la révolution de février
1848', *Cahiers d'histoire*, xiv (1969), 393–419.

[68] Stern, i. 320; Garnier-Pagès, vi. 43.

as certain elements in the military came to believe that the Republic would introduce a process of democratization within the army. Revolts by troops against non-revolutionary officers occurred in some regiments; on one occasion the soldiers of a certain unit even requested of the Minister of War the right to elect their own commanding officers. At times the rank and file took the revolutionary step of dismissing non-republican officers. On 16 March General Castellane, writing in his diary, bemoaned the fact that recently six ranking officers had been ousted by their men, one of them nearly being killed in the process.[69] As the Danish minister in Paris observed, French military discipline seemed to be breaking down and 'disorders had occurred in more than one regiment'; the army appeared to be 'in a state of demoralization which threatened it with complete dissolution by the relaxation of all lines of authority'.[70] The army had already been neglected and undermanned during the July Monarchy. After the Revolution of February the demoralization and agitation which occurred within its ranks rendered the army's reliability suspect, at least until late April. In fact, discipline and order would only be definitely re-established within the army in May.

In early March the Provisional Government took immediate steps to rebuild the army. The Ministry of War and the newly formed Commission of National Defence announced a programme on 13 March which proposed to expand French military strength from 101,000 to 247,000 men in one and a half months.[71] Despite the near bankruptcy of the Treasury measures were taken to finance the expansion of the army. These efforts to raise funds proved to be quite successful, for at the end of the month of March the Commission announced that within a short time the army would number 200,000 men. Efforts were also made to restore discipline in the ranks. As a concession to republican elements some eighty-four high-ranking officers, including seventy-five generals, were retired and pensioned off.[72]

There is no doubt that the Provisional Government's pre-

---

[69] Pierre Chalmin, 'La crise morale de l'armée française', *L'Armée et la Seconde République* ('Bibliothèque de la révolution de 1848', vol. xviii; La Roche-sur-Yon, 1955), pp. 50–1, 53, 56.

[70] Denmark, Rigsarkivet, Frankrig II (5, 11 Apr., E. C. L. Moltke to Knuth).

[71] Comité national du Centenaire de 1848, *Procès-verbaux . . .*, p. 64 (13 Mar.).

[72] Ibid., pp. 68, 110, 152 (15, 29 Mar., 15 Apr.); Chalmin, pp. 56–8.

occupation with the army was partly dictated by requirements of national defence and foreign policy. Lamartine had requested the formation of a 60,000 to 80,000 man Army of the Alps and of a 100,000 to 120,000 man army to cover the northern and eastern frontiers.[73] The Army of the Alps was to be an important military and diplomatic factor in the Republic's relations with Sardinia and Austria, while the army in the north and east was necessary because of commitments to Prussia concerning Poland. Nevertheless, it is possible that France's desire to deploy her army along the frontiers was simply meant to placate French public opinion. It seems that the French revolutionary tradition required troops to be sent off to defend the nation's borders.[74] Lamartine told the Belgian ambassador in Paris that the proposed Army of the East existed on paper only, that its creation was intended to 'flatter public opinion; in difficult circumstances Frenchmen demand army corps on the borders; this idea charms them'.[75] Finally, there was one other very important reason why it was necessary to expand the army: it could be used to establish and maintain order within France.

The Provisional Government had been having considerable difficulty containing the revolutionary elements in Paris. The army had been removed from Paris after the Revolution, and the National Guard was of doubtful loyalty. Moreover, the *gardes mobiles*, created at the instigation of Lamartine, were still in training. The police force of the July Monarchy had been dissolved and the new corps of *gardiens de la paix* and *garde civique*, formed late in March, were too few and too poorly trained to be of any real immediate assistance. Lamartine was no doubt exaggerating when he told the Belgian ambassador that he did not have four men at his disposal to protect the Belgian embassy, or when he insisted to Apponyi that he did not have 'one bayonet' available for use against the German refugees.[76] Still, the Provisional Government did not feel strong enough to use its scanty forces against the Paris populace until the middle of April, when the National Guard proved its loyalty.

[73] Comité national du Centenaire de 1848, *Procès-verbaux* . . ., p. 109 (29 Mar.).
[74] Zaniewicki, *Cahiers d'histoire*, xiv. 393, 397.
[75] Ridder, i. 385–6 (26 Apr., Ligne to Hoffschmidt).
[76] Normanby, *A Year of Revolution*, i. 237; Austria, HHS, Frankreich Korr. Kart. 337 (25 Mar., Apponyi to Austrian Chancellor of State).

Garnier-Pagès related how the Provisional Government perceived itself to be under continual pressure from the Paris populace:

If one compares the resources which the Provisional Government had at its disposal, resources which were doubtful, equivocal, elusive, with the powerful means of defence existing in calm and ordinary times—the army, national guard, policemen, secret police, innumerable agents of all sorts hidden in the shadows—it would seem that with the slightest popular murmur the entire structure would crumble. One understands the precautions, proceedings, interviews, conferences, concessions, conciliations, which in any other circumstance would have been futile, superfluous, and impolitical, but which at this time became a dire necessity and a clever move.[77]

Feeling insecure, threatened and stripped of all power, the Provisional Government looked longingly to the army as a force which could be used to establish internal order.

Throughout March and most of April the Provisional Government feared bringing the army openly into Paris. Lamartine, nevertheless, admitted that during the spring he had remained in constant contact with General Négrier, who commanded the 27,000 man Army of the North, so that the General could have been called upon to march on the capital if the governing council had been threatened and forced to flee the city.[78] As Louis Blanc caustically remarked in his work on 1848, Lamartine, the author of *L'Histoire des Girondins*, was planning to 'renew the manœuvre of the old Girondin party' by using the army and the provinces against Paris.[79] Furthermore, Lamartine informed the British ambassador in Paris that the Army of the Alps, whose purpose was supposedly to cover the Italian border, could also be used 'for the maintenance of order' in Lyons, the other great centre of working-class agitation in France. The presence of a strong army in the Rhône valley seems to have 'had an internal motive' as well as the obvious external one.[80]

In a meeting of the governing council on 29 March Lamartine insisted that up to 30,000 men be recalled from North Africa and stationed within metropolitan France, despite opposition from the army high command which argued that such a move

[77] Garnier-Pagès, vii. 232–3.
[78] Lamartine, *Œuvres complètes*, xxxix. 205.   [79] Blanc, ii. 11.
[80] Britain, PRO, F.O. 27/806 (1, 6 Apr., Normanby to Palmerston); Lamartine, *Histoire de la révolution de 1848*, ii. 45.

might seriously compromise the defence of Algeria.[81] Lamartine intended to use these troops to strengthen the Army of the Alps, which might be needed in Italy. However, the Provisional Government also envisaged using these contingents for internal purposes. On 31 March the Minister of the Army, François Arago, wrote a directive within his ministry, stating that the troops recalled from Africa would be used to restore order in the interior. Detachments of troops from Algeria were accordingly sent to the towns of Castres and Lunel, two communities where there was considerable disorder at the time.[82]

The use of troops to restore order at trouble spots in the provinces seems to have been a matter of general policy. When the Provisional Government inquired why the projected strengthening of the armies along the frontiers was proceeding more slowly than scheduled, the repeated reply by the military was that too many troops were needed for 'civil' purposes in the French countryside. A recent study of the army in 1848 has shown that during the spring so many troops were being used to maintain internal order in the provinces that it would probably have been difficult for the army to undertake any foreign adventures.[83] Although the army was being strengthened and rebuilt, it was being used primarily for suppressing disorders in the provinces. This fact obviously restricted the Provisional Government's foreign policy.

With the army proving its effectiveness in the provinces the members of the Provisional Government began to examine the possibility of reintroducing army units into Paris. Lamartine admitted that one of his main projects during the spring of 1848 was to:

Rehabilitate the army in the heart of the people of Paris and prepare the way for the troops' return to the capital. This return, patiently and prudently planned, was the principal thought of [François] Arago and the majority of the government. . . . The re-entrance of the army before the susceptibilities of the people had been calmed would have been the inevitable signal of a clash out of which a

---

[81] Comité national du Centenaire de 1848, *Procès-verbaux* . . ., p. 110 (29 Mar.).

[82] Suzanne Coquerelle, 'L'armée et la répression dans les campagnes, 1848', *L'Armée et la Seconde République*, pp. 141–2.

[83] Ibid., pp. 142, 151.

second civil war would have resulted. They [the majority] strongly began to want the army. Only the socialist and demogogic party spread the alarm and prepared sedition at any word of the return of our soldiers.[84]

As Lamartine suggests, Louis Blanc and Albert, the representatives within the government of what Lamartine referred to as 'the socialist and demogogic party', were resolutely opposed to returning the army to Paris. Ledru-Rollin, the radical republican Minister of the Interior, agreed, however, with the majority that it was absolutely necessary to re-establish the army in Paris.[85] Like most of his colleagues within the government, Ledru-Rollin showed a distinct fear of the revolutionary and socialistic clubs which were extremely active within the French capital. The Provisional Government believed the threat from the clubs to be so great that Lamartine devoted many of his energies from the middle of March to the middle of April to trying to approach the clubs, watch over them, influence them, and either win them over or sow dissension within them.[86] Until the latter part of April the Provisional Government lacked any means of enforcing order within the capital and showed its apprehension of the clubbists by taking elaborate clandestine measures to fortify the Hôtel de Ville during the first two weeks of April.[87] Lamartine's overriding concern with penetrating the Parisian clubs is demonstrated by the fact that he even used secret funds, allotted to him as Minister of Foreign Affairs, to finance the elaborate spy system which the Provisional Government had created to monitor the actions of the clubbists.[88] The foreign service could be neglected while the French foreign minister attempted to save the Republic from internal strife.

In late April Lamartine's government, powerless to do otherwise in light of the internal situation, allowed the actions of German refugees to compromise once again French foreign policy objectives, just as the exploits of the Savoyard and Belgian *corps francs* had done in late March and early April. Despite the crushing defeats inflicted upon the Belgian and Savoyard legions, in April the German republican refugees in France decided that the time had come for them to do battle with the

[84] Lamartine, *Histoire de la révolution de 1848*, ii. 287.   [85] Stern, i. 428.
[86] Lamartine, *Histoire de la révolution de 1848*, ii. 142–53.
[87] Stern, ii. 163–6.   [88] Garnier-Pagès, vii. 229–30.

German Rhineland princes. Like their Belgian and Savoyard counterparts, the German *émigrés* had begun to formulate their invasion plans as far back as the middle of March. The Germans too made little effort to dissimulate their intentions or conceal their preparations, with the result that the German diplomats in Paris were as aware as their Belgian and Sardinian colleagues had been of the imminent threat to their borders.[89]

The Société démocratique allemande, which organized the German workers in the French capital, made its existence known to the French public by a poster on the walls of Paris, requesting arms to enable the Germans to leave and 'proclaim the German Republic'.[90] This appeal for arms was seconded by certain elements of the French press, which saw the Germans going forth to liberate not only Germany but Poland as well.[91] At the same time the German refugees addressed themselves to all the clubs of Paris by sending a proclamation to club presidents which stated that even a few thousand men could succeed and 'assure the triumph of revolution in their fatherland' if they were allowed to organize on a military basis within France. They added, as if to entice support from those who might act out of more selfish motives, that by leaving Paris the German workers would yield their positions to their French brothers while departing 'to seek bread and freedom in their own country'.[92] Another chapter was being enacted in the drama of foreign workers emigrating under the pressures of unemployment in France.

There is some evidence to suggest that the German workers intended to leave France near the end of March at the same time as their Belgian and Savoyard brethren. A leftist Parisian newspaper announced on 26 March that the so-called 'German legion' had appealed to the French National Guard for arms, that one column of Germans had departed for the German border on the previous evening, and that another group was scheduled to leave on that day.[93] The German Rhineland states definitely felt an invasion of their territory to be imminent at this time. Fear spread through the towns of Baden near the Rhine, while a general panic reigned in the Hessian and Bavarian Rhineland.

[89] Austria, HHS, Frankreich Korr. Kart. 337 (25 Mar., Apponyi to Chancellor of State). [90] Paris, Bibliothèque nationale, Lb 53. 1605.
[91] *Le Bon Conseil*, 26 Mar. [92] *La Voix des clubs*, 19 Mar.
[93] *La République française*, 26 Mar.

The Grand Duchy of Hesse, along with Baden, Bavaria, and Wurtemberg, rushed contingents of troops to the frontier.[94] An examination of the diplomatic record shows, moreover, that at this time Lamartine forewarned at least two German states, Bavaria and Baden, of the impending departure of the legions, assuring them that German workers would not be allowed to depart armed.[95] Nevertheless, when the foreign minister of Baden suggested that the French government might be more co-operative and divide the legions into small detachments which could be peacefully admitted at specified border crossings, the French agent in Carlsruhe replied that: 'It is the Grand Duchy's right and duty to provide for its own security, but that for its part the Provisional Government has to humour public opinion in every way; that the government of Baden should take into account the difficulties we are facing.'[96] The French government informed Baden—just as it had done in the case of Belgium— that it had the right to use armed force in receiving the emigrat- ing workers, but that France, for her part, was not in a position to impede their departure in light of the Parisian radicals' show of strength on 17 March.

The German emigrants did not implement their invasion plans during the latter part of March, either because they were dis- heartened by the defeat of their Belgian and Savoyard counter- parts or because the internal uprisings in Germany which they were awaiting failed to materialize. Nevertheless, they remained congregated in Strasbourg and along the Rhine, threatening to overflow into Germany at any time. Under these circumstances the French government began negotiations with Baden concern- ing the possibility of peacefully expatriating the legions.[97] Encouraged by the German governments to take some decisive action, on 19 April the Provisional Government drew up a decree dissolving contingents of foreign workers near the French frontiers and providing for their internment far from the eastern

[94] FAAE, Corr. pol., Bade 84 (27 Mar., Liechtenberger to Lamartine); Corr. pol. des consuls, Mayence-Hesse-Darmstadt 1 (29 Mar., Englehardt to Lamar- tine); Corr. pol., Allemagne 805 (27 Mar., Salignac-Fénelon to Lamartine).

[95] Ibid., Corr. pol., Bade 84 (30 Mar., Lefebvre to Lamartine); Corr. pol., Bavière 224 (27 Mar., Bourgoing to Lamartine); Austria, HHS, Frankreich Korr Kart. 337 (17, 19 Mar., Apponyi to Metternich).

[96] FAAE, Corr. pol., Bade 84 (30 Mar., Lefebvre to Lamartine).

[97] Ibid. (15 Apr., Lefebvre to Lamartine).

borders. The French government felt confident enough to take this action, for on 16 April the Parisian radicals had suffered defeat and humiliation in another of the spring 'days'; an awesome clubbist demonstration had been intercepted and curtailed by the Parisian National Guard, which now rallied behind the government. However, internal pressure still weighed upon the Provisional Government; the decree was made, but the government refrained from publishing it until after the elections for the French National Constituent Assembly, which took place on 23 April.[98] The Provisional Government obviously feared defeat at the polls despite its victory in the streets on 16 April.

The German *corps francs* took advantage of the French government's vacillation and crossed the Rhine to invade Baden before the decree dissolving the legions was published. Lamartine had given the order that no armed contingents be permitted to cross the border, and, consequently, few of the workers who crossed the frontier were actually armed.[99] However, once again the legions failed to encounter any resistance from French authorities as they left France. It was quite apparent that the Republic had made no real concerted effort to interfere with their departure.

Some 1,200 workers, led by the German democrats Herwegh, Bornstedt, and Boernstein, entered Baden near the Swiss frontier on the night of 24 April. They met with little resistance at first and even managed to capture and hold momentarily the town of Zell. However, a unit of German troops closed in on them and they attempted to flee southward to seek asylum in Switzerland. With the Swiss border in sight, the legion stumbled upon a contingent of troops. The refugees fought gallantly until army reinforcements arrived, but then broke ranks and fled into Switzerland, leaving behind some 30 dead and 370 prisoners.[100]

The third and last attempt by foreign workers residing in France to export revolution to their homelands had ended in an utter fiasco. The French government had been well aware that in view of the military preparations taken in the Rhineland the

[98] Comité national du Centenaire de 1848, *Procès-verbaux* . . ., p. 165 (19 Apr.); Normanby, *A Year of Revolution*, i. 338–9; Circourt, ii. 47–8; Austria, HHS, Frankreich Korr. Kart. 337 (1 May, Thom to Ficquelmont).

[99] FAAE, Corr. pol., Bade 84 (15 Apr., Lamartine to Lefebvre).

[100] Louis Blaison, *Un Passage de vive force du Rhin français en 1848* (Paris, 1933), pp. 78–168.

German legion had no chance of success.[101] The incident, though, had served to rid France of undesirable elements. In the case of the German legion, as in the case of the Belgian and Savoyard refugees, the Provisional Government had been primarily motivated by the desire to cater to French public opinion and to attenuate internal pressures upon itself. The entire series of episodes with foreign *émigrés* in March and April of 1848 demonstrated the French government's overwhelming concern with internal difficulties and its willingness to relegate foreign policy considerations to a secondary position.

[101] FAAE, Corr. pol., Wurtemberg 72 (2 Apr., Fontenay to Lamartine).

IV

LAMARTINE'S DIPLOMATIC STRATEGY

THE attack on the Rhineland by German political refugees based in France caused some indignation in Germany, but it seems not to have substantially imperilled France's relations with the different German states. To be sure, Heinrich von Gagern, Prime Minister of Hesse-Darmstadt and later president of the Frankfurt Assembly, reacted to the invasion attempt by telling the deputies in the Hessian chamber that there was no difference between a state which declared war on another country and a state which permitted the formation of an expeditionary force of foreigners within its borders.[1] Such a statement brought the influential Parisian daily, *Le National,* to voice its astonishment at Germany's reaction to the invasion attempt. Still, for the most part the German states appeared to accept French assurances, such as those which appeared in *Le Moniteur,* that the Republic was in no way implicated in the German legion's exploits and that the French people desired the most cordial relations with Germany.[2] The French chargé d'affaires in Munich reported that in spite of German apprehension concerning the legion's activities the German and French peoples were still united in their desire to liberate the Italians and Poles.[3] The legion's invasion of the Rhineland did not seem to have interfered with the Franco-Prussian *entente* either. On the contrary, in spite of French internal difficulties and French embarrassment at the attacks upon neighbouring states by the *corps francs,* the Republic's diplomatic position *vis-à-vis* the other European Powers had been considerably enhanced during March and April by the revolutionary developments that shook the continent.

The Prussian decision to re-establish an independent Poland out of its holdings around Posen had not only alienated the Tsar, but had obliged Russia to withdraw from the Western European

[1] FAAE, Corr. pol. des consuls, Mayence-Hesse-Darmstadt 1 (29 Mar., Englehardt to Lamartine).　　[2] *Le National,* 3 Apr.; *Le Moniteur universel,* 4 Apr.
[3] FAAE, Corr. pol., Bavière 224 (30 Mar., Bourgoing to Lamartine).

　　　　　　　　　　　　　　　　　　　　　　　　F

diplomatic scene because of the probability of a revolt within her Polish provinces and the possibility of war with Prussia. A Belgian diplomatic observer remarked already on 24 March that two weeks earlier French intervention in Italy would have meant war with Russia and Prussia, but that this was no longer the case.[4] Then, as France and Prussia moved progressively closer as a result of Frederick William IV's decision to reconstruct Poland, Prussia withdrew entirely from the coterie of the 'Northern Powers' so dreaded by France. On 4 April France committed herself to come to the aid of Prussia if war broke out between Russia and Prussia over Poland.[5] Three days later the Prussian foreign minister, von Arnim, confidentially informed the Republic's chargé d'affaires in Berlin that if France became involved in Italy Prussia would remain neutral; moreover, von Arnim told Circourt that Prussia would try to influence the other German states to follow Prussia's example, as long as France did not go so far as to invade Austria proper.[6] Great Britain publicly proclaimed throughout the spring that Her Majesty's Government would not become involved in Italy even if France were to intervene beyond the Alps. The British made it known that they would guarantee the existence of Belgium, but that they did not feel bound by the treaties of 1815 to assist Austria in retaining her Northern Italian provinces.[7] In effect, France had a relatively free hand to exert her influence in her traditional area of interest, Italy. The spring revolutions had turned the diplomatic tables to the point where the Republic could consider resorting to force to implement a strong and ambitious Italian policy without being concerned about any real opponent except the diplomatically isolated and apparently crumbling Austrian Empire. Lamartine's contention that an adventuresome French foreign policy would have welded together a new coalition and resulted in invasion and defeat for France no longer really held true by April.[8]

Lamartine used several arguments in defending himself against those of his contemporaries who criticized his pursuit of a peaceful foreign policy at a time when it seemed that a more active policy on the part of France might have guaranteed the

---

[4] Ridder, i. 244–7 (24 Mar., O'Sullivan de Grass to Hoffschmidt).
[5] See above, p. 45.   [6] Circourt, i. 377–9.
[7] Ridder, i. 17–18, 143–4 (28 Feb., 7 Mar., Van der Weyer to Hoffschmidt); Garnier-Pagès, i. 465.   [8] Lamartine, *Histoire de la révolution de 1848*, ii. 23.

success of the European revolutionary movement and republicanized Europe.[9] On the one hand the French foreign minister argued that the state of France's army and economy made war unthinkable. On the other hand, he reiterated his contention that France's revolutionary example, her 'attitude and reserve fought peacefully for the Republic'.[10] Lamartine insisted that to declare a war against the princes of Europe would only have served to rally the people of Europe around their governments, while the pursuit of a peaceful foreign policy by France would win these peoples over to the revolutionary camp once they came to realize the advantages of the republican form of government.[11] However, the argument which Lamartine stressed the most when defending his pacific foreign policy was that he abhorred war in principle and was a dedicated pacifist. In his political writings Lamartine assured posterity of his profound conviction that:

War, far from meaning progress for humanity, is mass murder, which retards, afflicts, decimates, and dishonours humanity. Peoples who play with blood are the instruments of ruin and not the instruments of life in the world. They expand, but they expand against the will

[9] Leonard Gallois in his *Histoire de la révolution de 1848* ([8 vols.; Paris, 1849–51], i. 156–7) contended that with all of Europe aflame in the spring of 1848 France would certainly have been successful in a war of republican propaganda. Hippolyte Castille severely castigated the French foreign minister in his *Histoire de la Seconde République française* ([4 vols.; Paris, 1854–6], ii. 102–3). In assessing Lamartine's policy Castille remarked that 'no doubt the Second Republic had an army in disarray, that it lacked men, munitions, and funds; but what she lacked most of all was good faith' in failing to respond by armed action when the suppressed peoples of Europe called upon her for assistance.
Modern historians have also argued that the Second French Republic might have been able to save the revolutionary movement in 1848 by acting in support of the liberal and democratic forces which had emerged across Europe in the spring of that year. Émile Tersen (pp. 75–7) has asserted that France's failure to launch 'a revolutionary war' in the spring of 1848 had 'especially profited the European monarchies', that the Provisional Government's inaction had 'lost the battle of European liberty'. In a similar manner A. J. P. Taylor (*The Opening of an Era, 1848: An Historical Symposium*, François Fejto, ed. [London, 1948], p. xxvi) has remarked: 'All Europe had expected revolutionary France to march anew and to liberate, at least, the two martyred nations, Poland and Italy. Instead [France adopted a foreign policy which was] more resolutely pacific even than in the time of Louis Philippe. The failure to launch a general war for the sake of Poland or even to go to the assistance of Italy, in a word the foreign policy of Lamartine, marked the decisive step on the path that led to Munich and to French renunciation of her position as a Great Power.'
[10] See above, pp. 37–8.
[11] Lamartine, *Histoire de la révolution de 1848*, ii. 24–5.

of God, and finish by losing in one day of justice all that they had conquered by years of violence. Illegal murder is no less a crime for a nation than for an individual. National crime is a false foundation which does not sustain, but which engulfs it. From this philosophical, moral, and religious point of view, Lamartine did not want to give war as a tendency or even as a diversion to the new Republic. A diversion of blood is worthy only of tyrants or Machiavelians.[12]

French historians, tending to accept Lamartine's assurances at face value, have found numerous statements in the great poet's political writings to substantiate his contention that pacifism was a lifelong conviction on his part.[13] These scholars have pointed out, for example, that in 1841 Lamartine had extolled the virtues of peace in his poem 'La Marseillaise de la paix'.[14] Moreover, it is well known that, although Lamartine was a bitter critic of most aspects of the July Monarchy, he had lauded the pacifism of Louis Philippe's foreign policy. In a speech at a political banquet at Mâcon on 18 July 1847 Lamartine had ridiculed the July Monarchy and predicted 'a revolution of scorn', but at the same time he had credited it with preserving peace, something which, he believed, 'in the future will be the glorious amnesty of this government against all its other errors'.[15] Historians have also stressed the fact that Lamartine had denounced Thiers's aggressive attitude during the Egyptian crisis of 1840, quoting his famous article on 'La question d'Orient, la guerre, le ministère' which appeared at this time in order to illustrate Lamartine's abhorrence for war.[16] In this article Lamartine declared that:

those who clamour for war belong to a different century; they are impatient and retarded souls. . . . A mere soldier understands war: it is a brutal thing. . . . O people, always remember that from the very beginning of the great revolution of 1789 there were always two

[12] Lamartine, *Histoire de la révolution de 1848*, ii. 12; *Œuvres complètes*, xxxix. 13–14.

[13] Such recent Lamartinian scholars as Tersen and Guyard (Marius Guyard, 'Les idées politiques de Lamartine', *Revue des travaux de l'Académie des Sciences morales et politiques*, 1966, 2nd semestre, pp. 1–16) have stressed Lamartine's innate pacifism in explaining the French Provisional Government's major foreign policy decisions.

[14] Henry, *Revue historique*, clxxviii (1936), 202–3; Pouthas, 'La politique étrangère de la France sous la Seconde République et le Second Empire', pp. 20–1.   [15] Lamartine, *Œuvres complètes*, xxxviii. 15–22.

[16] Quentin-Bauchart, *Lamartine et la politique étrangère de la révolution de février*, pp. 45–6.

parties both within the revolution and outside it: the liberal, reform-ing party, and the warlike and agitating party, one party which strove to do everything by and for liberty, and the other party which tried to accomplish everything by and for war. . . . All the true friends, all the sincere fanatics of the liberal revolution from Lafayette to Fox have belonged to the party of peace. All the men insatiable for power, all the exploiters of circumstances, all the deceivers of the people, have belonged to the war party.[17]

Lamartine obviously placed himself within the former rather than the latter category.

In spite of numerous passages from Lamartine's writings and speeches during the period 1840–7 indicating a profound aver-sion to war and violence, it is interesting to note that elsewhere in this very article on the Eastern Question, Lamartine intimated that war for a just cause was acceptable, that 'the question is not if France will make war well, but why she will make it'. He then went on to argue that 'war at a well-chosen moment' could be tolerated if it were in France's interest.[18] It seems, therefore, that this oft-quoted article of Lamartine's was essentially a denuncia-tion of Thiers's specific projects rather than of war in general.

While Lamartine no doubt harboured pacifist sentiments, his actions after he came to power in 1848 suggest that he was not as adamant an opponent of war as he claimed and as he is usually assumed to have been. Everything indicates that he thought more in terms of traditional French diplomacy, a diplomacy which was prepared to use war as a tool of foreign policy, than many of his defenders among the staunch republican historians of the Third and Fourth Republics would like to admit. As an astute foreign observer in Paris remarked in 1848, Lamartine 'has generally been considered as a pacific foreign minister. . . . But we are constrained to say that the general tendency of his political feeling is not pacific but . . . ambitious.' Nassau William Senior then went on to explain that Lamartine had armed one out of every sixteen Frenchmen, had assembled an army on the frontier of Italy, and had attempted to use the war between Austria and Sardinia as a means of acquiring Savoy.[19] This contemporary

---

[17] Lamartine, 'La question d'Orient, la guerre, le ministère', *Vues, Discours et Articles sur la question d'Orient* (Brussels, 1841), pp. 18, 119–20.

[18] Ibid., p. 101.

[19] Nassau William Senior, *Journals Kept in France and Italy, from 1848 to 1852* (2 vols.; London, 1871), i. 60–1, 65.

observer had a certain amount of insight into Lamartine's diplomatic aims, for a close scrutiny of the French diplomatic position in the late spring of 1848 shows that Lamartine was prepared to take up arms to achieve certain traditional French foreign policy objectives. Like Napoleon III some ten years later, he coveted Nice and Savoy and hoped to gain these areas for France at the expense of Sardinia. These ambitions were curtailed only because he hesitated to associate himself with the expansionist foreign policy advocated by the Parisian radicals, because his colleagues in the government refused to support his projects, and because Sardinia, wary of France's intentions, refused to accept French assistance.

In examining the factors which influenced Lamartine's major foreign policy decisions in the spring of 1848 it is necessary to keep constantly in mind the situation in the French capital. One of the radical Parisian revolutionaries' primary aims was to introduce a policy of active republican propaganda on the European scene, a policy calling for overt assistance to repressed peoples and the launching of a republican holy war against kings. Lamartine was quite aware of these ideals of his political opponents. He informed Brignole, the Sardinian ambassador in Paris, for example, of the difficulties he was having containing 'the unrestrained demagogues and the partisans of aggressive war' within France. On another occasion he confided to the Austrian Apponyi that any war in Italy would permit 'the anarchic faction' within France which wanted a European conflict to 'compromise and overthrow' his government.[20] Similarly, in March he wrote—with his usual modesty—to a friend that 'God is helping me in my conduct of foreign affairs, but men would like very much to spoil them'. He was even more explicit when he wrote to another acquaintance some time later: 'You see how our foreign affairs are going, but you do not see everything. I am staying to prevent their being altered by an insensate exterior policy.'[21] Lamartine, the historian of the Great French Revolution who was ever aware of the course of events in 1792–3, feared the repercussions which the adoption of an adventuresome foreign policy might have upon the domestic scene in 1848, and

---

[20] Sardinia, AST, Lettere Ministri Francia (2 Mar., Brignole to Saint-Marsan; 11 Mar., Brignole to Pareto).

[21] Lamartine, *Correspondance de Lamartine*, vi. 309, 311.

undoubtedly believed that his presence alone was serving to hold back the radical onslaught which could destroy the moderate Republic by bringing war, and war's logical consequence, a new Reign of Terror, to France.

In 1840 Lamartine had already suggested in a letter to a friend that 'war is the enemy of liberty and democracy' as well as of humanity.[22] He was more precise in his Manifesto when he declared, after having referred to the events of the Great Revolution, that in war liberty was the greatest victim, that 'war means almost always a dictatorship'.[23] Lamartine best explained his thoughts on this subject when he wrote:

Lamartine knew by history and by nature that every war of a single people against all others is an extreme and desperate war; that every extreme war required in the nation that was carrying it on efforts and means of political upheaval as extreme and as desperate as the war itself; that efforts and means of this nature can only be employed by a government which is also extreme and desperate; and that its means are excessive taxes of gold and blood, forced loans, paper money, proscriptions, revolutionary tribunals and scaffolds. . . . To inaugurate the Republic with such a government would be to bring about tyranny instead of liberty . . . crime instead of public virtue, the ruin of the people instead of its well-being. Lamartine and his colleagues would rather have sacrificed their heads to the revolution than give it a drop of blood.[24]

To Lamartine, a nation in arms evoked images of the Terror. The great poet could already picture himself on the Jacobin scaffold of 1848.

The other members of the Provisional Government seem to have shared Lamartine's belief in the wisdom of avoiding war. Within the government the division between moderates and radicals was not nearly as pronounced concerning the question of war and peace as it was concerning domestic policy matters. Of all the members of the Provisional Government Ledru-Rollin, the Jacobin republican who served as Minister of the Interior, was most inclined to advocate an adventuresome foreign policy. Ledru-Rollin's private secretary during 1848 has asserted that he favoured a republican war against Europe and 'retained bellicose

[22] Ibid., v. 454.   [23] Le Moniteur universel, 5 Mar.
[24] Lamartine, Histoire de la révolution de 1848, ii. 24; Œuvres complètes, xxxix. 24.

memories of 1793', while the majority of the government dreaded these ideas. In the spring of 1848 Ledru-Rollin had proclaimed that 'the remains of thrones where idle kings slumbered will soon disappear under the popular surge'.[25] Despite these bellicose proclivities, however, Ledru-Rollin did not break with the official government policy of non-intervention in Europe. Even in the case of the Belgian refugees, Ledru-Rollin ended up by subscribing to his colleagues' cautious foreign policy. As his biographer remarked: 'That he would have been delighted to see a Belgian republic is undoubted . . . but from start to finish as a government official he refused anything that could be called official sanction.'[26]

Louis Blanc for his part seemed to pay little attention to questions of foreign policy while devoting all of his energies to the Luxembourg Commission for the workers in the spring of 1848. To be sure, in his *Histoire de dix ans, 1830–1840,* his *Histoire de la Révolution française,* and his journalistic efforts prior to 1848 he had advocated war as a necessary means of achieving both French expansion and the liberation of oppressed nations.[27] However, once he became a member of the government after the February Revolution he fully supported Lamartine's conduct of foreign affairs, holding that the Manifesto was 'the eloquent declaration of the only policy then possible'. According to Louis Blanc, France was wise not to go to war in 1848. He argued that most republicans realized that it was necessary first to consolidate the Republic at home 'against treason in the interior' before it was possible to contemplate making war.[28]

It is impossible to ascertain exactly what French public opinion in 1848 felt concerning the respective virtues of war and peace. For example, historians disagree concerning the foreign policy aims of such a large and heterogeneous segment of the population as the French working class. Georges Duveau has argued that the Parisian workers were extremely bellicose, while Daniel

[25] Elias Regnault, *Histoire de Gouvernement provisoire* (Paris, 1850), pp. 243–4; A.-A. Ledru-Rollin, *Discours politiques et Écrits divers* (2 vols.; Paris, 1879), ii. 14.
[26] Alvin Calman, *Ledru-Rollin and the Second French Republic* (New York, 1922), p. 102.
[27] Leo A. Loubère, 'Les idées de Louis Blanc sur le nationalisme, le colonialisme et la guerre', *Revue d'histoire moderne et contemporaine,* iv (1957), 33–63; *Louis Blanc: His Life and his Contribution to the Rise of French Jacobin-Socialism* (Evanston, 1961), p. 51.   [28] Blanc, i. 243, 263; ii. 76.

Stern believed that the workers did not desire war any more than the rest of the population.[29] As for the French population as a whole, Lamartine remarked in his *Histoire de la révolution de 1848* that the idea of peace 'had become popular' by 1848. However, elsewhere in his writings he contradicted this by saying that 'the people clamoured' for war, that 'the superabundance of an active and unoccupied population exerted pressure' for war.[30] Perhaps Daniel Stern was correct when she suggested that in reality only a minority within France 'spoke loudly' in favour of war.[31] Another keen observer of the French scene in 1848, Odilon Barrot, writing in his *Mémoires*, concurred in the belief that 'the immense majority of the government and of the nation' was 'very firmly resolved to remain at peace'.[32] Still, an examination of the Parisian press in the spring of 1848 clearly indicates that, while a majority of the French population might have preferred the preservation of peace, radical elements in France definitely favoured the adoption of an adventuresome, bellicose foreign policy.

Moderate and conservative newspapers, on the one hand, tended either to support the government's cautious foreign policy or to echo even more profound anti-war sentiments. Like the French foreign minister, *Le National*, which often acted as an unofficial organ of the government in 1848, assured Europe that conquests were things of the past. *L'Assemblée nationale* warned that war would bring 'the conflagration of Europe'; and the *Journal des débats* proclaimed that war would set Europe back one generation. Émile de Girardin's *La Presse* displayed its conservatism by admonishing the Republic to observe the strictest non-intervention in its foreign policy, not even aiding other peoples if they requested assistance.[33]

On the other hand, leftist clubbists and the radical or socialist Parisian press, spokesmen for the extreme revolutionary elements within France, were severe in castigating the moderate Republic's

[29] Georges Duveau, 'Les relations internationales dans la pensée ouvrière, 1840–1865', *Actes du Congrès historique du centenaire de la révolution de 1848* (Paris, 1948), pp. 278–81; Stern, i. 423–4.

[30] Lamartine, *Le Passé, le Présent et l'Avenir de la république*, p. 54; *Histoire de la révolution de 1848*, ii. 22.   [31] Stern, i. 419.

[32] Odilon Barrot, *Mémoires posthumes* (4 vols.; Paris, 1875), ii. 84.

[33] *Le National*, 11 Mar.; *L'Assemblée nationale*, 15 May; *Le Journal des débats*, 23 Mar.; *La Presse*, 28 May.

foreign policy. The clubs, it seems, were primarily interested in domestic affairs.[34] However, the radical clubs tended to be staunch supporters of the foreign legions which were organized in Paris in March. Blanqui's club was furious about Lamartine's speech to the Irish delegation, and the clubs as a whole seem to have been hostile to Lamartine because he refused to aid the legions.[35] Moreover, the radical clubs favoured positive action on the part of France on behalf of the oppressed peoples of Europe. *La Commune de Paris*, the organ of the clubs, remarked in an article entitled 'the Republic will spread around the world' that it was an inspiring spectacle to see the foreign legions depart to liberate their homelands. The departure of these volunteers was a noble effort to republicanize Europe.[36]

Not only did the radical press support the departing legions, but it also pressed the French government to implement a belli-cose foreign policy. *La Propagande républicaine* encouraged Frenchmen to march to the aid of other peoples, and *La Montagne de la fraternité* exhorted the government to declare 'an eternal war against despotism'. *Le Bon Conseil* admonished the government to smash the treaties that restrained and humiliated France, to regain France's 'natural frontiers', to liberate the peoples of Europe.[37] The leftist, bonapartist *La Liberté* called for war now that the peoples of Europe were ready for it and while their princes were still off their guard; war was necessary, for liberty would sweep the world 'only when pre-ceded by trumpets and followed by squadrons and numerous battalions'.[38] *La Réforme* rejoiced that kings were in flight, but declared that one last war was necessary to republicanize Europe. If Russia became involved, then 'republican France would be happy to fight for the salvation of the world, and leave the sword of war plunged into the heart of the last king'.[39] *Le Père Duchêne, gazette de la révolution* proclaimed that 'the sword of France should shine wherever there is a people to emancipate'. The Republic's role should be to ally herself 'with peoples who gnaw at their chains' and assist them; 'war, the most

---

[34] Suzanne Wassermann, *Les Clubs de Barbès et de Blanqui en 1848* (Paris, 1913), p. 166.   [35] Normanby, *A Year of Revolution*, i. 294, 307.
[36] *La Commune de Paris*, 26 Mar., 1 Apr.
[37] *La Propagande républicaine*, 30 Mar.; *La Montagne de la fraternité*, 5 May; *Le Bon Conseil*, 3–4 Apr.   [38] *La Liberté*, 28 Mar., 6 Apr.
[39] *La Réforme*, 20, 24 Mar.

glorious, the most sublime, the most holy war' should be declared.[40]

As reaction gained strength on the European scene by late spring, radical sheets began to ask why the government did not act to preserve the European revolutionary movements. These dailies often ended up by censuring Lamartine personally for the course that he was setting for French foreign affairs. *Le Bon Conseil* accused Lamartine and his colleagues of having shrunk from their responsibility of liberating Europe, adding: 'Certainly France had the right to expect something different from those chosen on the 24th of February' to govern the Republic.[41] *La Vraie République*, the organ of Pierre Leroux, George Sand, and Barbès, sarcastically remarked that:

We understand that with his diplomatic background the illustrious Minister of Foreign Affairs believed it necessary to humour the susceptibilities of the European aristocracy in his Manifesto; but we feel that it would be treason to the peoples of Europe to remain today in relations of neutrality and indifference [toward the floundering revolutionary movement].[42]

Early in April Raspail's paper, *L'Ami du peuple,* admonished the Republic to march to Poland's assistance and then asked whether the government might not be planning to continue following Louis Philippe's policy of refusing to assist that unfortunate country. Later in the same month Raspail's sheet declared that the Republic should act to aid the Italians rather than 'permit everything' on the part of the victorious reactionary forces; it exclaimed that 'this system of national humiliation is the system of Louis Philippe'.[43] Finally, *La Vraie République* voiced with bitter invective the radical reproach to Lamartine's foreign policy when it remarked that France should die of shame for remaining inactive during the advance of reaction. 'But alas, what can be done? We have chased out the minister of corruption [Guizot] only to install the minister of impotence.'[44] If the radical Parisian press can be taken as representative of radical circles, it seems that the Parisian radicals had become just as disenchanted with the Republic's foreign policy as with its internal policy. In their view the new Republic seemed to have

[40] *Le Père Duchêne, gazette de la révolution,* 4 May.
[41] *Le Bon Conseil,* 30 Mar.
[42] *La Vraie République,* 25 Apr.
[43] *L'Ami du peuple,* 6, 27 Apr.
[44] *La Vraie République,* 20 June.

adopted the defunct July Monarchy's foreign policy of pursuing peace at all costs.

Radical criticism of the Republic's pacific foreign policy was just another aspect of the internal division and instability which rendered the French government insecure, thereby obliging it to be discreet in its relations with Europe. Nevertheless, the favourable diplomatic circumstances which gave the Republic a relatively free hand *vis-à-vis* the Italian peninsula by April encouraged Lamartine to consider waging a limited war on the Italian scene. His objective was twofold: to aid Italy, and at the same time, by making France's diplomatic and military presence felt in the Peninsula, to acquire Nice and Savoy without involving the Republic in a major European conflict. The Parisian radicals were wrong in their judgement of the French foreign minister, for he was not simply continuing Louis Philippe's supposed policy of peace at any price. Lamartine, the former Legitimist, was instead planning to reopen a chapter of traditional French diplomacy by exerting French influence in Italy in the hope of improving France's strategic position.

French historians have often vouched for Lamartine's pure and altruistic intentions toward Italy in 1848. Georges Bourgin, for example, has insisted that Lamartine's dispatch of 21 March to the French Minister of the Navy requesting that a French fleet under Admiral Baudin be sent on a goodwill mission to Italian waters provides ample evidence of Lamartine's friendly and fraternal attitude toward Italy. In this note Lamartine had stressed France's 'profound sympathy' for the Italian cause and had reiterated the altruistic sentiments put forth in his Manifesto.[45] Ferdinand Boyer, a prolific writer on Franco-Italian relations in 1848, is an even more staunch defender of the purity of Lamartine's Italian policy. In a series of articles and later a book Boyer has firmly asserted that the French foreign minister simply wanted to assist Italy to liberate herself without harbouring any selfish or hidden intentions on his own part; and he has quoted numerous dispatches from Lamartine to French agents in Italy which express Lamartine's good intentions toward the Peninsula in an attempt to demonstrate this. Boyer's principal argument is that no French diplomatic document in the early

---

[45] Georges Bourgin made this point in his introduction to Circourt, *Souvenirs d'une mission à Berlin*, i, p. liv.

spring of 1848 makes any direct reference to France's desire for territorial compensation, thus supposedly proving that Italian historians had been 'in grave error' in suspecting the Republic of having designs on Nice and Savoy.[46]

The diplomatic dispatches which Lamartine sent to French agents in Italy seem at first glance to substantiate Boyer's contention. On 29 March Bixio, the French envoy to Turin, wrote that Sardinia had gone to war with an 'audacity' that contrasted with her 'insufficient military means'. When Lamartine received this dispatch, he wrote in the margin: 'Reply that this information seems to conform with our predictions. It is necessary to insist upon the need to complete Sardinia's forward movement now that she has engaged herself; France will not intervene unless Italy calls her.'[47] Shortly thereafter Lamartine assured Brignole, the Sardinian ambassador in Paris, that the formation of the Army of the Alps in no way implied French hostility toward Sardinia, for whom the Republic expressed 'sentiments of sincere friendship'.[48] Finally, on 28 April Bixio reiterated his assurances to Turin that France would not 'intervene in the affairs of the Peninsula until that day when the cause of Italian independence were imperilled and the assistance of our army were invoked'.[49]

Lamartine's diplomatic dispatches seem imbued with benign

---

[46] These contentions are advanced by Ferdinand Boyer in 'Le problème de l'Italie du Nord dans les relations entre la France et l'Autriche, février–juillet, 1848', *Rassegna storica del Risorgimento*, xlii (1955), 206–17; 'Lamartine et le Piémont', *Revue d'histoire diplomatique*, lxiv (1950), 37–57; 'Les entretiens franco-autrichiens de juin 1848', *Revue des travaux de l'Académie des Sciences morales et politiques* (1953), 15–24. Boyer has recently united his findings from these articles in the first section of his recent book, *La Seconde République, Charles-Albert et l'Italie du Nord en 1848* (Paris, 1967). In these works Boyer attempts to refute the arguments of late nineteenth- and early twentieth-century Italian historians, such as Bianchi, Manzone, Barbieri, and Adami, who, rightly it seems, had impugned France's intentions toward Italy in 1848 (Nicomede Bianchi, *Storia documentata della diplomazia in Italia dall'anno 1814 all'anno 1861* (8 vols.; Turin, 1865–72); B. Manzone, 'L'intervento francese in Italia nel 1848', *Rivista storica del Risorgimento*, ii (1897), 553–8; V. Barbieri, 'I tentativi di mediazione anglo-francese durante la guerra del 48', *Rassegna storica del Risorgimento*, xxvi (1939), 683–726; Vittorio Adami, 'Dell' intervento francese in Italia nel 1848', *Nuova Rivista storica*, xii (1928), 136–68).   [47] FAAE, Corr. pol., Turin 321 (29 Mar., Bixio to Lamartine).
[48] Ibid. (12 Apr., Lamartine to Brignole); Sardinia, AST, Lettere Ministri Francia (4 Apr., Brignole to Pareto).
[49] FAAE, Corr. pol., Turin 321 (28 Apr., Bixio to Lamartine).

concern for Italy, but these dispatches alone do not preclude the possibility that Lamartine was 'playing a double game' in his relations with Italy.[50] Lamartine, like Napoleon III, tended to engage in personal diplomacy, and his fondest diplomatic designs were not necessarily outlined in standard diplomatic communications. Accordingly, an examination of Lamartine's foreign policy must be based upon a thorough study of personal memoirs and foreign archival material as well as French diplomatic documents, for the former contain a considerable amount of incriminating evidence as to Lamartine's desire to acquire Nice and Savoy. Moreover, upon close examination even Lamartine's diplomatic correspondence with French agents in Italy is less innocent than his apologists might like to admit.[51]

Charles Albert of Sardinia had gone to war against the Austrian Empire, but as the marginal note on Bixio's dispatch of 29 March indicates, Lamartine was sceptical of Sardinia's chances of success. The Sardinian ambassador in Paris himself noted Lamartine's doubt concerning Sardinia's military capabilities.[52] This doubt, as well as the diplomatic situation in Europe at the time, led Lamartine to consider French intervention in Italy. Early in April he informed Normanby that the Republic had

. . . no desire to interfere in the internal concerns of any other country; but since the late expedition of the King of Sardinia [attacking Austria], it was impossible not to feel that events might occur which it would be difficult for the French Government to view with indifference. If in consequence of any defeat of Charles Albert, he was in difficulties, and Italy likely to be exposed to prolonged warfare on the part of its population against an Austrian army, [Lamartine] should then think it was a case, not for any isolated step on the part of France, but for the intervention of an armed diplomacy; that his first object, if the case arose, would be to consult with [England], and endeavour to come to an understanding with the British Government, and if possible, with Europe, as to a settlement of the Italian question.[53]

[50] Quentin-Bauchart suggested this in his *Lamartine et la politique étrangère de la révolution de février*, p. 279.

[51] Part of the following discussion is drawn from my article, 'Lamartine's Italian Policy in 1848: A Reexamination', and reprinted with the permission of *The Journal of Modern History*.

[52] Sardinia, AST, Lettere Ministri Francia (14 Apr., 1 May, Brignole to Pareto).   [53] Britain, PRO, F.O. 27/806 (7 Apr., Normanby to Palmerston).

Lamartine assured the British ambassador that the Provisional Government would not act alone in intervening in Italy. It seems, though, that he was either not frank or that he soon changed his mind, for on 11 April he sent a dispatch to Bixio inquiring about the possibility of French intervention in Italy. Lamartine wrote:

The developments in Italy trouble us enough to make us think of the eventuality of sending an army corps as observers into Sardinia, with the prior consent of the Sardinian government, or if necessary, by anticipating their request. Do not mention these fears to the government in Turin, but attempt to find out by way of conversation or otherwise indirectly whether in the case of the advance of a French army corps through Savoy the [Sardinian] forts on the road to Maurienne, like Brumont and others, would fire upon us.[54]

In light of this dispatch, it seems that in his conversation of early April with Normanby Lamartine had simply been sounding out Great Britain to see how Her Majesty's Government might react to French intervention in Italy. He had already formulated a concept of French 'armed mediation' which meant that France would come to the aid of a defeated Sardinia and demand territorial compensation from a victorious Sardinia.[55] In early April Sardinia was victorious, but Lamartine already anticipated her eventual defeat. Accordingly, he was envisaging an attempt to exert French influence in Italy and claim his prize of Nice and Savoy either as payment for French assistance or as compensation for Sardinian aggrandizement.

Lamartine's apologists have suggested that his letter of 11 April to Bixio was not bellicose, although they admit that France was fortifying her coasts and that the Army of the Alps had been placed on the alert. Boyer contends that the letter was a mere 'sounding of opinion' which put forth two possibilities for intervention, both of which supposedly required 'the negotiated or tacit consent of the government of Turin'. Upon close examination of the letter, however, it becomes quite clear that Lamartine was considering the possibility of intervening before Sardinia requested such action. Moreover, Boyer's

---

[54] Garnier-Pagès, i. 239–40. Although this incriminating communication can no longer be found in the French diplomatic archives, it has been preserved by Garnier-Pagès, himself a member of the Provisional Government, in his work on 1848.   [55] See above, pp. 40–1.

contention that 'it was not a question of an army of invasion, but of an army of assistance' is not entirely correct, for Lamartine had asked if the Sardinian forts would fire upon French troops.[56] Lamartine was definitely weighing the possibility of intervening in Italy despite Sardinia's apparent opposition to such a move. Furthermore, Lamartine's desire to aggrandize France territorially at Sardinia's expense is also evidenced by the Italian policy which he was to pursue in May and June.

In April Lamartine's plans concerning Italy were frustrated by Sardinia's resolute opposition to French intervention under any circumstances. Sardinia had already displayed considerable antipathy toward France in late March and early April.[57] During April and May Sardinia's victories on the battlefield combined with her government's growing suspicions of French intentions to deepen the estrangement between the two Powers to the point where no co-operation would be possible, even against Austria. Lamartine was prepared to intervene in Italy, but he was not as yet ready to engage in a war against Austria without the concurrence of Sardinia.

In the spring of 1848 it appears that not all of the Italian states were as antagonistic towards France as Sardinia. At the end of March the Provisional Government of Lombardy made an indirect reference to French assistance in an address sent to the French government. However, when the contents of this address were made public, Lombardy was severely reprimanded by the Sardinian and Tuscan governments, which demanded that Milan should immediately retract any reference to French aid. At the same time the Sardinian ambassador in Paris was instructed once again to inform Lamartine that French intervention in Italy was not 'required, or even wished by the Italian governments'.[58]

Sardinia's concern about French intentions was clearly demonstrated by her reaction to Milan's initiative. Bixio warned Lamartine in a dispatch dated 15 April, which has been preserved by Garnier-Pagès, that the advance of a French army into Italy at this time could prove disastrous:

[56] Boyer, *Revue d'histoire diplomatique*, lxiv. 51–2.   [57] See above, pp. 41–3.
[58] Curato, *Le relazioni diplomatiche fra la Gran Bretagna e il Regno di Sardegna*, i. 158–60 (14 Apr., Abercrombie to Palmerston); Garnier-Pagès, i. 223–33; Sardinia, AST, Lettere Ministri Francia (14 Apr., Brignole to Pareto).

The developments in Milan and Savoy and the Austrian retreat before the Sardinian army have given public sentiment a very high degree of confidence and excitement.

French intervention in Italy, without that aid having been requested and in spite of the oft repeated Sardinian protestations, would be regarded by all parties as an act of unworthy disloyalty on the part of France.

There are in Savoy only four thousand soldiers, but the forts are armed and their commanders, alerted by a recent example [the attempt on Chambéry], will defend them with energy. They will be supported by the population, which the constitution, the difference in taxes and a recent success have made anti-French at this time. . . .

French intervention at this time would no doubt be the signal for a general war, and will certainly have on Italy the effect that the surprise of 1808 produced on Spain. The influence and the honour of the Republic are at stake.[59]

Bixio had obviously understood Lamartine's letter of 11 April to be a prelude to armed intervention against Sardinia's wishes. He predicted that such an intervention—especially following the attack on Chambéry by the Savoyard legion—would not be accepted by Sardinia and would result in the general war that Lamartine was not at all prepared to wage.

Sardinia adamantly opposed French military involvement in the Peninsula and this opposition to French intervention was encouraged by English diplomacy. Despite the Anglo-French *entente*, a cardinal principle of English foreign policy in 1848 was to keep France out of Italy. Working in this sense, immediately after the February Revolution in France Great Britain had encouraged Sardinia and Austria to concert their efforts for the common defence of Italy against the Republic. At the same time the British had also tried to discourage Sardinia from attacking Austria.[60] When hostilities did break out Palmerston warned the Sardinians that war with Austria might necessitate French involvement in Italy and a subsequent loss of territory by Sardinia.[61] In April Great Britain went further in her efforts to dissuade Sardinia from appealing to France by guaranteeing the integrity of Sardinian territory proper if the tide of battle

---

[59] Garnier-Pagès, i. 240–1.

[60] See above, p. 4; *Parliamentary Papers*, lvii. 189–90 (20 Mar., Ponsonby to Palmerston); Ashley, 90–1.

[61] See above, pp. 41–2.

were to turn and Austria were to emerge victorious.[62] Sardinia had much to gain and little to lose in her war with Austria over Northern Italy. She had no need to seek French assistance, especially since French involvement in Italy might endanger Sardinian holdings along the French border.

The tenor of other dispatches from Bixio in Turin made it quite clear to Lamartine that French intervention in Italy was not only unwanted but vehemently opposed by the Italians. On 20 April Bixio wrote that:

The essential character of the movement which is agitating Italy, what profoundly distinguishes it from all former movements is that it is before everything else Italian . . . nobody has the idea of substituting France for Austria.

France must realize that if the army of the Republic crosses the Alps without being called here by the events, the interests, and the hearts of Italy, French influence and ideas in Italy will have come to an end in Italy, and this for a long time.

Bixio added, however, that if France were only to wait for an Italian military reversal, French troops would be as welcome in Italy as they were now feared.[63]

Faced with Sardinia's unyielding objection to intervention of any kind, Lamartine decided to demur. In a conversation with Normanby he remarked that if Sardinia were defeated 'there would be a great cry' within France 'for assistance to the Italians' and that France 'might be obliged at least to make a diplomatic demonstration'. Still, Lamartine promised that his government would take no move without England's concurrence. Lamartine finished by proposing to England that some 'sort of a Congress or Conference' be held to settle the Italian question.[64] Lamartine was quite aware that French interests could also be served at a general conference in which Italian boundaries were redrawn.

At the end of April Bixio abruptly changed his attitude toward French intervention in Italy. On 24 April he reported that he suspected England, Austria, and Sardinia to be surreptitiously negotiating an Italian settlement without taking French interests

---

[62] FAAE, Corr. pol., Turin 321 (20 Apr., Bixio to Lamartine); George Sand, *Souvenirs de 1848* (Paris, 1880), p. 303.

[63] FAAE, Corr. pol., Turin 321 (20 Apr., Bixio to Lamartine).

[64] Britain, PRO, F.O. 27/806 (24 Apr., Normanby to Palmerston).

into consideration. Because of the altered diplomatic situation, Bixio insisted that France must quickly decide

between two important possibilities: observation or action. The continuation of the simple role of observer resembles more and more an abdication.

As for action, it can be either military or diplomatic.

Militarily, it would be easy in a few days to have Italy call upon us. A panic in Milan, or the rumour of a treaty will suffice.[65]

Shortly thereafter the French envoy in Turin sent off another dispatch in which he admonished Lamartine either to support Charles Albert and 'immediately demand engagements which attach him in an irrevocable manner to the policies of the French Republic' or to support republican elements in Italy against the Sardinian king and prepare to send a French army to assist them.[66] Bixio was moving towards Lamartine's original position of intervening in Italy to force Sardinia's hand and make French presence felt in the Peninsula.

Lamartine seems to have been deeply moved by Bixio's arguments. Fearing a secret agreement among the Powers, he confronted the British ambassador in Paris with France's demands concerning Italy. On 1 May he informed Normanby that France would not object to a settlement of the Italian question in which Sardinia would acquire Lombardy, 'but that then France might well expect some small compensation in the way of security, if so powerful a neighbour as Sardinia would then become, was established upon her Eastern Frontier within forty miles of Lyons'. Normanby, shocked by the bluntness of the French proposal, denied that England was taking part in any covert negotiations and countered by asking whether Lamartine had already envisaged requesting territorial compensation when he had proposed the calling of a European congress one week earlier. Lamartine's reply was that 'the Treaties of 1815 had left so untenable a position for France on the side of Lyons ... that it could

---

[65] FAAE, Corr. pol., Turin 321 (27 Apr., Bixio to Lamartine). French suspicions about collusion among the Powers seem to have been ill-founded. Austria had sent a delegate, Hartig, to Northern Italy in an attempt to deal directly with the Lombards. England supported Austria's efforts to obtain a peaceful settlement of the Italian question, but there was no attempt by the Powers to bring about a secret armistice agreement. In fact, both Lombardy and Sardinia refused to treat with Hartig, whose mission was a complete failure.   [66] Ibid. (2 May, Bixio to Lamartine).

not be thought unreasonable, if, when the independence of Italy was assured with the free consent of France, she should expect some addition in that quarter which would not amount in all to half a million souls'.[67] Lamartine announced that if Sardinia were defeated France would make only a 'demonstration', then open negotiations, in concert of course with Great Britain. On the other hand, if the Venetian Republic fell to Austria,[68] 'it would be impossible to restrain French feeling on the subject, and an intervention would become inevitable. After the efforts which the Italians had made within the last few weeks no French government could resist the national impulse. [Lamartine] knew what he could attempt and what he could not, and though no one was a more determined advocate of the "status quo" and a more ardent lover of peace, he could not earn the character of the Guizot of the Republic.' Lamartine declared that he had received requests from Venice to intervene on her behalf, and that France would have to act. To Normanby's consternation, Lamartine admitted that, even though French intervention was opposed by the Sardinian king, 'it was [Charles Albert's] frontier he would have to violate'.[69]

Normanby fired off his report to Palmerston, who warned France the following day that the sending 'of a French army into Italy would bring on in all probability that general war in Europe which he himself [Lamartine] as much as Her Majesty's Government would deprecate'.[70] At the same time Palmerston forewarned Sardinia and Austria of France's intentions, encouraging them to come to an agreement over Italy in order to preclude probable French intervention.[71]

[67] Britain, PRO, F.O. 27/807 (1 May, Normanby to Palmerston). French historians, such as Ferdinand Boyer (*La Seconde République, Charles-Albert et l'Italie du Nord en 1848*, pp. 48, 79, 90, 99), argue that no French diplomatic documents for the period of the Provisional Government have as yet been found to prove that Lamartine coveted Nice and Savoy. The British document, however, shows conclusively that Lamartine's interest in Italy went beyond altruism.

[68] Already on 17 Apr. the French consul in Venice had warned that Austrian troops were massing for an attack on the city (FAAE, Corr. pol. des consuls, Venise–Autriche 8, 17 Apr., Limpérani to Lamartine).

[69] Britain, PRO, F.O. 27/807 (1 May, Normanby to Palmerston).

[70] Ibid., F.O. 27/798 (2 May, Palmerston to Normanby).

[71] Curato, *Le relazioni diplomatiche fra la Gran Bretagna e il Regno di Sardegna*, i. 180–1 (8 May, Palmerston to Abercrombie); *Le relazioni diplomatiche fra il Regno di Sardegna e la Gran Bretagna*, p. 131 (12 May, Revel to Pareto).

Faced with opposition from both Britain and Sardinia, Lamartine was not ready to press the soon-to-be disbanded Provisional Government, which was preparing to hand over its powers to the newly elected Constituent Assembly, to intervene in Italy. Already on 3 May he retreated somewhat from his previous position, informing Normanby that if Venice fell 'the French army would then make a demonstration but would not enter Italy', a demonstration which Normanby feared might entail the occupation of Savoy.[72] The French foreign minister was apparently temporarily shelving his plans to intervene in Italy. However, by 19 May a combination of diplomatic developments and internal pressures within France would make Lamartine consider more seriously than ever the possibility of imposing French intervention or armed mediation on Italy. And once again, he would be prepared to demand Nice and Savoy as necessary compensation for France.

In April Lamartine's plans to exert French influence by intervening in Italy were frustrated by British diplomacy and by the steady deterioration in Franco-Sardinian relations. In late April and early May Franco-Prussian relations also took a turn for the worse. Prussia began to espouse a retrogressive policy in Poland and at the same time display aggressive nationalism in Germany's dispute with Denmark. Lamartine realized that his hopes for a liberal Prussia, a revitalized Poland, and a French alliance system embracing the German states were being dashed. Moreover, this alteration in Frederick William IV's policy toward Poznań evoked a virulent protest by the Parisian radicals which caused Lamartine considerable concern by developing into a threat against the French government.

In early April Frederick William IV appeared to be fully implementing his decision to liberate Prussian Poland. This development led the French to believe that they and the Prussians were partners in the holy cause of resuscitating Poland. On 6 April the Prussian Landtag voted for Poznań's exclusion from the German Confederation. The German Diet seemed to concur fully in the Prussian decision to liberate Poznań; a minister of the Diet intimated to the French agent in Frankfurt that Prussian Poland was not an integral part of Germany and that it

---

[72] Britain, PRO, F.O. 27/807 (3 May, Normanby to Palmerston).

would be best for Germany to renounce her claims to Poznań.[73] The French government, confident in Germany's intentions, informed the Polish legion that was about to march off to serve in Poland that the Germans would supply them with arms once they crossed the border and entered Germany.[74] A Parisian newspaper saluted the Poles as they left France, believing that Germany was committed to the liberation of Poland.[75]

It soon became evident, however, that Prussia and Germany were not as sincere in their endeavour to aid Poland as France had assumed. Already on 8 April a French newspaper, *La Réforme*, proclaimed Frederick William IV to be a traitor to Poland; the Polish legion was not being armed after it left France and the number of Prussian troops in the Duchy of Poznań was being augmented.[76] Then matters came to a head in Poland as the German minority there protested against its separation from Prussia. Frederick William's government decided to retain certain enclaves in Posnania in which the population was predominantly German. The Poles resorted to arms to defend their national unity, and Prussian troops went into action against the Poles. The division between Poles and Germans in Poznań was apparent, as was the fact that the Prussians were supporting their fellow Germans in the Duchy.[77] The French chargé d'affaires in Berlin, Circourt, himself unfavourable to the Polish cause, correctly analysed the situation when he remarked on 1 May that a month earlier the German people were well-disposed toward Poland, but that now they displayed only hatred for the Poles.[78]

French relations with both Prussia and the government in Frankfurt were adversely affected by the events in Poland. A French agent in Germany observed that, although France and Germany had been quite close to each other in March, by the beginning of May German sentiment toward France was less friendly. He remarked that republicanism no longer seemed to be important in Germany, that 'one idea dominates in Germany, that of the formation of national unity'.[79] Already in early April

---

[73] FAAE, Corr. pol., Allemagne 805 (26 Mar, Salignac-Fénelon to Lamartine).
[74] Garnier Pagès, vii. 275–7.   [75] *L'Atelier*, 8 Apr.   [76] *La Réforme*, 8 Apr.
[77] FAAE, Corr. pol., Hambourg 149 (18 Apr., Groux to Lamartine).
[78] Circourt, ii. 108.
[79] FAAE, Corr. pol., Bade 84 (10 May, Klein to Lamartine). The German Diet and then the Frankfurt Vorparlament and Parliament were vigorous

the French had taken notice of a remark made by a deputy during the opening session of the Frankfurt Vorparlament to the effect that, because Germany was freeing Poland, France should surrender Alsace-Lorraine.[80] With the turn of events in Poland in May, Lamartine sent a polite but candid protest to Prussia, reminding Frederick William's government that France would 'like to see the Cabinet of Berlin, faithful to its earlier inspirations, listen to the voice of fraternity and justice concerning Poland and Poles . . . and to abstain from rigorous actions like those that it had not feared to order despite its promises'.[81] A much more vehement protest against Prussia's policies in Poland was made by the revolutionary elements in Paris and voiced in the liberal and radical press.

The Parisian press was as aware of the changing tide in Germany and Poland as were French diplomatic agents. In the middle of April Le National remarked that it was 'bothered' by 'Germany's susceptibility' concerning Poland. It also openly admonished 'free Germany' not to resort to violence in its dispute with Denmark.[82] Le Courier français, for its part, denounced the King of Prussia's 'dishonesty' in dealing with Poznań. Another Parisian daily, La Liberté, suggested that a French alliance was indispensable for Germany, but that before France would commit her sons to defending her neighbour against Russia, Germany would have to formally renounce any pretensions to Alsace-Lorraine or the sole possession of the Rhine.[83]

In early May, when reports of Germans massacring Poles began to reach Paris, the Parisian press's criticism of Germany's actions reached its crescendo. La Commune de Paris bluntly declared that France should not allow Italy and Poland to be crushed.[84] At the same time Lamennais in Le Peuple constituant

defenders of the rights of German nationals in both the Polish and Schleswig-Holstein questions. In fact, the pressure of public opinion, as voiced through the Frankfurt government, was instrumental in inducing Prussia to champion the German cause in both of these questions. France's awareness of Frankfurt's stance on these issues caused French disillusionment with the Frankfurt governments and, consequently, resulted in a progressive estrangement between the French Republic and Frankfurt, as well as between France and Prussia.

[80] Garnier-Pagès, ii. 311.
[81] FAAE, Corr. pol., Prusse 302 (7 May, Lamartine to Circourt).
[82] Le National, 16, 20 Apr.
[83] Le Courrier français, 30 Apr.; La Liberté, 10 Apr.
[84] La Commune de Paris, 9 May.

reprimanded the French people for being too preoccupied with their own affairs and forgetting about oppressed nationalities. Then, in an article entitled 'German hypocrisies' he bitterly denounced German ambitions which infringed upon the liberties of other peoples:

War is ravaging at this moment part of Europe. German ambition is at the heart of this combustion. . . . Can Europe consent to such encroaching plans of conquest? She owes it to herself . . . to combat such falseness, such hypocrisy on the part of Germany, which, to satisfy her aggressive inclinations, disguises herself in the North under national sympathies, while there as well as in the East and South, she does nothing other than to ride roughshod over the Danish, Polish, and Italian nationalities.[85]

La Liberté and *L'Atelier* adopted a bellicose attitude toward Germany, declaring that the French Army of the North should march to save Poland from reaction; France should aid Poland in spite of Germany. *La Commune de Paris* published a decree by the Club des amis du peuple calling for an ultimatum to Prussia over Poland.[86]

Part of the radical vitriol was reserved for Lamartine personally. Raspail's paper proclaimed that Lamartine would have to answer to posterity for his policy of cowardliness in not aiding Poland.[87] *La Réforme* attacked him for having acted in such a manner as to preserve the kings on their thrones and the aristocracy of Europe in its privileges. *La Vraie République* encouraged Lamartine's government to adopt the policies of 1792 and not to continue looking on the struggle of peoples with indifference.[88]

Lamartine strove to ward off criticism of his foreign policy with a speech delivered before the Assembly on 8 May in which he eloquently defended his actions. He proclaimed once again that the French Revolution of 1848 was one 'of ideas' and not 'of territory'. He argued that the Republic's 'attitude of disinterested devotion to the democratic principle of Europe combined with respect for the material inviolability of territories, nationalities, and governments' had brought about a profound transformation in Europe, having encouraged revolutionary movements

---

[85] *Le Peuple constituant*, 3, 8 May.
[86] *La Liberté*, 13 May; *L'Atelier*, 7 May; *La Commune de Paris*, 11 May.
[87] *L'Ami du peuple*, 4 May.
[88] *La Réforme*, 11 May; *La Vraie République*, 9 May.

throughout the continent. Lamartine exalted that without a single battle 'France, instead of marching at the head of 36 million people was already marching at the head of 88 million confederated and friendly peoples, including in its system of allies Switzerland, Italy, and the emancipated peoples of Germany!'[89]

The French foreign minister was obviously exaggerating French diplomatic accomplishments. His critics called him to task. Raspail countered Lamartine's optimistic assessment of France's diplomatic achievements with his own appraisal of French foreign policy: Lamartine had dissolved the foreign legions, kept the Army of the Alps out of Italy, and turned his back on Poland. In a word, Lamartine had adopted the policies of Louis Philippe.[90] *La Réforme* attacked Lamartine's basic premise that the French Republic's peaceful dispositions had advanced the revolutionary cause; Lamartine could speak of the victories of France's pacific foreign policy, but he neglected to mention that reaction was well under way across Europe. After a similar speech by Lamartine before the Assembly on 23 May, *La Réforme* scornfully remarked that Lamartine should have espoused the revolutionary cause throughout Europe instead of simply reading diplomatic dispatches before the Assembly in an attempt to demonstrate his good intentions.[91]

Perhaps the radical press was over-harsh with Lamartine. Still, there is no doubt that he had misrepresented the Republic's true diplomatic position in his discourse of 8 May. Switzerland had long previously spurned a French alliance, while France's relations with Italy were embittered and those with Germany estranged. Lamartine's desire to exert French influence in Italy and to re-establish Poland through co-operation with Prussia was also frustrated, and he was definitely indulging in polemics when he declared before the Assembly that his foreign policy had been a remarkable success. Lamartine had managed to preserve the peace, but even this was more the result of Italian opposition to his projects and of complications caused by French internal difficulties than of any deliberate decision on his part.

[89] *Le Moniteur universel*, 9 May.
[90] *L'Ami du peuple*, 11 May.
[91] *La Réforme*, 9, 24 May.

V

DENOUEMENT OF LAMARTINE'S ITALIAN POLICY

In March and April domestic politics had frequently curtailed Lamartine's freedom of diplomatic action or preoccupied him to the point where he was obliged to relegate his diplomatic duties to a secondary position. In May pressures on the French internal scene were about to erupt once again into another of the spring 'days' of 1848. By mid May the internal grievances of the Parisian radicals would merge with their dissatisfaction on foreign policy issues, threatening to topple the moderate Republic and replace it with a revolutionary government which might perhaps have been willing to institute a Committee of Public Safety and proclaim a war against kings.

In early May radical elements within Paris were angered by their defeat in the streets on 16 April and embittered by their setback at the polls during the general elections of 23 April. The elections had been a catastrophe for the radicals. The newly elected French National Constituent Assembly was dominated by moderate republicans and monarchists in republican guise.[1] Moreover, the five-man Executive Commission which was chosen by the Assembly in early May to exercise the executive powers in place of the Provisional Government was controlled by moderate republicans. To be sure, Ledru-Rollin joined Arago, Garnier-Pagès, Marie, and Lamartine as a member of the executive council, but he had little influence upon his more conservative colleagues. As Louis Blanc aptly remarked, the election of the Executive Commission amounted to a continuation of the

---

[1] The most satisfactory studies of the elections of 23 Apr. have been made by George W. Fasel, 'The French Election of April 23, 1848: Suggestions for a Revision', *French Historical Studies*, v (1968), 285–98; Frederick A. de Luna, *The French Republic under Cavaignac* (Princeton, 1969), pp. 100–7; A. Chaboseau, 'Les constituants de 1848', *La Révolution de 1848*, vii (1910), 287–305, 413–25; viii (1911), 67–80.

Provisional Government with the exclusion of its socialist and more radical members.[2]

Radical discontent with the political situation in France was clearly expressed by the leftist Parisian press. *Le Représentant du peuple* declared that 'universal suffrage has lied to the people'; civil war now seemed inevitable. *La Vraie République* warned that 'if the Constitution deceives the people, the sovereign people will again climb upon its throne of paving stones'.[3] At the same time the radical press was savagely attacking the government's foreign policy, demanding that France should undertake a crusade to save Poland. The Parisian radicals had little reason to rejoice at the situation which prevailed in France and Europe, for reaction seemed to be gaining ground on both the European and domestic scene. They decided to strike out in desperation at their seemingly universal foe. The Polish question provided the occasion for them to act.

With reaction under way in Poznań, the radical Parisian clubs, heeding pleas for support issued by Polish refugee groups within the French capital, fully espoused the Polish cause. Certain French radical elements also seem to have envisaged using the Polish cause as a means of challenging and exerting pressure upon the new moderate government.[4] Already on 13 May clubbists staged a demonstration which advanced toward the National Assembly, shouting support for the Poles. Then, on 15 May, a day on which the Polish question was scheduled for debate in the Assembly, a massive crowd, advancing to the cry of 'long live Poland', marched on the Assembly, broke through the cordon of troops protecting the Palais Bourbon, and invaded the legislative chambers. Amid the confusion within the Palais Bourbon a clubbist leader, Huber, declared the Assembly dissolved; and, subsequently, a new provisional government was set up by clubbist leaders at the Hôtel de Ville. The entire episode ended in fiasco when the National Guard chased the mob from the chambers and then advanced upon the Hôtel de Ville to seize the radicals who had attempted to institute a revolutionary

---

[2] Blanc, ii. 71.

[3] *Le Représentant du peuple*, 4 May; *La Vraie République*, 6 May.

[4] For a detailed account of 15 May see the recent article by Peter Amann ('A "Journée" in the Making: May 15, 1848', *The Journal of Modern History*, xxxxii [1970], 42–70), as well as the standard works by Garnier-Pagès (ix. 54–341) and Stern (ii 241–86).

government there. Once again the outnumbered Parisian radicals suffered a substantial setback at the hands of the forces of order, and conservatives could rejoice that the moderate Republic, and the social order, had been preserved.

The 'day' of 15 May was a resounding victory for the government as well as for the moderate and conservative elements in France. Nevertheless, this triumph did not resolve the difficulties which the Executive Commission faced. On the one hand, the radicals' defeat had only deepened the rift between the conflicting factions within France, and class animosities were increased to the point where civil war now seemed to loom as a distinct possibility in the not too distant future. On the other hand, the immediate threat from the left had been diminished, but now the government was more vulnerable to attacks from its enemies to the right. And the monarchists and ultra-conservatives were becoming increasingly vociferous in their criticism of the Executive Commission.

The five members of the Executive Commission had been elected to their positions by the solemn vote of the Constituent Assembly. However, by 20 May it was evident that many of the ultra-conservative members of the Assembly regretted their decision and had second thoughts about the desirability of conferring the reins of government on the remnants of the Provisional Government. The composition of the Executive Commission was not conservative enough to satisfy many members of the Assembly. Monarchist and conservative deputies intimated that they lacked confidence in their government, that the Executive Commission did not provide the leadership that France needed during such trying times.[5] The events of 15 May had served not to remove the pressure upon the Executive Commission, but only to change the direction from which it came.

Lamartine was especially sensitive to the demands of both left and right, for he saw his ideal of reconciling different factions in a united front to preserve the Republic being shattered. The nation seemed to be sliding steadily toward the abyss of civil war. In view of the radicals' defeat on 15 May which rendered them temporarily incapable of gaining the ascendency in France, Lamartine seems to have overcome his fear of war leading to an

[5] Garnier-Pagès, ix. 77–8, 321; Stern, ii. 286–7; Lamartine, *Histoire de la révolution de 1848*, ii. 457–8; *Le National*, 17 May; *Le Constitutionnel*, 17 May.

internal reign of terror. In a dramatic meeting in council of the five man Executive Commission on 19 May he boldly proposed that the French Republic should go to war in Italy as a diversionary measure which he hoped would serve to unite all of France behind its government. With the government under monarchist pressure and faced with a possible civil war, Lamartine once again decided to sacrifice foreign policy considerations to internal necessity.

Lamartine was no longer foreign minister under the Executive Commission, but as a member of the Commission he retained considerable influence over foreign policy. In fact, it seems that Lamartine, and not his successor in the Ministry, Bastide, dominated the conduct of French foreign affairs until the June Days.[6] Therefore, his proposals in council on 19 May had the weight of an important policy decision. The former foreign minister was well aware of the evolution of events in Italy: the Austrians were gaining strength, the Pope and the King of Naples seemed to have abandoned the Italian cause. On the other hand France was ready to act, for the government had had no difficulty in financing the expansion of the Army of the Alps to 60,000 men. Furthermore, Lamartine realized that a sizable contingent of deputies in the Assembly was not averse to war.[7] The proposal that Lamartine put forth was clear and precise. He suggested to his colleagues that:

The moment has come to give the Army of the Alps the order to advance. It is necessary to save Italy and give security to France by a patriotic diversion offered to hostile passions. To prevent Italy from falling once again under the dreaded yoke of the Hapsburgs, and to prevent the Republic from expiring by being torn up in a fratricidal struggle, the Executive Commission should take the vigorous initiative by giving the generals the order to cross the Alps, then, the act accomplished, present itself before the National Assembly and request of her either a bill of indemnity or an act of impeachment. The Executive Commission would rise or fall nobly.[8]

Lamartine believed that France's entrance into the Italian war at this time could serve to aid Italy, gain Nice and Savoy for

[6] Circourt, ii. 63-4.
[7] François-Saturin-Léonide Babaud-Laribière, *Histoire de l'Assemblée nationale constituante* (2 vols.; Paris, 1850), i. 23-4.
[8] Garnier-Pagès, x. 6.

France, and act as a panacea to cure France's internal ills. A war in Italy would answer those deputies who charged the Executive Commission with indecision and either enhance the government's position or bring about its noble demise. Lamartine might have claimed that he would not consider taking France to war even as a diversionary measure, but his acts in secret council on 19 May contradicted this. Once again he not only contemplated but actually planned going to war.

Lamartine was not alone in contemplating the possibility of going to war as a diversionary measure in the spring of 1848. In March the socialist theoretician Proudhon predicted that 'they would go to war to keep 50,000 workers occupied'.[9] Odilon Barrot, a former leader of the left opposition under the July Monarchy, held that in 1848 war could have been an 'all powerful diversion' to alleviate 'interior dangers, dangers which became more and more menacing every day'.[10] Garnier-Pagès believed that war would have improved France's internal situation, providing a diversion which would make France easier to govern. War could solve the problem of the National Workshops by sending men 'from misery to glory'.[11] Then, on 15 May, the Parisian daily *La Liberté* suggested 'that a foreign war for the holy cause of peoples was alone capable of holding in check internal dissension'. *La Gazette de France* and Alfred de Nettement's *L'Opinion publique* also noted that war rumours were spreading; and *L'Opinion publique* expressed its fears that the government would seek 'to escape the internal dangers which menace it' by engaging in 'the hazards of a European struggle'.[12] The members of the Executive Commission were probably not taken aback by Lamartine's proposal, for the course of action which he proposed was not a novel one.

The diplomatic situation prevailing in Europe in May discouraged the Executive Commission from adopting the course of action suggested by Lamartine. Europe seemed to sense that French intervention in Italy was imminent. Austria dreaded French intervention and tried to obviate this possibility by informing the Republic that she would defend herself if attacked,

---

[9] Quoted by Charles Moulin, *1848: le livre du centenaire* (Paris, 1948), p. 326.
[10] Barrot, ii. 85.
[11] Garnier-Pagès, i. 254–5.
[12] *La Liberté*, 15 May; *La Gazette de France*, 15 May; *L'Opinion publique*, 15 May.

requesting the assistance of all of Germany if necessary.[13] Great Britain was as concerned as Austria, and in early May Normanby was convinced that French public opinion was persuading Lamartine to intervene in Italy despite the opposition of Sardinia to such a move. Normanby bemoaned the fact that Lamartine did not seem to be 'fully alive to the impropriety of forcing assistance where it is not sought, and attacking those who are only defending their own rights, merely for the sake of satisfying a discontented army and an impetuous people'.[14] On the eve of the demonstration of 15 May Normanby suspected that France was about to invade Italy and take possession of Savoy as a diversionary measure to satisfy the French populace.[15] A day before the secret council meeting of the Executive Commission on 19 May, he prophetically remarked that, in light of the internal difficulties facing the French government, 'many think it not unlikely that the official representatives of the young Republic may fancy they would find a sort of impunity and protection in a foreign war'.[16] Fearing a French invasion of Italy to be forthcoming, the British government encouraged both Sardinia and Austria speedily to settle the Italian problem themselves.[17]

The Sardinians needed little encouragement to be suspicious of their powerful neighbour on the borders of Savoy. In April the Sardinian ambassador in Paris surmised that the French government under Lamartine 'was somewhat taking umbrage at the progress of the King's [King of Sardinia's] army in Italy and of the probable future [territorial] growth of our Monarchy'. Then, after Bastide had replaced Lamartine as foreign minister, Brignole remarked that Bastide also seemed to be 'not at all favourable' to the 'probable future growth of the Sardinian monarchy in Italy'.[18] Sardinia's anxiety concerning France was intensified when General Oudinot, the French commander of the Army of the Alps, addressed his men on 28 April and suggested that they might soon be called upon to descend into Italy.[19] Oudinot's proclamation brought a repudiation of French assistance by the

---

[13] FAAE, Corr. pol., Autriche 435 (8 May, Delacour to Lamartine; 12 May, Delacour to Bastide).

[14] Britain, PRO, F.O. 27/807 (5 May, Normanby to Palmerston).

[15] Ibid., F.O. 27/808 (14 May, Normanby to Palmerston).

[16] Ibid. (18 May, Normanby to Palmerston).   [17] See above, p. 90.

[18] Sardinia, AST, Lettere Ministri Francia, 6 Apr., 20 May, Brignole to Pareto).   [19] Le Moniteur universel, 2 May.

Milanese and Genoese press.[20] The French special envoy to Turin, Bixio, reported that 'General Oudinot's proclamation to the Army of the Alps produced a very distressing impression here. This impression bears witness once again to the fact that the day when the French appear in Italy without having been called there, they [the French] should count only upon themselves.'[21]

By May the Sardinian government had become extremely concerned about the possibility of French intervention beyond the Alps. On 1 May, when Lamartine was actively considering the possibility of intervening in Italy, Brignole seemed to sense what was in the air. He noted that France's belief in Sardinia's military weakness might bring the Republic to declare war on Austria if Sardinia were to suffer a severe defeat. In that case, he believed, France would send an army across Sardinian territory, even if she were not requested to intervene by the Turin government.[22] Brignole's suspicions to this effect seem to have been confirmed on 2 May when Normanby informed him of Lamartine's remarks on the previous day to the effect that France would have to go to war if Venice were to fall to Austria. Brignole was now convinced that 'if the Italian cause were to experience a reversal, the French government would not hesitate to engage actively in the quarrel, and I can give no guarantee that, despite the assurances that were made to me to the contrary, this government would not, under the pretext of coming to our aid, ignore the respect due to our independence and, generally speaking, to the principle of non-intervention'.[23] An apprehensive Sardinian government once again asked France for assurances that she would not intervene in Italy unless requested to do so by Turin; and Lamartine once again replied with the necessary verbal pledges.[24]

Brignole's dispatches of early May seem to have reinforced Sardinia's determination to defer from calling upon French armed assistance under any circumstances. On 12 May Charles Albert's foreign minister announced to the Sardinian Chamber, which was becoming increasingly uneasy about France's designs

[20] *Le Siècle*, 23 May.
[21] FAAE, Corr. pol., Turin 321 (10 May, Bixio to Lamartine).
[22] Sardinia, AST, Lettere Ministri Francia (1 May, Brignole to Pareto).
[23] Ibid. (2 May, Brignole to Pareto).   [24] Ibid. (6 May, Brignole to Pareto).

upon Italian territory, that Savoy was safe, for 'the French army will not enter Italy unless we call it, and because we will not call it, it will not enter'.[25] Charles Albert's government had obviously been somewhat reassured by Lamartine's verbal pledge to Brignole in early May. Still, Bixio could write on 15 May that Sardinia 'has come to fear the French Republic and the soldiers of the Army of the Alps as much as the armies of Austria'.[26] As far as the Sardinians were concerned, French intervention was as unwelcome in May as it had been in April.

The Executive Commission realized that if France were to intervene in Italy against Turin's wishes French troops might have to enter into action against both Sardinian and Austrian forces. In their secret sessions of 19–20 May members of the governing council argued against Lamartine's proposal to intervene in Italy, insisting that Europe was revolutionizing itself and that French military action would only interfere with this process. The question posed by members of the council was whether France had the right to save Italy in spite of herself.[27] As the sessions progressed each member of the Executive Commission elaborated in great detail upon his particular point of view concerning Italy:

According to Ledru-Rollin the Republic owed its support to Italy and not to the King of Sardinia. . . . A Republic should defend peoples and not serve to raise up a king. Ledru-Rollin inclined toward the idea of having the Army of the Alps cross the frontier before it had been called upon to deliver Italy, but with great reservations concerning the Sardinian King.

Arago and Marie were revolted at the idea of penetrating into Italy before having been called there. . . . What orders should be given to the soldiers? If they were opposed with a semblance of resistance, should they fire on the Italians while they were supposedly going to the Italians' aid? . . .

Garnier-Pagès was struck by the grandeur of these latter arguments. He yielded to them, while at the same time affirming the necessity of having the army quickly cross the Alps in the interest of the Republic, Italy, and the peoples of Europe. The Republic had an excess of life and strength which had to be spilled on the exterior if it were not to devour her on the interior. They would soon be

---

[25] *Parliamentary Papers*, lvii. 459. Quoted from the *Gazzetta piemontese* of 13 May.   [26] FAAE, Corr. pol., Turin 321 (15 May, Bixio to Bastide).
[27] Garnier-Pagès, x. 7–8.

obliged to choose between a glorious war on the plains of Lombardy or a bloody and baneful internal struggle. Blood spilled to liberate Italy would affirm the Republic, while blood spilled in a civil war would weaken it.

Lamartine . . . as a statesman, had to foresee the results of the formation of a strong kingdom [in Northern Italy], allying itself later on with Austria against France, in control of all the passes of the Alps, the doors of France, as a result of the treaties of the second invasion [1815], and freeing them to enemy armies overflowing into France. It was therefore impossible to consent to the concentration of several Italian states, without claiming back what had even been left to us by the first treaties of 1814, a line of frontiers which would be defensive, not offensive, for the two nations, which would assure to each, by loyally established boundaries, complete security.[28]

Lamartine, for his part, was certain that France was justified in requesting such indemnities and that this request could not be refused by a people which France would have liberated in the process of her intervention. Later on in the summer Lamartine would justify his Italian policy in the Foreign Affairs Committee of the Constituent Assembly as a farsighted policy by which the Republic could have gained Nice and Savoy as compensation for French recognition of a Kingdom of North Italy.[29] However, in light of the repugnance which Sardinia was displaying toward France the other members of the five-man council disagreed with Lamartine's arguments, and even Lamartine finally conceded that the time had not yet come to intervene. It was decided to wait with intervention until Italy requested it after her probable defeat at the hands of Austria.[30] As a token of France's readiness to intervene upon Italy's call the Executive Commission did unanimously support Lamartine's plan to mobilize 300 battalions of the National Guard, bringing the Republic's armed forces to a total of 832,000 men.[31]

His plan for intervention in Italy having been disapproved of by his colleagues in the Executive Commission, Lamartine made a speech in the Assembly on 23 May in which he affirmed that the Republic would not intervene in Italy unless the Italians requested such assistance. The Assembly, for its part, passed a moderate-inspired resolution on the following day, calling for 'the independence of Italy' and thus putting on record the Repub-

[28] Garnier-Pagès, i. 440–3.   [29] See above, p. 41.
[30] Garnier-Pagès, x. 9.   [31] Ibid. i. 438; x. 9.

lic's long-publicized sympathy for the Italian cause.[32] The British ambassador in Paris felt reassured after these developments, for the Assembly's resolution did not reveal 'a warlike attitude' and indicated instead that France had committed herself to simple 'diplomatic exertions' in favour of Italy and Poland.[33] The Sardinian ambassador in Paris, whose government was even more directly involved in the question, was equally reassured, and probably considerably relieved by the French Assembly's proceedings.[34]

Lamartine had proposed a concrete plan of action to intervene in Italy, aid the Italian liberation movement, and acquire Nice and Savoy in the process, only to have his project blocked by the opposition of his colleagues. Still, Lamartine's entire Italian strategy in the spring of 1848 did not reflect poorly upon his abilities as a diplomat. Everything points to the fact that during his tenure as foreign minister Lamartine was not the naïve poet-diplomat that he is sometimes thought to be.[35] Nor was he the pure, republican diplomat who would not think of violating Italy and who had only the best of intentions concerning the Peninsula. To the contrary, Lamartine was a quite capable, traditionalist-minded diplomat who was concerned with further-ing French national interests and improving France's strategic position *vis-à-vis* Italy. In fact, Lamartine anticipated the course of action for the liberation of Italy from Austrian rule which Napoleon III and Cavour would put into effect some ten years later. It is tempting to conjecture that perhaps Northern Italy could have been freed from Austrian domination already in the spring of 1848 if Charles Albert had been a Cavour.

---

[32] *Le Moniteur universel*, 24, 25 May. The Assembly's resolution of 24 May also called for a 'fraternal pact with Germany' and 'the reconstruction of an independent and free Poland'.

[33] Britain, PRO, F.O. 27/808 (27 May, Normanby to Palmerston).

[34] Sardinia, AST, Lettere Ministri Francia (24 May, Brignole to Pareto).

[35] In his literary biography written some sixty years ago René Doumic referred to Lamartine as 'the René of politics' (René Doumic, *Lamartine* (Paris, 1912), p. 91). The coining of this phrase by Doumic reinforced a certain popular tradition which has tended to portray Lamartine as a romantic dreamer, and, thus, as an incompetent diplomat. This unjustifiable characterization of Lamartine as an inept, poet-diplomat has been refuted by most serious historians. Still, the myth seems to have survived. See, for example, the recent, largely hypothetical and unconvincing study by James Garvin Chastain ('French "Kleindeutsch" Policy in 1848', Ph.D. dissertation, University of Oklahoma, 1967).

It was at the end of May that the pre-Napoleonic Second French Republic came nearest to going to war. From this time on French foreign policy would turn away from the possibility of intervention and move toward a policy of negotiation and mediation in Italy. Faced with increasing internal difficulties as well as with the determined opposition of Sardinia, from **May onwards** the French Republic would try to assert its influence in Italy via the conference table. Nevertheless, until the June Days and the fall of the Executive Commission French aims did not basically change. Lamartine also wished to be able to gain Nice and Savoy as territorial compensation for successful French mediation in which Sardinia would be aggrandized.

Attempts by France to settle the Austro-Sardinian war by negotiation or mediation had been made as early as one week after the outbreak of the conflict. On 1 April the French agent in Vienna offered Austria the good offices of the French government as mediator if the occasion should arise in which mediation would be desirable.[36] The French, it seems, proposed to Austria a 'project for settling affairs in Lombardy by some pecuniary transaction, as an indemnity to the Austrians for giving up the country'.[37] The Austrians, however, were suspicious of French intentions and preferred to deal directly with Sardinia, using the good offices of Great Britain to facilitate this.[38] On 5 April Fiquelmont, Austrian foreign minister succeeding Metternich, requested England to assist in arranging direct Austro-Sardinian negotiations. Palmerston responded two weeks later by recommending that Charles Albert should order a cease-fire so that an Austrian delegation to Italy could make its peace proposals. Nevertheless, the victorious Sardinian government refused to negotiate with Vienna as long as a single Austrian soldier remained on Italian soil.[39] The war continued in Northern Italy with the Sardinians on the offensive and the Austrians withdrawing to their strongholds of the famous Quadrilateral, the fortresses of Mantua, Verona, Peschiera, and Legnano.

[36] FAAE, Corr. pol., Autriche 435 (1 Apr., Delacour to Lamartine).
[37] *Parliamentary Papers*, lvii. 290–1 (2 Apr., Ponsonby to Palmerston).
[38] FAAE, Corr. pol., Autriche 435 (8 Apr., Delacour to Lamartine).
[39] Sand, 303 (5 Apr., Ficquelmont to Dietrichstein); Ashley, 101–3 (21 Apr., Palmerston to Ponsonby); FAAE, Corr. pol., Turin 321 (2 May, Bixio to Lamartine).

Given the estranged state of Franco-Austrian relations after the February Revolution, it is quite understandable that Austria should have refused France's mediation proposal of early April. On 8 March Lamartine had openly avowed to Apponyi that his government was sympathetic to the oppressed peoples of Italy— in other words, to the Italians who lived under the yoke of Austrian rule in the provinces of Lombardy and Venetia—and had intimated that France would assist the Italians in any war against Austria.[40] Although France had not carried out her threat to join the Italians against the Austrians when war broke out between Sardinia and Austria in late March, in April Vienna still had good reason to believe both that France supported the Italian cause and that the Republic might intervene on Sardinia's behalf. In early April, Thom, who had replaced Apponyi as the Austrian representative in Paris, felt convinced that one of the primary aims of French foreign policy was the expulsion of Austria from Italy.[41] In April Austria, like its antagonist Sardinia, was deeply concerned about the formation of the French Army of the Alps, for it was obvious that this army was intended for use in Italy against Austrian forces. Thom was so suspicious of France's intentions toward Italy at this time that he placed little faith in the assurances which Lamartine gave the papal nuncio in Paris about the Republic's desire not to become involved in the Austro-Italian conflict.[42]

As Austria's military and diplomatic fortunes worsened in late April and early May, however, the Austrian government became more amenable to the possibility of accepting French mediation. By early May the Austrian military situation appeared so bleak everywhere except on the Venetian front that Austria seemed prepared to compromise on the Italian issue in the hope of extricating herself from an unsuccessful war with as little loss of territory and face as possible.[43] Then, too, by late April it had become obvious that England's diplomatic efforts had failed to persuade the Italians to treat directly with Vienna. Faced with military defeat and no viable diplomatic alternative, the Austrian government decided to approach France about the

[40] See above, p. 28.
[41] Austria, HHS, Frankreich Korr. Kart. 337 (6 Apr., Thom to Ficquelmont).
[42] Ibid. (9, 26 Apr., Thom to Ficquelmont).
[43] FAAE, Corr. pol., Autriche 435 (2 May, Delacour to Lamartine).

possibility of employing her good offices to work for an Italian settlement. It seems that on 1 May, when Apponyi took leave of Lamartine before returning to Vienna, the Austrian ambassador inquired whether the French government might work for a settlement in which Lombardy's fate would be open to negotiation.[44]

Vienna was now prepared to accept the mediation offer which Delacour, the French chargé d'affaires in Vienna, had made to no avail one month earlier. But now it was France that demurred. For one thing, Lamartine knew that Austria's proposal concerning Lombardy fell far short of what a victorious Sardinia would be willing to accept. More important yet, Lamartine was aware of the fact that in early May French public opinion was unlikely to accept the sort of settlement which Austria hoped France would facilitate. At this time French public opinion was already highly critical of the Republic's Polish policy; and public pressures made it impossible for Lamartine to engage in negotiations with the arch enemy of revolution, Austria.[45] Indeed, at this time Lamartine was considering intervening in Italy on Sardinia's behalf.[46]

Lamartine had felt obliged to decline Vienna's overtures for mediation in early May because of internal policy considerations, but when events in mid May brought a decrease in radical strength as well as the defeat of Lamartine's project to intervene in Italy, the French Republic could wholeheartedly espouse the role of a mediator, discarding entirely its proclivities for intervention. Less than a week after the secret council meeting of the Executive Commission on Italy, the French chargé d'affaires in Vienna offered His Majesty the Emperor's government the Republic's good offices to end the war in Italy. The French made it quite clear that their mediation proposal was based upon the condition that Austria must entirely evacuate Italy, freeing both Lombardy and Venetia.[47] This offer had little appeal to Austria, however, for her military position *vis-à-vis* Venice was steadily improving and she now had no desire to divest herself of her prize Italian possession. Austria preferred once again to try to deal with Great Britain.

---

[44] Britain, PRO, F.O. 27/807 (3 May, Normanby to Palmerston).
[45] Ibid.   [46] See above, pp. 89–90.
[47] FAAE, Corr. pol., Autriche 435 (25 May, Delacour to Bastide).

On 23 May the Austrian Baron Hummelauer, who had been sent to London on a special diplomatic mission, made his first peace proposal to Palmerston. Austria informed the British that she was willing to grant 'separate and entirely national institutions' to Lombardy and Venice while keeping these areas within the Empire. Hummelauer added—as if to intimidate Britain to act on Austria's behalf—that were France to intervene in Italy, Austria 'would not accept battle' but would withdraw behind her Alps, leaving Northern Italy in France's hands and thus disturbing the continental balance of power. Palmerston, though, flatly refused to be associated with negotiations on these grounds, and Hummelauer replied with his second memorandum concerning peace terms the following day. In his memorandum of 24 May Hummelauer announced that Austria was prepared to give Lombardy, but not Venice, complete independence.[48] Once again Palmerston declined Hummelauer's proposal as a basis for negotiations, insinuating that he himself saw the wisdom in such a proposal, but that the British cabinet absolutely refused it as a basis for mediation.[49] It was obvious that at this time Great Britain was not prepared to support any negotiation project which did not call for the liberation of all of Italy from Austrian rule. But this in turn was entirely unacceptable to Austria. Hummelauer remarked that Austria was 'not yet dead' and that Italy would soon see 'signs of effective life' in the Venetian war theatre. Palmerston, for his part, replied that 'Her Majesty's Government would not consent to become involved in a negotiation which, in her opinion, offered no chance of success'.[50]

Throughout June Palmerston let it be known in Vienna that his government refused to be a party to any negotiations which would not result in the complete independence of Lombardy and of at least a part of Venetia. In fact, this seems to have meant that Austria would be called upon to surrender all of Venetia, for Palmerston was well aware that the Italians would not countenance an agreement in which Austria retained any part of

---

[48] *Parliamentary Papers*, lvii. 470–1, 447; Sand, p. 297; Garnier-Pagès, i. 454–5, 457–9; F. Planat de la Faye, ed., *Documents diplomatiques et pièces authentiques laissés par Daniel Manin* (2 vols.; Paris, 1860), i. 237.

[49] A. J. P. Taylor, *The Italian Problem in European Diplomacy, 1847–1849* (Manchester, 1934), pp. 106–7 (29 May, Hummelauer to Lebzeltern).

[50] *Parliamentary Papers*, lvii. 480–1 (26 May, Hummelauer to Palmerston); lvii. 532–3; Planat de la Faye, i. 238–9 (3 June, Palmerston to Hummelauer).

Italian soil.[51] Palmerston firmly believed that Italy was 'Austria's Achilles' heel', and he argued that the Austrian government should take advantage of the present opportunity to remove herself entirely from the Italian scene and retire behind the Alps.[52]

England had been unreceptive to Austria's proposals. Nevertheless, Austria felt compelled at least to affect a willingness to negotiate, for her military position was still precarious and she was under considerable internal pressure to resolve the Italian question. In reality Austria was above all trying to gain time until reinforcements could reach Marshal Radetzky's army in the Quadrilateral and turn the tide of battle in favour of the Empire. Under these circumstances Vienna reconsidered Paris's mediation proposals at the same time as she sought once again to deal directly with Lombardy. Austria was willing to entertain French peace proposals because she hoped that France could persuade Lombardy to accept the second Hummelauer memorandum as a basis for negotiation. Moreover, France was now applying considerable pressure upon Austria to accept her good offices.

On 6 June Bastide wrote to his chargé d'affaires in Vienna, Delacour, instructing him to inform the Austrian government that France was still offering her good offices as mediator between Austria and Italy if Vienna were willing 'to sacrifice what she still retains' in Italy. The French foreign minister suggested that the Republic might be able to arrange 'financial and commercial' concessions in Austria's favour if the Empire were to 'abandon' its Italian provinces, territories which it was bound to lose anyhow.[53] The following day Delacour reported from Vienna that he was trying to cultivate Austrian fear of French intervention in order to bring Austria to the bargaining table.[54] When it became evident that Austria was more interested in dealing directly with Lombardy than in accepting France's offer to facilitate Vienna's abandonment of Northern Italy, Delacour continued to menace Austria with the possibility of French inter-

[51] *Parliamentary Papers*, lvii. 597–8, 623–4 (20, 28 June, Palmerston to Ponsonby); Russell, i. 338 (8 June, Palmerston to Lord Russell).

[52] Ashley, i. 98–9 (15 June, Palmerston to King Leopold of Belgium); Russell, i. 327–8.

[53] FAAE, Corr. pol., Autriche 435 (6 June, Bastide to Delacour).

[54] Ibid. (7 June, Delacour to Bastide).

vention south of the Alps. He warned the Austrian government that if the war were to continue Lombardy 'would not fail to call for French assistance', thus placing France 'in a position where it would be impossible to refuse Lombardy'. France did not wish to go to war, and it was also not in Austria's interest to expand the conflict; therefore, negotiations should be started at once. While the Austrian government seemed determined to retain Venice, Delacour insisted that the aim of eventual negotiations should be the independence of both Lombardy and Venice, for to liberate Lombardy alone 'was doing things only half-way and consequently running the risk of doing nothing'.[55] As of early June France seemed no more willing to abandon the Republic of Venice than was Great Britain.

Although the French Republic had evidently been favourable to the liberation of all of Northern Italy from Austrian domination throughout the spring of 1848, it seems that by mid June France might have been wavering in her insistence that Venice as well as Lombardy should receive complete independence from Austria. It is interesting to note, for instance, that by June Venetian diplomats suddenly began to doubt France's commitment to liberating Venice. The Venetians were especially suspicious of Lamartine whom they feared might be prepared to compromise with Austria by abandoning Venice's cause in exchange for assurances that Austria would grant independence to Lombardy. Throughout the late spring of 1848 the Venetians dreaded the possibility that Lamartine might be ready to accept an Italian settlement similar to Napoleon's Treaty of Campo Formio (1797) by which France handed Venice to Austria. Lamartine might have reassured the Venetians somewhat when he personally guaranteed Venetian diplomats in Paris in mid May that he would never accede to another Campo Formio-like settlement. Still, the consternation of these same diplomats was great when less than two weeks later Lamartine seemed to do an abrupt about-face by suggesting 'that a new Treaty of Campo Formio will perhaps become necessary'.[56] From this time on the Venetians were prepared to expect the worst from Lamartine and from the Republic in which he was still a dominant figure.

[55] Ibid. (13 June, Delacour to Bastide).
[56] Planat de la Faye, i. 212, 214, 262 (27 Apr., 8 May, Zanardini to Manin; 5 June, Aleardi and Gar to Manin); Garnier-Pagès, i. 444.

An examination of the French and Austrian diplomatic records indicates that by the middle of June France had become willing to consider the liberation of only part of Northern Italy from Austrian rule, although this evidence is inconclusive. In mid June Baron Wessenberg, who had just become Austrian foreign minister, sent a dispatch to Paris in which he requested that France should adhere to the second Hummelauer memorandum as a basis for mediation.[57] It seems that Palmerston's refusal to accept the Hummelauer memorandum—with its basic contention that Lombardy be given full independence while Venice only be granted autonomy—had decided the Imperial government to turn once again to France for mediation on this basis. When the Austrian proposal was put to Bastide by Thom on 21 June, the French foreign minister expressed his satisfaction with Austria's willingness to liberate Lombardy, a move which Bastide characterized as being 'wise and moderate' and in Austria's own best interest. But, when Thom tried to sound out Bastide about the French government's reaction to the Venetian clause of the memorandum, that is, the stipulation that Venetia must be retained by Austria, Bastide would in no way commit himself.[58] At the same time the Austrian representatives in both Paris and London asked the British and French governments if they would use their good offices to encourage Lombardy once again to deal directly with Austria.[59] When Bastide replied to this overture by stating that he would bring up his proposal in council, Thom came to the conclusion that the French foreign minister was quite well-disposed toward Austria and that he might not be opposed to Venice remaining under Austrian domination.

The June Days completely preoccupied the French government during the last week of June and Thom did not have the opportunity to speak again to Bastide about either the Hummelauer memorandum or direct negotiations with Lombardy until the very end of the month. By this time any chance of

---

[57] *Parliamentary Papers*, lvii. 596 (12 June, Ponsonby to Palmerston).

[58] Austria, HHS, Frankreich Korr. Kart. 337 (23 June, Thom to Wessenberg).

[59] Ibid.; *Parliamentary Papers*, lvii. 619, 623-4 (16 June, Wessenberg to Dietrichstein); Curato, *Le relazioni diplomatiche fra la Gran Bretagna e il Regno di Sardegna*, i. 237-9 (28 June, Palmerston to Abercrombie); FAAE, Corr. pol., Autriche 435 (15 June, Gabriac to Bastide; 13 June, Delacour to Bastide).

successful mediation had been quashed by Lombardy's absolute refusal to come to a separate agreement with Austria and by the Empire's subsequent decision to launch a new offensive in Italy, a decision which meant that Austria would now try to settle the issue by force of arms rather than by negotiation.[60] Still, Thom had the distinct impression early in July that Bastide was not adverse to Venice remaining under Austrian control. In all of their recent discussions the French foreign minister had displayed 'no trace of jealousy regarding His Majesty the Emperor's determination to force the Venetian provinces to return once again under his domination'.[61] It seems that by June the French government might have been influenced by its growing antipathy to Sardinia to consider accepting a peace settlement in which Venice would remain under Austrian control.

Once again Lamartine's personal writings afford some insight into France's intentions concerning Italy in general and Venice in particular. They indicate that perhaps the Venetian diplomats had been correct after all, that Lamartine at least had been ready to come to an agreement with Austria in which Venice's interests would have been sacrificed. In his work published in 1849 Lamartine wrote:

The Austrian envoys unofficially appealed to [Lamartine] concerning offers that the Emperor's Cabinet was disposed to make to Sardinia. It was a matter of abandoning Lombardy and the Duchies of Parma, of a constitution given to Venice under the independent viceroyalty of a prince of the House of Austria. Lamartine did not hesitate to recognize that these propositions largely satisfied Italy's legitimate ambitions of liberation, and he encouraged the Austrian Cabinet to negotiate on these bases. Twice these semi-official overtures were made to [Lamartine], and twice he spoke in the same sense. He would have been neither a statesman nor a patriot if he had rejected them; for the conclusion of such an arrangement would allow the Republic to rectify one of its frontiers broken after the Hundred Days and the second Treaty of 1815; and he had been thinking of this for a long time.[62]

Besides shedding light upon Lamartine's intentions concerning

[60] Austria, HHS, Frankreich Korr. Kart. 338 (29 June, Wessenberg to Thom).
[61] Ibid., Frankreich Korr. Kart. 337 (1 July, Thom to Wessenberg).
[62] Lamartine, *Histoire de la révolution de 1848*, ii. 282–3; *Œuvres complètes*, xxxix. 248–9. Lamartine was obviously referring to the Austrian overtures of 1 May and 21 June.

Venice, this passage again stresses his deep-seated desire to improve France's strategic position in the Alps. To be sure, there is no doubt that France's desire to mediate a conclusion to the Austro-Sardinian war rested in part upon unselfish motives. On 24 May the Constituent Assembly had passed a resolution calling for a foreign policy based upon 'the liberation of Italy' and the government was now attempting to realize the aim of this directive through negotiations.[63] Moreover, both Lamartine and Bastide had considerable sympathy for the Italians and would have liked to be able to assist this oppressed people liberate itself. Still, in the spring and early summer of 1848 the French government under Lamartine's influence also conceived of negotiations as a means of advancing France's strategic interests.

There is other evidence which corroborates Lamartine's assertions and also suggests that in a diplomatic settlement of the Northern Italian question France hoped to receive Nice and Savoy as compensation for the aggrandizement of Sardinia. Italian sources indicate that when France made her mediation proposal to Austria in late May, Lamartine had asserted that France would request compensation in Savoy if the parts of Northern Italy liberated by Austria were annexed by Sardinia.[64] Then, too, the Italian patriot Mazzini insisted that Bixio's secretary visited him in Milan to try and persuade him to accede to the incorporation of Savoy into France. According to Mazzini, one faction of the Sardinian government had agreed to cede Savoy as compensation for French recognition of a Kingdom of North Italy. Supposedly, this sort of a settlement was so near realization that secret Sardinian maps no longer showed Savoy as belonging to the future Italy.[65]

What is certain is that in the Constituent Assembly on 16 June the French Minister of the Interior, Recurt, proposed the mobilization of 300 battalions of the National Guard, the measure which Lamartine had suggested as early as 20 May. Recurt explained that the primary purpose of this measure was to allow the regular army to be reduced in size and thus to economize on the military budget. He added:

[63] *Le Moniteur universel*, 25 May.
[64] Costa de Beauregard, *Les Dernières Années de Charles-Albert* (Paris, 1890), p. 272.   [65] Sand, pp. 299–300.

Nevertheless, there is another reason which should attract your attention. The Executive Commission maintains the firm hope of preserving the peace. However, France could not possibly look on without precautions to redistributions of territories. She could not tolerate that an increase in power of her neighbours, without compensaton for her, should reduce her own power.[66]

The neighbour that Recurt referred to was obviously Sardinia.

Shortly after Recurt made his speech in the Assembly, *Le Bien public*, a Parisian sheet which the diplomatic community recognized as 'passing for the organ of Monsieur Lamartine', offered the same sort of explanation for the Republic's decision to strengthen the National Guard.[67] *Le Bien public* went even further than Recurt in arguing that France 'could not permit' the King of Sardinia to absorb all of Austria's possessions in Northern Italy, to annex Lombardy and to move to within 'a few steps of Lyons and Toulon' an army which would then number from 100,000 to 200,000 men. The paper proclaimed that if Sardinia were to remake the map of Northern Italy France would have to request diplomatically 'guarantees, indemnities, compensation for this new extension of territories'; and, the article added, 'diplomacy does not speak well to armies in the field unless it has other armies behind it'.[68]

Quite understandably, the Sardinian ambassador in Paris was 'astonished' by Recurt's speech.[69] Already in early June Brignole had come to the conclusion that Lamartine 'coveted' Nice and Savoy and might ask that these provinces be ceded to France in exchange for any assistance which the Republic accorded Italy.[70] Now Recurt's statements seemed to confirm his suspicions. Brignole immediately asked Bastide for an explanation of Recurt's assertions; and the French foreign minister replied by attesting to his government's 'peaceful and friendly dispositions' toward Sardinia and by affirming that France wished no territorial compensation for any services which she might render Italy. Still, Bastide did admit that, once a Kingdom of North Italy had been established, France's 'interests' might require the French

---

[66] *Le Moniteur universel*, 17 June.
[67] Austria, HHS, Frankreich Korr. Kart. 337 (23 June, Thom to Wessenberg).
[68] *Le Bien public*, 20 June.
[69] Sardinia, AST, Lettere Ministri Francia (19 June, Brignole to Pareto).
[70] Ibid (3 June, Brignole to Pareto).

government to ask that Savoy, 'which touches upon [France's] borders, be declared a neutral area'.[71] Brignole seems to have been somewhat reassured by Bastide's professions of friendship, but he could not have been pleased by the French foreign minister's reference to Savoy. It is interesting to note that at this time the Sardinian ambassador seems to have advised Turin to transfer troops from the Austrian front to the French borders if this were militarily possible.[72]

After the publication of Recurt's statement Charles Albert, who was not ready to surrender Savoy, had ample reason to be suspicious of France's objectives regarding Italy. The French consul in Genoa could justly reprimand his government and:

deplore the ministerial discourse which pictured France as being on the verge of receiving territorial aggrandizement in proportion to that of her neighbour. It is a grievous heresy which no French discourse should ever have contained. Sardinia is not aggrandizing itself as a Power, but as a nation reconstituting itself, and the ministerial speech is an anti-republican contradiction of the principle of resurrection so nobly proclaimed by our revolution to the applause of the civilized world. I deem it urgent for the Executive Commission to intervene in order to give back to France her original role of mediator for the holy cause of peoples who are shaking off their fetters. Besides, the government would be committing a grave mistake by publishing in advance, so to say, the conditions of aid which it is disposed to give. The surest way to obtain a lot is to demand nothing but have others make offers. Italy will offer us Savoy, which is a burden to her and whose presence in the Italian League is an anomaly, and if the [French] government refuses it, Italy will then offer the County of Nice, pay the price of the war, and conclude a commercial treaty. Here lies the real interest of France. As for Savoy, it will throw itself into our arms owing to the force of circumstances and we will accept it as a bonus.[73]

When Normanby inquired whether France was now prepared to depart from her professed policy of friendship for Italy and 'ask for compensation from some supposed injury to her material interests', Bastide denied that his government had any set policy concerning the matter, but conceded 'that it was true they might feel, when Piedmont [Sardinia] was no longer a

---

[71] Sardinia, AST, Lettere Ministri Francia (19 June, Brignole to Pareto).
[72] Boyer, *Revue d'histoire moderne et contemporaine*, v. 135.
[73] FAAE, Corr, pol. des consuls, Turin 5, Gênes (24 June, Favre to Bastide).

second-rate Power but had monopolized the greatest part of Italy, that France could hardly view with the same unconcern her entrance into [France's] very centre within forty miles of Lyons'. The French foreign minister admitted that 'he did not think it would have been unreasonable if France had asked for some augmentation to her Frontier on the side of Nice or of Savoy; but he disclaimed any intention of putting such a feeling into the shape of a demand, still less of moving any army to enforce it'.[74] The French Republic was definitely inclined to seek compensation for an enlarged Sardinia; the French foreign minister had openly displayed his distrust of Charles Albert's Kingdom.

In view of France's attitude toward Nice and Savoy the Sardinian government was becoming increasingly determined not to seek French assistance for the liberation of Italy. Already in mid May the Sardinian cabinet had assured the Parliament in Turin that Charles Albert's government would not request French intervention in Italy.[75] Then in early June Brignole had admonished his government not to request either military or diplomatic assistance from France, suggesting that this was the best means of preventing France from claiming Nice and Savoy.[76] Now in late June the disclosure of France's ulterior motives for intervening in Italy seems to have resulted in increased estrangement between the Republic and Sardinia, rendering any future co-operation for the liberation of Italy virtually impossible.

In June the French government's attention shifted once again from the external sphere to the domestic scene. The 'day' of 15 May had strengthened the hand of the moderates and conservatives, but had not destroyed the power of the radicals. Internal pressures built up steadily after 15 May and on 23 June French society was profoundly shaken by civil war, the Parisian June Days. Lamartine's proposal on 19 May to invade Italy as a diversionary measure certainly suggests that already in May internal problems were so great as to eclipse foreign policy considerations. A statement made at that time by Champeaux, Lamartine's private secretary, corroborates this probability. On 22 May Champeaux wrote to the French chargé d'affaires in Berlin and Lamartine's personal friend, Circourt, explaining that

[74] Britain, PRO, F.O. 27/809 (19 June, Normanby to Palmerston).
[75] See above, pp. 102–3.
[76] Sardinia, AST, Lettere Ministri Francia (3 June, Brignole to Pareto).

he would not immediately communicate to Lamartine Circourt's most recent disconcerting dispatch on Poland, for: 'Lamartine has more work concerning the interior than the twenty-four hours of the day allow, and no matter how important the external question might be, that of the interior is one hundred times more so at the moment and does not permit a single moment of distraction.'[77] In a similar manner Bastide wrote to his agent in Copenhagen, concerning the Schleswig-Holstein problem, that 'grave interior complications have not as yet permitted the government of the Republic to consider this question as seriously as it would have liked to'.[78] In late May and throughout June French foreign policy would continue to be severely cramped and restricted by the overwhelming internal problems facing the Executive Commission.

With the increasing polarization of French society in May and June, several perceptive observers foresaw the apparent inevitability of an armed contest between left and right. In late May the Austrian chargé d'affaires in Paris, Thom, informed his government that the threat from the radicals was so great that a clash between this group and the government appeared to be 'inevitable in the near or not too distant future'.[79] Another foreign observer, Prince Albert of England, remarked in a letter written on 9 June that 'France is on the eve of bankruptcy, and of a Parisian massacre'.[80] In early June George Sand confided to de Tocqueville that she foresaw the possibility of civil war and told him: 'Try to persuade your friends, Monsieur, not to force the people into the streets by alarming or irritating them. I also wish that I could instill patience into my own friends; for if it comes to a fight, believe me, you will all perish.'[81] Lamartine intimated that the Executive Commission itself realized that a clash would result if the National Workshops were dissolved.[82]

---

[77] Circourt, ii. 192.

[78] FAAE, Corr. pol., Danemark 211 (7 June, Bastide to Dotézac).

[79] Austria, HHS, Frankreich Korr. Kart. 337 (24 May, Thom to Lebzeltern).

[80] Gooch, p. 102.

[81] Alexis de Tocqueville, *The Recollections of Alexis de Tocqueville* (New York, 1949), p. 149.

[82] Lamartine, *Histoire de la révolution de 1848*, ii. 459. By early June the National Workshops contained some 100,000 idle men. Increasing pressure was exerted upon the government by the propertied classes to dissolve the Workshops in which workers received a daily dole for doing little or no work. The book by McKay affords a detailed study of the National Workshops.

Anticipating the approaching storm, the government began taking precautionary measures shortly after 15 May.

Lamartine claimed that he took the initiative in demanding that military preparations be taken to protect the government against what he perceived to be a growing threat from both the National Workshops and Bonapartism.[83] On 20, 22, and 27 May the Executive Commission began to take an inventory of the military forces at its disposal in Paris; and on 27 May a plan of battle was devised whereby in case of threatening disturbances troops would be concentrated at the place de la Concorde and the Hôtel de Ville.[84] It was decided by the government that more troops were needed in Paris, and in the latter part of May the Minister of War, General Cavaignac, was ordered by the Executive Commission to build up the Paris garrison to a total of 45,000 men.[85] Of the total of 45,000 one-third was to consist of *gardes mobiles* and another 5,000 were to belong to the Republican Guard or the *gardiens de Paris*.[86] But most important of all, 10,000 men were to be called in from the 60,000 man Army of the Alps. Moreover, other elements of the Army of the Alps were dispatched to Lyons to keep order in France's second largest and second most revolutionary city.[87] Once again the army was being used to preserve order within France. The French government was preparing itself to do battle in the streets of Paris rather than on the plains of Northern Italy.

[83] Ibid., ii. 471–2. Large public gatherings on the Boulevards of Paris in late May and early June appeared to be partly inspired by Bonapartist circles. Moreover, Louis Napoleon's election to the Assembly by four different departments in the by-elections of early June also seemed to indicate that the Prince's star was on the rise.   [84] Garnier-Pagès, x. 32.

[85] This and the following was revealed on 25 Nov. 1848 in the course of interpellations of General Cavaignac in the National Assembly concerning his actions during the June Days (*Le Moniteur universel*, 26 Nov.).

[86] *Le Constitutionnel*, 6 June.

[87] Ferdinand Boyer, 'L'armée des Alpes en 1848', *Revue historique*, ccxxxiii (1965), 87.

VI

FRENCH DIPLOMACY FOLLOWING
THE JUNE DAYS

On 24 June the Austrian chargé d'affaires in Paris began his dispatch to Vienna thus: 'There was never any doubt that the dissolution of the National Workshops would be a moment of crisis for the tranquillity of Paris, that it would start a conflict between the workers and the armed forces.'[1] The publishing of an order by the French government on 22 June calling for the enrolment of workers from the Workshops into the army resulted in the building of barricades in Paris the next day. The bitter fighting which shook Paris between 23 and 26 June was aptly described by Lamartine as a 'servile war', a battle between the most determined elements of an impoverished artisan–worker class and the forces of order.[2] The June Days, the bloodiest insurrection in nineteenth-century Europe with the exception of the Paris Commune, had a profound effect upon French internal politics.[3] They also brought about a temporary hiatus in French diplomatic activity, although they did not appreciably alter the course of French foreign policy.

During the June Days 'order' had been the cry of the hour. Shortly after the insurrection broke out, the monarchist group within the Assembly, the rue de Poitiers coterie, now self-styled as the 'party of order' or as 'honest and moderate republicans', had worked for the demise of the discredited Executive Commission and the conferring of executive powers upon General Cavaignac. Cavaignac, the republican general who had been

---

[1] Austria, HHS, Frankreich Korr. Kart. 337 (24 June, Thom to Wessenberg).
[2] Lamartine, *Histoire de la révolution de 1848*, ii. 475.
[3] The best scholarly analyses of the June Days and of the period leading up to this uprising are afforded by the works of Stern, Garnier-Pagès, McKay, and Schmidt (Charles Schmidt, *Les Journées de juin, 1848* (Paris, 1926); *Des Ateliers nationaux aux barricades de juin, 1848* (Paris, 1948)). Rémi Gossez is now preparing a *doctorat d'état* thesis which promises to be the definitive work on the topic.

Minister of War under the Executive Commission and who had been entrusted with emergency dictatorial powers during the June Days, emerged after the June uprising as the champion of order, as the man to whom a fear-stricken France turned for leadership. As Daniel Stern wrote, it seemed that 'society as a whole, which remained despite its victory victim to a feeling of terror comparable to nothing since the invasion of Rome by the barbarians, saluted its liberator with a unanimous acclamation'.[4] Cavaignac would act as executive head of the French Republic until the elections of December 1848 brought Louis Napoleon Bonaparte to the French presidency.

There is no doubt that General Cavaignac was a sincere republican who wanted to defend and preserve the Republic.[5] However, the fact still remains that the General was above all a military man devoted to the cause of order, who would, both consciously and unconsciously, abet the advance of reaction within France after the June Days. During the uprising a state of siege had been proclaimed and several newspapers seized. On 26 June the clubs were summarily closed; on 27 June the Assembly proposed that the arrested insurgents be transported to the colonies; on 28 June the National Workshops were closed. National Guard units which had not answered the call to arms were disbanded. Cavaignac personally dissolved the National Workshops by decree on 3 July; and four days later he proclaimed the necessity of prolonging the state of siege. On 11 July the Cavaignac government proposed legislation to severely restrict the clubs and to require a deposit on the press, a move which occasioned Lamennais to remark caustically 'silence to the poor' when he suspended the publication of his *Le Peuple constituant*. Finally, the Assembly established an Investigation Commission to probe the causes of the 15 May and the June uprisings. The result was a political inquest, supported by Cavaignac himself, which unjustly proclaimed Louis Blanc and Caussidière guilty of subversion.[6] After the June Days reaction in France was fully under way with the forces of order at the helm.

[4] Stern, ii. 472–3.

[5] A much needed and interesting, if somewhat controversial, reinterpretation of Cavaignac's role in 1848 has recently been given by Frederick A. de Luna in his book, *The French Republic under Cavaignac, 1848.*

[6] Stern, ii. 486–93; Pierre de la Gorce, *Histoire de la Seconde République française* (2 vols.; Paris, 1887), i. 407–32; de Luna, pp. 200–19.

The Cavaignac ministry, composed entirely of republicans, did on occasion try to temper some of the more reactionary and anti-republican measures of the monarchist-dominated Assembly, such as those concerning the deportation of prisoners taken during the June Days.[7] However, the government often acquiesced in the Assembly's demands, for the republican ministers shared the Assembly's interest in preserving order and restraining the Parisian radicals. The Cavaignac government was, in fact, composed entirely of republicans of the *National* faction, or in other words, of the same moderate republican elements which had dominated the Provisional Government and Executive Commission. But now the radical republicans of the Executive Commission, such as Ledru-Rollin, had been removed from the government, and the moderate republicans were sharing power with the monarchist-inclined Assembly. Both groups viewed the radicals as their primary enemy. A radical-inspired foreign policy of revolutionary propaganda in favour of suppressed peoples had even less chance of being implemented by the conservatively inclined Cavaignac regime than by the moderate-dominated Executive Commission or Provisional Government. The composition of the different French governments of 1848 was far different from that of the fire-eating Jacobins of 1791–2. Despite their sonorous phases, Europe should not have expected the moderate French forty-eighters to follow the foreign policy aims of their revolutionary predecessors.

The Cavaignac government would in some ways alter the course of French foreign policy, especially in regard to Italy and Germany. Still, in certain matters continuity was apparent between the foreign policies of pre-June Days and post-June Days France. The internal and external problems facing the Cavaignac government, like the composition of the government itself, had not abruptly changed. Radical power had been destroyed in June, but the general fear of radical machinations lingered on, or even increased, after the June Days, obliging the 'government of order' still to devote most of its energies to internal policy considerations. Moreover, the Cavaignac government was bound by some of the basic republican foreign policy principles of Lamartine's Manifesto and by the Assembly's resolution of

[7] Stern, ii. 487–8; de Luna, pp. 220–2.

24 May, because its very existence depended upon its identification with republicanism. The moderate republicans within the Cavaignac ministry were under continual pressure from the monarchists, so they could neither entirely negate the revolutionary principles of February nor abandon the support of the small hard-core republican group within the Assembly.

The continuity in policy between the Executive Commission and the Cavaignac regime is illustrated by the fact that Jules Bastide continued to serve as French Minister of Foreign Affairs under the new government. Under the Executive Commission Lamartine had managed to dominate external policy decisions, even though Bastide had become foreign minister in May. Now, with Lamartine's disappearance from the scene, Bastide emerged for the first time as a figure of real consequence in formulating and implementing policy.

Bastide, a former wood merchant who had been active in the secret societies during the 1830s, had served as editor of *Le National* and then as a collaborator with Buchez in publishing *La Revue nationale*, which first appeared in 1847. Although Bastide had had no previous experience in diplomacy, he had specialized in writing articles dealing with foreign affairs for *La Revue nationale*, and thereby had gained the reputation of being something of an expert on diplomacy. As a prominent member of the *National* clique, Bastide had emerged as one of the leading spokesmen for the republican cause in the 1840s. During his tenure as foreign minister he clearly displayed his strong republican convictions when he personally reprimanded a French diplomat for using the anti-republican phrase 'courting a monarch' in one of his dispatches to Paris.[8] Moreover, the former secret society member seemingly retained many of his gruff republican habits after occupying the Foreign Ministry. Much to the despair of seasoned diplomats, Bastide often seems to have received dignitaries with his feet on his desk and a cigar in his mouth.[9] In fact, Bastide's staunch republicanism, his unorthodox manners and his lack of previous experience in foreign affairs brought such an experienced and aristocratic diplomat as Gustave de Beaumont, de Tocqueville's friend, to bemoan Bastide's incapacities as foreign minister in a series of

[8] FAAE, Corr. pol., Bade 34 (20 Aug., Bastide to Lefebvre).
[9] Henri Malo, *Thiers, 1797–1877* (Paris, 1932), p. 384.

letters which he wrote in the autumn of 1848 to de Tocqueville from his diplomatic post in London.[10]

Despite his gruff manners and diplomatic inexperience, it seems that Beaumont's evaluation of Bastide's ability as foreign minister was jaundiced and unjustified. A thorough examination of the diplomatic record indicates that Bastide, like Lamartine, was a competent minister who was well aware of France's traditional foreign policy objectives. Even before he had assumed control of the French Foreign Ministry Bastide had demonstrated that he was aware of France's national interests by seemingly acquiescing in Lamartine's plan to receive Nice and Savoy as compensation for the aggrandizement of Sardinia. As foreign minister throughout the summer and autumn of 1848 Bastide was fully cognizant of the threat which a united Italy or Germany posed to France. Bastide's diplomatic inexperience and fervent republican convictions seem to have in no way blinded him to France's traditional diplomatic interests.

As French foreign minister Bastide naturally played an important role in the conduct of French external affairs after the June Days, writing most of the diplomatic dispatches and profoundly influencing French policy *vis-à-vis* Italy, Germany, and Austria. However, he was not alone in formulating French foreign policy, for Cavaignac, as head of the government, had as deep an interest in foreign affairs as in every other important area of ministerial responsibility. The General took a personal hand in several important diplomatic discussions, actually drafted a few policy statements, and seems to have played a major role in conducting foreign policy.[11] Immediately after the June Days he had

---

[10] Alexis de Tocqueville, *Œuvres complètes*, vol. viii, part 2: *Correspondance d'Alexis de Tocqueville et de Gustave de Beaumont* (J.-P. Mayer, ed.; Paris, 1967), pp. 55–9, 66, 102, 111–12.

[11] In his recent book Professor de Luna has come to the conclusion that Cavaignac was 'the ultimate architect' of French foreign policy after the June Days (p. 339). De Luna bases this conclusion upon the fact that Cavaignac's personal archives, preserved in the Château d'Ourne, but also available for consultation on microfilm in Le Mans (Archives départementales de la Sarthe, Documents des archives privées de M. Eugène Cavaignac, reels 24–6), which he had studied in detail, contain several major foreign policy directives drawn up in the General's own hand. However, an examination of the Cavaignac archives in light of the entire diplomatic record shows that Cavaignac's autograph diplomatic documents often seem merely to summarize rather than to formulate the general lines of French policy. In fact, these recently opened archives, which many historians had surmised would be of utmost importance in

even planned to install General Bedeau in the Foreign Ministry and shift Bastide to the Ministry of the Navy. Nevertheless, Bastide was retained as foreign minister when Bedeau was obliged to refuse the appointment because of the wounds that he had received in June; and he served as interim foreign minister from 2 to 17 July, when he was confirmed as official foreign minister once again.[12] In reality it would seem that Cavaignac and Bastide shared responsibility for conducting foreign affairs after June, with the latter having a free hand in most minor policy decisions.

While Bastide and Cavaignac formulated the major lines of French foreign policy from June to December, all major policy questions were also discussed and decided upon in the council of ministers, where a simple majority vote of all of the ministers appears to have decided most issues.[13] Moreover, the Cavaignac government was responsible to the Assembly in all matters, including foreign affairs. Though the Assembly allowed the Cavaignac government considerable liberty in both determining and implementing foreign policy, its ultimate authority had to be taken into consideration. In reality, then, Bastide's authority over foreign affairs was considerably restricted by other members and branches of the government. Bastide, himself no radical, acted under the restraint of even more moderate influences as he tried to resolve the problems confronting French diplomacy in the summer of 1848.

One of the principal realities facing French diplomacy in the summer of 1848 was the fact that throughout Europe the forces of reaction and aggressive nationalism were steadily gaining impetus while liberalism was on the wane. As spring turned to summer it became increasingly evident that the revolutionary spark which France had struck was dying out in Europe as quickly as in France herself. Austria was recouping her forces,

---

evaluating French foreign affairs in 1848, are disappointing to the diplomatic historian. Apart from a few directives drawn up by Cavaignac in line with the general precepts of French diplomacy and a few personal diplomatic communications of no great importance, much of the material in the Cavaignac archives is duplicated by dispatches available in the Quai d'Orsay.

[12] *Almanach national annuaire de la République française pour 1848–1849–1850* (Paris, 1850), p. xiii.

[13] This was the case, for example, in the decision not to land troops in Venice in September (Stern, ii. 522–3).

while Poland and Italy were once again sinking into subjugation. Even more distressing for France was the realization that in the German Confederation, where liberal elements had supposedly come to power with the advent of the Frankfurt Assembly, the policies of the so-called liberals were more threatening and aggressive than those of the German princes.[14] By the summer of 1848 nationalism and not liberalism was the dominant force on the European scene. Republican France saw her visions of a republican and liberal Europe vanish, while she herself was unable to influence this transformation in any way short of war. And the Cavaignac ministry was convinced that war was not in France's national interest.

Despite the Republic's disappointment with Germany's position toward Poland, in the late spring of 1848 France still entertained hopes of establishing close relations with the Frankfurt Assembly, the self-appointed spokesman for all Germany, which the French government felt would build a united, republican Germany friendly to France. In his speech before the French Constituent Assembly on 23 May Lamartine proclaimed France's peaceful intentions toward Germany. On the following day the Constituent Assembly passed its resolution calling for 'the reconstruction of a free and independent Poland, the liberation of Italy', and 'a fraternal pact with Germany'. By this resolution France testified to her continued faith in Germany. The French agent in Frankfurt communicated France's desire for a 'fraternal union with Germany' to the German Assembly, assuring this body that France had never had hostile intentions toward Germany, that France's 'greatest glory would be to win Germany over only to the cause of liberty, the only and last conquest which [France] desired'.[15] As Bastide told his chargé d'affaires in Munich, 'the time of rivalries and national pretensions is passed' and France was deeply sincere in her desire for 'relations of friendship and fraternal union with Germany'.[16]

Germany as a whole seemed reassured by the French expressions of friendship. Prices rose sharply on the Hamburg Stock

[14] The Frankfurt Parliament has been the topic of a recent impressive work by Frank Eyck, *The Frankfurt Parliament, 1848–1849* (London, 1968).

[15] FAAE, Corr. pol., Allemagne 805 (30 May, Savoye to Bastide). Savoye had replaced Salignac-Fénelon in Frankfurt.

[16] Ibid., Corr. pol., Bavière 224 (3 June, Bastide to Humann). Humann had succeeded Bourgoing in Munich.

Exchange when news of Lamartine's discourse of 23 May reached Germany.[17] On 24 June the Frankfurt Parliament saluted the French Assembly for its proclamation of 24 May and expressed its sympathy in turn for France.[18] However, in the meantime another French agent in Germany had reported that German sentiment toward France 'left something to be desired', for the German people still thought of their neighbour across the Rhine as a hotbed of revolution.[19] Frankfurt's reservations concerning France were to become increasingly clear on 3 July, when the Frankfurt Assembly refused a proposal for a French alliance, despite the possibility which existed throughout the summer of war between Germany and Russia over Denmark.

Russia's staunch support of Denmark and her menacing protests to both Prussia and Frankfurt over the Schleswig-Holstein crisis had made diplomatic observers believe that a Russo-German war was possible or even imminent throughout May, June, and part of July.[20] Bastide had placed enough credence in these reports to order all French agents in Eastern Europe to report immediately any definite knowledge of Russian troop movements toward Poland.[21] The possibility of a war with Russia seems to have made the German Powers somewhat receptive to French alliance overtures.[22] However, by July reassuring reports began to reach Germany that Russian troop concentrations were being made only to preclude the possibility of internal difficulties within Russian Poland.[23] On 3 July it was already quite obvious that the Frankfurt Assembly mistrusted republican France as much as it feared reactionary Russia.

---

[17] Ibid., Corr. pol., Hambourg 149 (28 May, Bernard des Essard to Bastide).

[18] Ibid., Corr. pol., Allemagne 805 (24 June, Savoye to Bastide).

[19] Ibid., Corr. pol., Hesse Cassel 34 (18 June, Rothan to Bastide).

[20] Ibid., Corr. pol., Suède 324 (5 July, Lobstein to Bastide); Ridder, ii. 94 (3 June, Comte de Briey to Hoffschmidt).

[21] FAAE, corr. pol. des consuls, Russie 6, Varsovie (14 July, Bastide to French consuls in Bucharest, Varsovie, Tassy, and Danzig).

[22] Ibid., Corr. pol., Prusse 302 (1 July, Arago to Bastide); Corr. pol., Allemagne 805 (11 June, Savoye to Bastide); Ridder, ii. 111–13 (17 June, Hoffschmidt to Nothomb); La Réforme, 17 June. Emmanuel Arago, the son of François Arago and the Republic's commissar in Lyons in the early spring, had been appointed minister in Berlin by Bastide, replacing Circourt, who had served there as chargé d'affaires under Lamartine.

[23] FAAE, Corr. pol., Belgique 30 (13 July, Quinette to Bastide); Corr. pol., Angleterre 670 (27 June, Tallenay to Bastide). Tallenay had left Hamburg to assume the post of French minister in London.

France, for her part, was becoming increasingly disenchanted with both Frankfurt and Prussia by late spring because of the aggressive tendencies which these Powers displayed toward Denmark and Poland. France's attitude toward the Danish conflict with Germany over the duchies of Schleswig-Holstein clearly reflects the Republic's growing disappointment with Germany.[24] In April and early May the French government and French public opinion alike, favourable to a Germany which seemed to be republicanizing herself and liberating Poland, tended to back the Duchies and Germany in their war against Denmark. Lamartine, who hoped to implement his alliance with Germany, refused to support Denmark or 'become involved in any way' in the Schleswig-Holstein crisis.[25] The French press, from such liberal Parisian dailies as *La Réforme* and *Le National* to such conservative sheets as *Le Journal des débats* and *Le Constitutionnel*, chastized Denmark for her supposed dependence upon Russia and lauded Germany for liberating the Duchies from monarchical Denmark.[26] In May, however, the French became aware of the aggressive character of German nationalism as a result of Prussia's and Frankfurt's moves against Poznań. Papers which had been unfavourable to Denmark in April, now made a complete about-face and printed articles in support of Denmark and critical of Germany.[27] When Bastide replaced Lamartine as French foreign minister, the French government's position toward Denmark and the Duchies question also altered, for Bastide

[24] For a detailed discussion of France's policy toward Denmark and the Schleswig-Holstein question in 1848, a policy which is most revealing as to France's attitude toward Germany, see my article, 'French Diplomacy and the First Schleswig-Holstein Crisis', *French Historical Studies*, vii (1971), 204–25. Prior to 1848 the Elbe Duchies had been connected to Denmark as personal possessions of the Danish monarch, but by 1848 a Danish national movement was pressing for the complete incorporation of Schleswig into Denmark proper. The Schleswig-Holstein crisis of 1848, a series of events which highly resembled and set the stage for the well-known crisis of 1863–4, erupted in late March, when German nationalists in the Elbe Duchies took up arms to oppose the incorporation of Schleswig into Denmark proper, established a provisional government in Kiel, and appealed to the Frankfurt Diet for military assistance. The German states, and Prussia especially, executed Frankfurt's mandate to assist the Kiel government by sending troops into the Duchies—and for a brief time into Denmark proper—to oppose Danish attempts to occupy Schleswig.

[25] Denmark, Rigsarkivet, Frankrig II (2 April, E. C. L. Moltke to Knuth).

[26] *La Réforme*, 1, 19 April, 5 May; *Le National*, 16 April; *Le Journal des débats*, 11 April; *Le Constitutionnel*, 19 April.

[27] *La Réforme*, 8 May; *Le Journal des débats*, 7, 16 May.

was more suspicious of Germany's territorial designs than his predecessor had been.

By late spring Bastide was offering the Danish crown France's wholehearted support in its struggle with Germany over Schleswig-Holstein. The reasons that motivated him to support Denmark are clear. Following Bastide's first discussion with the Danish minister in Paris, E. C. L. Moltke could report to his government: 'The territorial invasions which Germany is contemplating in all directions was the object of the conversation which I had yesterday with M. Bastide; and M. Bastide told me that he had seen a new map of Germany on which Alsace and part of Lorraine were indicated as part of Germany, something which did not strike my interlocutor as pleasing.'[28] Bastide himself wrote a dispatch to Emmanuel Arago in Berlin denouncing 'the unjust aggression of Germany' toward Denmark and adding: 'As far as nationality is concerned, one cannot reasonably say that Schleswig is German simply because [the German] language has been introduced there . . . German is also spoken in Alsace, in Lorraine, in Switzerland, in Courland, and in Livonia. Will this be a reason for Germany to want to incorporate Alsace and Lorraine, the German areas of Switzerland, Courland, and Livonia? Such a principle would lead to the absurd.'[29] While Bastide could not realize how prophetic his words had been, by the late spring and summer of 1848 the French foreign minister was definitely aware that an expansionist, aggressive German nationalism might pose an eventual direct threat to France's German-speaking provinces, Alsace and Lorraine, just as this same force was menacing Denmark's German-speaking provinces, Schleswig-Holstein.

In support of Denmark Bastide sent letters to the French ministers in London, Berlin, Copenhagen, and Frankfurt, instructing them to censure Germany's procedures toward both Denmark and Poland. The dispatches cast additional light upon the suspicions that the French foreign minister had developed toward Germany. In mid June Bastide informed Tallenay in London that 'we cannot possibly remain indifferent to these tendencies of Germany which under the pretext of constituting German unity are aimed at nothing less than the absorption

---

[28] Denmark, Rigsarkivet II (15 May, E. C. L. Moltke to Knuth).
[29] FAAE, Corr. pol., Prusse 302 (29 June, Bastide to Arago).

within the German Confederation of all territories in which there is a population of German origin'.[30] Bastide also sent a letter to Savoye, French chargé d'affaires in Frankfurt, in which he began by reminding his agent that the French government still wished to realize the 'fraternal alliance' with Germany prescribed by the Constituent Assembly, but then went on to complain about

... all that is unjust and contrary to the treaties in Germany's pretension to annex Schleswig because a fraction of the German population is located there. As for us, Sir, we consider Schleswig to be a Danish province. . . . We applaud the energetic and courageous Danish resistance and . . . in conformity with the guarantee stipulated by France in the Treaty of 14 June 1720, we consider it our duty to declare ourselves strongly in favour of right and justice, which were offended by the high-handed conduct of Germany toward Denmark. Germany's desire to build herself according to the principle of national unity is no doubt very legitimate. But this tendency should not be pushed to usurpation. All countries where there exists a population of German origin do not belong to Germany by this alone. And yet it is in this abusive sense that Schleswig and the Duchy of Poznań have been dealt with. . . .[31]

On another occasion Bastide informed Savoye that 'without a doubt, Sir, it is in our interest to cultivate Germany and conciliate her to us, and we are entirely disposed to do this. . . . But our sympathies and considerations for her should not, however, go so far as to blind us to the acts of manifest usurpation, to the digressions of this spirit of German nationality which drives Germany to invade territories which never belonged to her. . . .'[32] The contradiction between France's desire both to cultivate German friendship and discourage German territorial pretensions was becoming apparent. As the French government grew progressively aware of what Bastide himself referred to as 'acts of manifest usurpation' of other territories by Germany, Franco-German relations were bound to deteriorate. And as the year advanced Bastide's wariness of Germany's territorial ambitions would increase to the point where, by late summer, the French government had lost all sympathy for Germany and would actually try to impede the German unification movement.

[30] FAAE, Corr. pol., Angleterre 670 (12 June, Bastide to Tallenay).
[31] Ibid., Corr. pol., Allemagne 805 (8 June, Bastide to Savoye).
[32] Ibid. (16 June, Bastide to Savoye).

France viewed German subjugation of Poland in the same light as Germany's invasion of Schleswig-Holstein.[33] In fact, French diplomatic protests to Germany often drew parallels between Poznań and Denmark. It is interesting to note, for example, that on the very day the Frankfurt Parliament proclaimed its friendship for France the French representative in Frankfurt delivered a protest against Germany's unjust actions toward Denmark and Poland, something which could not make the Frankfurt parliamentarians more favourable to the French Republic.[34] As far as Poland was concerned, the Constituent Assembly's resolution calling for 'the reconstruction of a free and independent Poland' provided the basis for France's Polish policy in the early summer of 1848; and the Cavaignac government followed its predecessor's example of pleading Poland's cause in the capitals of Germany and taking the Frankfurt Assembly to task for sanctioning Prussia's actions in Poznań. However, it is interesting to note that the wording of the 24 May resolution concerning Poland was much milder than a radical proposal that would have 'demanded' the reconstruction of Poznań and thereby served as an ultimatum to Germany.[35] The Parisian demonstration of 15 May which had used Poland as a pretext to invade the Assembly seems to have had the effect of tarnishing the Polish cause in the eyes of many Frenchmen. As Fouquier, the reactionary editor of the *Annuaire historique*, aptly remarked, the Polish question 'had everywhere made common cause with demagoguery. The reaction against the disorder [of 15 May] was the signal for its defeat. In Paris the enthusiasm for this cause, previously so cherished, changed into repulsion when the name of Poland served as pretext for a ridiculous and criminal attempt at insurrection.'[36] Moreover, Poznań's uprising was crushed by Prussian troops in May and her plight was a *fait accompli*. France was sympathetic to Poland, but she would not champion the Polish cause to the point of rupturing relations with Prussia, Frankfurt, and even Russia.

In early June Bastide ordered Emmanuel Arago, who had just replaced Circourt as French representative in Berlin, the latter having been recalled because of his lack of sympathy for the

---

[33] See above, pp. 91–5, 97, for an analysis of France's reaction to Prussia's suppression of the Poles in Posen.

[34] FAAE, Corr. pol., Allemagne 805 (24 June, Savoye to Bastide).

[35] *Le Moniteur universel*, 24 May.   [36] Cited by Tersen, p. 67.

Polish cause, to protest to Frederick William's government about the annexation of Poznań on the pretext that it contained a large German population. To Bastide this Prussian action amounted to nothing less than 'a fourth partition of Poland'. Berlin should be informed that:

France would not remain a passive spectator to the incorporation of half of the Grand Duchy of Poznań into the German Confederation. The government of the Republic . . . therefore considers it a right and a duty to protest strongly against an action as evidently contradictory to the stipulations of the treaties as to the rights of the Polish nationality which has been threatened only too often.[37]

A few days later Bastide sent a similar note to Frankfurt, Prussia's accomplice in incorporating Poznań into the German Confederation.[38]

When Emmanuel Arago delivered France's protest to Berlin, Arnim, the Prussian foreign minister, was taken aback by what he called France's 'new position on Poland' and the discrepancies between Circourt's understanding attitude and Arago's threatening tone.[39] It seemed that Franco-Prussian relations had momentarily taken a turn for the worse. However, Bastide suddenly adopted a more conciliatory stance at the end of June. Bastide informed Arago that 'we do not intend to go beyond our protest against the division of the Grand Duchy of Poznań. This protest stands: It is enough for now.'[40] Bastide had obviously not expected Arnim to react as he did and had therefore decided to demur, not wishing to strain Franco-Prussian relations any further. Another factor influencing the modification of France's position was undoubtedly the Tsar's assertion that Russia would regard the reconstruction of Poland as a *casus belli*.[41] France did not want to sacrifice her relations with both Prussia and Russia for what Lamartine had candidly called a 'sepulchre'.

French hopes for Poland were briefly revived in early July when the formation of a Prussian commission to investigate the division of Poznań led Arago and Bastide to believe that an independent Poland might be established after all.[42] On 21 July

[37] FAAE, Corr. pol., Prusse 302 (9 June, Bastide to Arago).
[38] Ibid., Corr. pol., Allemagne 805 (16 June, Bastide to Savoye).
[39] Ibid., Corr. pol., Prusse 302 (15, 17 June, Arago to Bastide).
[40] Ibid. (29 June, Bastide to Arago).   [41] Ibid. (20 June, Arago to Bastide).
[42] Ibid. (4, 6 July, Arago to Bastide; 11 July, Bastide to Arago).

Bastide suggested that his agent in Frankfurt 'plead the Polish cause' so that Frankfurt too might reconsider the moves that she had taken to incorporate Poznań into the German Confederation.[43] Nevertheless, shortly thereafter he ordered Arago not to accede to Polish pressures and publish certain French notes reprimanding Prussia for her Polish policy; France did not want the situation to become 'more heated'.[44] Then, at the end of July, French hopes for Poland's re-establishment were shattered and the Polish cause seemingly 'lost' when the Frankfurt Parliament voted irrevocably to incorporate part of the province of Poznań into the German Confederation.[45]

Bastide quickly faced up to diplomatic reality and told Arago that, in view of Germany's 'regrettable' resolution to annex Poznań, France could console herself with the fact that

... she had done all that she could to prevent it. We have protested in advance to Berlin; we have acted in the same sense and with the same aims in Frankfurt. ... In the general situation in Europe and in relation to other questions, the question of the Duchy of Poznań is of secondary interest. Let us not place more stress on it than is necessary, and without deserting the principle to which it is related, let us not forget that our action could exert itself upon a matter of more direct interest to us.[46]

By late summer Poland had become a decidedly 'secondary' issue in French foreign policy. France no longer championed the Polish cause because the Republic did not wish to exacerbate her relations with Germany at the very moment when the Italian question was coming to a head. France did not want to reject Germany and push her into Austria's outstretched arms. Moreover, an important Russian diplomat in Naples, Chreptovitch, the son-in-law of Nesselrode, had intimated to the French agent in that city that if France were to 'renounce' her efforts to reconstruct Poland Russia would remain neutral even if France were to become involved in Italy.[47] By the end of July France feared that she might be obliged to intervene in Italy and in this event a friendly attitude on the part of the Tsar would be highly

[43] Ibid., Corr. pol., Allemagne 805 (21 July, Bastide to Savoye).
[44] Ibid., Corr. pol., Prusse 302 (22 July, Arago to Bastide).
[45] Ibid., Corr. pol., Allemagne 805 (27 July, Savoye to Bastide).
[46] Ibid., Corr. pol., Prusse 302 (1 Aug., Bastide to Arago).
[47] Ibid., Corr. pol., Naples 176 (22 July, Sain de Boislecomte to Bastide).

beneficial to her. The Polish cause was seemingly being sacrificed because of France's overriding concern with the Italian question.

The Italian problem was the Second Republic's primary foreign policy interest throughout the summer and autumn of 1848. In Italy, as in Germany, the forces of reaction were gaining the upper hand by June and July. And in Italy these forces presented themselves in the form of a rejuvenated Austrian army which was preparing to take to the offensive. The Austrian commander in Northern Italy, the octogenarian Marshal Radetzky, had suffered a significant defeat at Peschiera on 31 May; however, on 11 June he stunned Italy and the diplomatic world with an Austrian victory at Vicenza in Venetia. The tide of battle was turning. On 24 June Radetzky informed Vienna 'that if he could be reinforced by 25,000 men he would be in a position to dislodge Charles Albert so that peace could be made on Sardinian soil'. The Austrian Minister of War duly replied that the reinforcements would be sent. Two days later Wessenberg, the Austrian foreign minister, told the Austrian Council of Ministers that 'Austria had the alternative either to continue the war or surrender all her Italian possessions, in return for financial compensation'. Faced with these alternatives 'the Council resolved to carry on the war with all possible energy'.[48]

Austria now announced that Radetzky had refused to obey orders to cease fire and carry on negotiations; therefore, the Emperor's government felt obliged to continue the war even while efforts to initiate negotiations continued.[49] Delacour, the French minister in Vienna, reported at this time that Austria, buoyed by her victory at Vicenza, was suddenly less peacefully disposed than previously. In the Austrian capital there were now 'few sincere partisans of peace'.[50] Then, in late June word arrived in Vienna that Lombardy would not negotiate with the Emperor's representatives.[51] This made Austria decide to cease all attempts to deal diplomatically with the Lombards. The Austrians now made it clear that they meant to settle their dispute with Italy on the field of battle.[52]

[48] Taylor, 124–5 (Ministerialprotokoll, 24, 26 June).
[49] FAAE, Corr. pol., Autriche 435 (25 June, Delacour to Bastide).
[50] Ibid. (29 June, Delacour to Bastide).
[51] Austria, HHS, Frankreich Korr. Kart. 338; Planat de la Faye, i. 299; *Parliamentary Papers*, lviii. 36 (18 June, Casati to Wessenberg).
[52] Austria, HHS, Frankreich Korr. Kart. 338 (29 June, Wessenberg to Thom).

Austria immediately informed Great Britain that no mediation had any chance of success, for Austria must first experience some military successes.[53] As the Austrian diplomatic position became less flexible, Delacour reported from Vienna that Austria was increasingly bellicose, that sincere negotiations with Italy were no longer contemplated by the Viennese government. In fact, the papal envoy who had arrived in Austria in June to offer his good offices in an attempt to settle the war by negotiation had been requested to return to Italy. It was no longer a question of just continuing the struggle to avenge Austrian honour, as Vienna had claimed to be doing in May. There was now talk in Vienna of Radetzky dictating peace terms to Charles Albert in Turin, the Sardinian capital.[54]

The French government was fully aware of the turning tide of battle and the grave implications which this had for French foreign policy. The French had had little faith in Sardinia's chances of defeating Austria from the very beginning of the conflict.[55] Then, in late June reports began to flow out of Italy predicting the imminent defeat of Charles Albert's forces. The French consul in Milan, Denois, wrote that in view of the Austrian victory at Vicenza the republican element in Italy, which had previously rejected any French intervention, now impatiently awaited French armed assistance.[56] On the same day the French consul in Genoa, Léon Favre, wrote that the Italians still rejected French intervention in principle, but that 'the coming of the French, while not desired, has been considered a fatal necessity for two days now', that is, ever since word had arrived of Austria's victory at Vicenza.[57] The following day Reiset, who as chargé d'affaires had replaced Bixio in the Sardinian capital, reported that the Italians were becoming disillusioned with Charles Albert. Reiset had been informed that Italian republicans had written letters to members of the French Constituent Assembly encouraging them to interpellate their government on the necessity of intervening beyond the Alps.[58]

---

[53] *Parliamentary Papers*, lviii. 32–3 (5 July, Wessenberg to Thom).

[54] FAAE, Corr. pol., Autriche 435 (10 July, Delacour to Bastide).

[55] See above, pp. 84–5.

[56] FAAE, Corr. pol. des consuls, Autriche 10A, Milan (16 June, Denois to Bastide).

[57] Ibid., Mémoires et Documents, Italie 36 (16 June, Favre to Bastide).

[58] Ibid., Corr. pol., Turin 321 (17 June, Reiset to Bastide).

On 20 June Reiset informed his government that news from the front was extremely discouraging. Austria was becoming stronger every day and 'without French intervention, the Italians will never manage to chase the enemy from this country. . . . The fact is that anxiety reigns here and people know less than ever what will become of Italian affairs if one day France does not come to Italy's rescue.'[59] Three days later Reiset reported that French intervention was generally unpopular in Turin, but that he himself believed Charles Albert to be incapable of defeating Radetzky. He added: 'If French intervention would not result in a general European war, it is now or never the moment to aid, without losing any time, our [Italian] brothers who are fighting for the independence of their country.'[60]

Bastide fully realized that another major Italian defeat would necessitate French intervention in Italy. The Milanese were already suggesting that France might at least loan the Italians a French general to supply them with necessary military leadership; and the Sardinians seemed to concur in this.[61] Bastide was certainly not comforted by a report from the French ambassador to Rome to the effect that French intervention was so unpopular in Italy that

If the situation becomes worse, it is possible that Italy will open her arms to France, but what I have seen convinces one that, sooner or later, we will only find ingratitude and disappointment, and that our situation would not be very different in this country from what it was in Spain from 1807 to 1812. I believe it is in France's interest to insist upon this point to you.[62]

It was evident that many Italians feared French intervention but thought it to be practically inevitable. Reiset reported that, although French intervention was extremely distasteful to most Italians, they would be obliged to request French assistance if Austria took Venice.[63] And in the light of Radetzky's advances in the Venetian war theatre, while Charles Albert's forces lay paralysed and inactive, the fall of Venice seemed to be a definite possibility. Bastide could envisage French troops being obliged

[59] FAAE, Corr. pol., Turin 321 (20 June, Reiset to Bastide).

[60] Ibid. (23 June, Reiset to Bastide).

[61] Ibid., Corr. pol. des consuls, Autriche 10A, Milan (25 June, Denois to Bastide).

[62] Ibid., Corr. pol., Rome 988 (24 June, Harcourt to Bastide).

[63] Ibid., Corr. pol., Turin 321 (3, 5 July, Reiset to Bastide).

to cross the Alps at any moment, much to his and Sardinia's dismay. On 10 July Bastide wrote stoically and ruefully that 'in Milan and even in Turin, French intervention is regarded as a necessity'.[64] France did not wish to be dragged into a war against her will. By early July France was already seriously considering joint mediation with England to preclude the possibility of being forced to intervene in Italy.

Throughout the spring and early summer of 1848 France and England had maintained the close and friendly relations which Lamartine had striven to achieve, but any co-operation between the two Powers concerning Italy had been impeded by mutual suspicion of each other's motives. In May France had suspected Palmerston of being favourable to Austria and of seeking an Italian settlement with Austria to the exclusion of France. Moreover, Bastide was ignorant of the fact that Palmerston had refused the Hummelauer proposals in June, believing quite falsely that Britain was ready to support Austria's claims to Venice. He was convinced that Palmerston's only concern was to keep France from sending troops across the Alps, and he believed that England might be prepared to deal directly with Austria to prevent this. Bastide clearly displayed his suspicions of Great Britain when he remarked to Tallenay in London that 'the British cabinet has shown itself to be especially preoccupied with the need to make it impossible for our Army of the Alps to enter Italy'.[65]

It is true that Austria had continued to hope for British support after Palmerston's rejection of the Hummelauer memorandum. In early summer Austria made several approaches to England to try to convince Palmerston that she was on the road to victory and would never agree to liberate Venetia.[66] Palmerston, nevertheless, bound by ministerial decisions, continued to insist that he would not encourage Venice to retain her ties to the Empire unless the Venetians were themselves willing to do so.[67] Finally, on 17 July Palmerston broke off the discussions with Austria, informing that Power that he would no longer occupy

---

[64] Ibid., Corr. pol., Angleterre 670 (10 July, Bastide to Tallenay).

[65] Ibid. (31 May, Bastide to Tallenay; 12 June, Tallenay to Bastide).

[66] *Parliamentary Papers*, lviii. 32–3 (5 July, Wessenberg to Ponsonby); lviii. 30 (7 July, Ponsonby to Palmerston).

[67] Curato, *Le relazioni diplomatiche fra la Gran Bretagna e il Regno di Sardegna*, i. 237–9 (28 June, Palmerston to Abercrombie).

himself with a problem to which a peaceful solution seemed impossible.[68]

French suspicions that England was in collusion with Austria, then, were largely groundless. Britain, for her part, had doubted France's intentions concerning Italy just as much as Bastide had suspected England's. Bastide was correct in assuming that throughout the late spring and early summer—and for the rest of the year too for that matter—Palmerston feared above all a French occupation of Italy and the establishment there of a French sphere of influence. Palmerston had made this apparent not only by having encouraged an Austro-Sardinian understanding to avert French intervention, but also by having bluntly informed France that Her Majesty's Government would 'seriously oppose' any territorial changes in the treaties of 1815 and 'would not be indifferent to a French army crossing the Alps and even simply occupying Savoy'. The French minister in London was correct in concluding that England feared French ambitions in Italy and was refusing to recognize officially the Republic because of this.[69]

Mutual suspicions and recriminations had divided France and Great Britain over Italy, and it was only in late June and early July that France's fear of being obliged to intervene in Italy made Bastide decide to capitalize upon England's motives and try to arrange a basis for joint mediation in Italy with Palmerston. Such an arrangement would satisfy both Powers. Joint mediation would alleviate England's fear of French involvement in Italy at the same time as it would assure the Cavaignac government of a restraining force against military intervention in Italy, something which the French government now wished to avoid. As a result of unfavourable developments on both the domestic and foreign scenes, the Cavaignac government was abandoning Lamartine's flamboyant Italian policy and adopting a conservative policy of strict non-intervention south of the Alps.

Already in late June Bastide and Normanby had held a discussion which led to some clarification of each nation's policy toward the Sicilian problem.[70] In the spring French diplomats

---

[68] *Parliamentary Papers*, lviii. 44 (17 July, Palmerston to Ponsonby).

[69] FAAE, Corr. pol., Angleterre 670 (2 June, Tallenay to Bastide).

[70] For a discussion of France's attitude toward the Sicilian question, following the revolt of Sicily from the Kingdom of Naples (Kingdom of the Two Sicilies)

had tended to suspect England of attempting to exploit the discord between the Kingdom of Naples and Sicily in order to establish an English protectorate over sulphur-rich Sicily.[71] Accordingly, the French government had demurred from recognizing Sicily's independence from Naples. On 29 June, however, Bastide informed the British ambassador in Paris that France had adopted England's position regarding the Sicilian question. Bastide now expressed 'a perfect readiness to recognize the independence of Sicily as soon as the [Sicilian] government should be definitely established'.[72] This modification in France's policy caused Palmerston to profess 'the sincere gratification of Her Majesty's Government at finding that the two Governments [England and France] are likely to act in unison and to have the same views and objects in regard to the affairs of Italy and Sicily'.[73] By late June France and Great Britain seem to have come to an understanding on at least one aspect of the Italian question, thus preparing the way for a general Anglo–French *entente* on this subject.[74]

In early July the British minister in The Hague remarked to the French chargé d'affaires there, de Lurde, that 'the Italian question could only be settled at a conference; and Europe would certainly give Austria the military frontier which she absolutely needs'. Bastide replied to de Lurde that the British minister's words 'reflected the thought of his [the British] government, which, by the way, has not as yet made overtures concerning this question'.[75] On the same day Normanby wrote that 'Bastide told me

in January 1848, see the article by Ferdinand Boyer, 'La marine de la Seconde République et la révolution sicilienne de février à juillet 1848', *Études d'histoire moderne et contemporaine*, ii (1948), 184–203.

[71] FAAE, Corr. pol., Naples 174 (8, 13 June, Baudin to Bastide); Naples 175 (24 Mar., Montigny to Lamartine; 14 June, Sain de Boislecomte to Bastide); Corr. pol. des consuls, Palerme–Messine 1 (27 Mar., 12 Apr., Bresson to Lamartine).

[72] Britain, PRO, F.O. 27/809 (29 June, Normanby to Palmerston).

[73] Ibid., F.O. 27/799 (4 July, Palmerston to Normanby).

[74] Donald M. Greer notes that the preliminaries to the Anglo-French *entente* on Italy in 1848 date back to late June. Greer, however, simply mentions this fact without elaborating upon it. In fact, Greer gives the impression that Bastide and Normanby had spoken about Italy in general, while the diplomatic record indicates that at this time they had only discussed the Sicilian question (Donald M. Greer, *L'Angleterre, la France et la révolution de 1848: le troisième ministère de Lord Palmerston au Foreign Office* (Paris, 1925), p. 242).

[75] FAAE, Corr. pol. Pays-Bas 650 (4 July, de Lurde to Bastide; 10 July, Bastide to de Lurde).

this morning, that, in Council yesterday, he had pressed much upon Cavaignac and his colleagues the importance of acting in accord with England upon all foreign affairs, and particularly upon everything relating to Italy. He added that he was happy to say there seemed a general agreement in these views.'[76]

By early July the Cavaignac government had made its decision to co-operate with England for an Italian settlement.[77] Palmerston was alert to the French propensity to mediate. On 18 July he wrote to Normanby suggesting further communication with Bastide in an attempt to find 'a common policy' on Italy.[78] On the very same day that Palmerston wrote of his willingness to come to an understanding with France over Italy, Bastide proposed the possibility of joint Anglo-French mediation orally to Normanby and in written form to Tallenay. In his conversation with Normanby he professed that, motivated by his government's desire to avert a general European war, 'he [Bastide] was anxious . . . to see if we could hit upon any means by which we might prevent so incalculable an evil'.[79]

---

[76] Normanby, *A Year of Revolution*, ii. 103.

[77] The general course of Anglo-French mediation of the Italian question in 1848, the problem of European diplomacy which was of foremost concern to France from July to December, has been discussed in the books by Boyer, Greer, and Pouthas and in the article by César Vidal, 'La France et la question italienne en 1848', *Études d'histoire moderne et contemporaine*, ii (1948), 162–83. Unfortunately, though, the works by Greer, Pouthas, and Vidal do little more than outline the problem; they also suffer from the fact that they are based on a limited examination of the diplomatic record. The most detailed study of Anglo-French mediation was made by Boyer (*La Seconde République, Charles-Albert et l'Italie du Nord en 1848*), but Boyer's work is openly apologetic for France. Basing his work upon a selection of French and Sardinian diplomatic documents, Boyer tries to deny the relevance of Austrian and English archival material, which he did not consult, while also systematically neglecting even those French documents which contradict his theory that France was well disposed toward Italy and most willing to assist Sardinia. Probably the most accurate analysis of the mediation process is contained in the brilliant work by A. J. P. Taylor (*The Italian Problem in European Diplomacy, 1847–1849*). Taylor's book, based upon an examination of the French, Italian, English, and Austrian diplomatic records, correctly analyses the role of French diplomacy. However, this work simply offers an analysis of the Italian problem in general and it does not deal with the mediation question in the detail which this most important aspect of French diplomacy merits. Then, too, even Taylor was unaware of some of the most revealing French and English diplomatic documents which shed considerable light upon French diplomacy *vis-à-vis* this problem.

[78] Britain, PRO, F.O. 27–799 (18 July, Palmerston to Normanby).

[79] Ibid., F.O. 27/810 (19 July, Normanby to Palmerston); FAAE, Corr. pol., Angleterre 670 (18 July, Bastide to Tallenay).

Both internal and external developments probably determined Bastide to propose mediation on 18 July. First of all, Bastide was very 'much embarrassed by the prolonged discussion' which was going on in the French Assembly's Committee of Foreign Affairs concerning 'the question of Italy'.[80] The Committee was preoccupied with examining and discussing the Cavaignac government's Italian policy on ten different days in July and early August.[81] Observers' accounts indicate that members of this influential committee clearly denounced the timidity of French foreign policy towards the Peninsula.[82] The French government, for its part, was deeply concerned that this would give rise in the Assembly to criticism of the government's inaction in Italy—as it inevitably did. As Bastide intimated to Thom in mid-July, pressure within the Committee in favour of France intervening militarily to assist Sardinia was so great that Bastide feared any signal military success by Austria in the Italian theatre might oblige France to undertake 'armed intervention beyond the Alps'.[83] Then, too, the French foreign minister was distressed by the war news from Italy. Austria, which had once been willing to surrender Lombardy, now seemed to want to preserve all of her holdings and press on with the war.[84] Bastide realized that France, bound by her publicly stated commitment to assist Italy, would have to react in some manner or other if Northern Italy were reconquered by Austria. As Bastide avowed to Normanby, if Sardinia were defeated, 'from the language which had been held in the Committee of Foreign Affairs, and from his knowledge of the character of his countrymen, he [Bastide] was afraid it would be difficult for the government under such circumstances to resist a strong expression of the popular will'.[85] The best way to resist pressure to intervene in Italy was to come to a mediation accord with Her Majesty's Government.

While several factors might have had some influence upon his

[80] Normanby, *A Year of Revolution*, ii. 179; Britain, PRO, F.O. 27/810 (10, 21 July, Normanby to Palmerston).

[81] Archives nationales, C926, 3, procès-verbaux du comité des affaires étrangères. As mentioned above, p. 41, the minutes of the Assembly's Committee of Foreign Affairs simply indicate what topics were discussed on a given day, but provide no detail concerning these discussions.

[82] Sardinia, AST, Lettere Ministri Francia (21 July, Brignole to Pareto).

[83] Austria, HHS, Frankreich Korr. Kart. 337 (19 July, Thom to Wessenberg).

[84] FAAE, Corr. pol., Naples 176 (19 July, Bastide to Sain de Boislecomte).

[85] Britain, PRO, F.O. 27/810 (19 July, Normanby to Palmerston).

decision, probably the deciding factor which determined Bastide to seek joint mediation was his distrust of Charles Albert and the Sardinian government. By the middle of July Sardinia seemed prepared to recognize the French Republic; this, along with repeated suggestions from Italy that Sardinia would like to borrow the use of a French general, undoubtedly led Bastide to feel that a Sardinian request for French assistance was imminent.[86] And Bastide was convinced that it was not in France's interest to aid the Sardinian monarchy aggrandize itself and thereby constitute an eventual threat to France.

Bastide's suspicions of Sardinia had been provoked by the decisions of Lombardy (13 June) and Venice (4 July) to fuse with Sardinia. As a result of these developments, Sardinia now seemed prepared to assimilate all of the former Austrian provinces in Northern Italy. Moreover, in mid-July Bastide had ordered Reiset to protest in Turin about Sardinia's project to annex the cities of Roquebrune and Menton, two free cities which had previously belonged to Monaco but which were now requesting amalgamation with Sardinia.[87] He was also convinced that Sicily's recent election of the Duke of Genoa as king was 'a new success' for the Sardinian royal house. Bastide clearly did not want to intervene in Italy to enhance the position of Charles Albert, and although he insisted that France still 'desired the liberation of that country', he believed Charles Albert's domination of Italy to be 'perhaps more disquieting for the Peninsula than that of Austria herself'.[88]

France's suspicions of Sardinia brought Bastide to propose mediation to England on 18 July. Charles Albert, he argued,

was not pursuing the war with much determination, was stirring up Italy by his intrigues and was aiming at nothing less than becoming [Italy's] sovereign. . . . As far as we [France] are concerned, we could not remain passive spectators to this overflowing of Sardinian ambition: we find it already a grave enough fact for France and Italy that a great Power, of ten million people, having at its head a monarchical house nourished in the ideas of conquest, is forming at the foot of the Alps . . . without other sovereign parts of Italy being

[86] FAAE, Corr. pol. des consuls, Autriche 10B, Milan (12 July, Denois to Bastide).

[87] Ibid., Corr. pol., Turin 321 (15 July, Reiset to Bastide); Sardinia, AST, Lettere Ministri Francia (17 July, Pareto to Brignole).

[88] FAAE, Corr. pol., Naples 176 (19 July, Bastide to Sain de Boislecomte).

absorbed by this house and this new kingdom besides. It would be desirable that France and England come to an agreement to exercise a joint mediation with the aim of hastening the pacification of Italy on more reasonable bases.[89]

Bastide wished to enter into a mediation agreement which would serve both to preclude the possibility of French intervention and to curtail Sardinia's influence over Northern Italy.

England, for her part, was seriously concerned about the possibility of French intervention in Italy and most eager to avert a general European war.[90] To co-operate with France was an effective means of restraining her. Palmerston showed a 'visible satisfaction' with Bastide's proposed mediation; he briefed Tallenay on the Hummelauer mission and asked what terms Bastide envisaged for the mediation.[91] With both Powers desirous of mediating the Italian question, only the basis for joint mediation now remained to be established.

Bastide had definite ideas as to what sort of basis for joint mediation the two Powers should propose to the belligerents. On 19 July Normanby reported to London Bastide's words to the effect that he 'did not consider it impossible to propose such a division of the North of Italy as should leave under the separate Government, as a distinct state, of an Austrian Archduke, such a portion of the Venetian States as would comprise every assumed interest of Germany'.[92] When Normanby remarked in answer to this that Lamartine, as foreign minister of the Provisional Government, had seemingly committed the French Republic to supporting Venetian independence, Bastide replied that 'circumstances had much changed since then: that the events which were threatening in the East of Europe had given greater importance to the maintenance of the national strength of Austria'.[93] Then, on 22 July Bastide made a proposal which underlined the Republic's willingness to compromise with Austria. The French foreign minister suggested that Lombardy should be allowed to unite

[89] Ibid., Corr. pol., Angleterre 670 (18 July, Bastide to Tallenay).
[90] Ibid. (16 July, Tallenay to Bastide); Britain, PRO, F.O. 27/810 (19 July, Normanby to Palmerston).
[91] FAAE, Corr. pol., Angleterre 670 (21 July, Tallenay to Bastide).
[92] Britain, PRO, F.O. 27/810 (19 July, Normanby to Palmerston).
[93] Ibid. The allusion to 'events which were threatening in the East of Europe' referred to the advance of Russian troops into the Danubian Principalities. For an analysis of France's reaction to this Russian move, see below, Chapter IX.

with Sardinia now that this was a *fait accompli*, while Venetia should remain an Austrian possession, though autonomous under an Austrian Archduke. He also remarked that such an arrangement would be more conducive 'to the real independence of Italy than the erection of a large Kingdom extending from Venice to Genoa under the King of Sardinia, which would in point of fact be a great alteration in the present territorial arrangement of Europe'. There were, he argued, 'two extremes which it would be very difficult' for France 'to admit without opposition: the restoration of Lombardy to the dominion of Austria on the one side, and the union into one powerful state under King Charles Albert of all the Principalities into which the North of Italy has hitherto been divided' on the other.[94] Deeply apprehensive about Venetia fusing with Sardinia, Bastide was prepared to leave at least part of the Venetian province in Austrian hands. This, then, was the 'more reasonable bases' which Bastide had in mind for an Italian settlement.

Austrian diplomatic documents tend to corroborate the assumption that Bastide was so antagonistic toward Charles Albert that he would just as soon have seen Austria retain a part of Italy as have it gravitate into Sardinia's possession. In late spring Bastide avowed to Thom that France had no desire to see Sardinia absorb even Lombardy. Thom reported to 'his government that on 21 June

M. Bastide told me that the French government would see in the union of Lombardy with the states of the King of Sardinia enormous inconveniences and great dangers for the political situation of the south of Europe, that this would constitute an agrandizement for the King of Sardinia which would render him the master of the future fate of all of Italy, and that consequently it would be difficult for France to give her consent to this, France pronouncing herself instead for a free and independent Lombardy.[95]

Then in mid-July Bastide admitted that he would prefer to have Austria rather than Sardinia retain control over Northern Italy. He told Thom that 'we have no interest in seeing Sardinia aggrandized, and we sincerely desire that you retain the greater part of your possessions in Italy'.[96] Again at the end of July, at

[94] Britain, PRO, F.O. 27/810 (22 July, Normanby to Palmerston).
[95] Austria, HHS, Frankreich Korr. Kart. 337 (23 June, Thom to Wessenberg).
[96] Ibid. (12 July, Thom to Wessenberg).

a moment when it seemed as though France might shortly be called upon to intervene in Italy, Bastide exclaimed to Thom: 'Believe me that I, for my part, do not at all desire to see France intervene in Italy in King Charles Albert's favour. I do not hide the way that I feel about this, and thus the Piedmontese party here in France, and which is very numerous, accuses me of following in the footsteps of Guizot.' Bastide made it clear that 'he cared little about the outcome of the war between Austria and Sardinia, as long as France was not obliged to become involved in it'.[97] It might be added that Normanby, for his part, was also convinced that 'in all the policy of France on this subject, one cannot conceal from oneself that jealousy of the aggrandizement of the House of Savoy is a powerful ingredient, and on this common ground she [France] is ready to meet Austria'.[98]

It was quite obvious that France's desire to end the war 'speedily' and thereby obviate any need for intervention by France in favour of Sardinia meant that Venice would be sacrificed and receive something less than the 'independence' from Austria which the French Constituent Assembly's resolution of 24 May had prescribed for Italy. In fact, Bastide's animosity toward Charles Albert's realm had brought him to consider Northern Italy's 'independence' from Sardinia to be at least as important as her liberation from Austrian rule. Still, the terms for the mediation were not as yet definitely established, for Palmerston refused the basis proposed by Bastide on the ground that it was too anti-Italian. Palmerston replied to Bastide's proposal with the remark that Austria would probably accept the terms that he had in mind, but that Britain doubted whether Italy would accept them.[99] Tallenay explained to Bastide that Palmerston was unwilling to accept a basis for negotiation such as the French proposal, which was identical to the second Hummelauer proposal refused by Palmerston in late May. Palmerston would prefer to see Austria retain only a small portion of Venetian territory, exclusive of the city of Venice, and set the Austrian boundary at the Piave instead of at the Adige [the border between Lombardy and Venetia] as France had

[97] Ibid. (28, 31 July, Thom to Wessenberg).
[98] Britain, PRO, F.O. 27/810 (19 July, Normanby to Palmerston).
[99] Ibid., F.O. 27/799 (28 July, Palmerston to Normanby).

proposed. France, for her part, Tallenay remarked, would prefer Austria to retain Venetia all the way to the Adige, an arrangement which 'would have the great advantage of conciliating our respect for the Italian nationality and our own political interests which counsel us not to favour except in a certain measure the ambitious views of King Charles Albert'. Tallenay suggested, though, that Britain would not be adverse to giving independence to both Lombardy and Venice, to the establishment of a Lombard-Venetian state, or to the formation of a Venetian state separate from Lombardy. An arrangement such as the latter, he intimated, could also be to France's advantage, for it too would remove Venice from Charles Albert's control.[100] Bastide and his agent in London concurred in the belief that France should above all act to circumscribe Sardinia's ambitions in Northern Italy. In July the French government was largely indifferent as to whether Venice should gain her independence or simply achieve a certain amount of autonomy under Austria. French antagonism toward Sardinia had developed to the point where the Republic's real concern was keeping Venice out of Sardinia's possession.

[100] FAAE, Corr. pol., Angleterre 670 (30 July, Tallenay to Bastide).

VII

CEMENTING THE MEDIATION *ENTENTE*

By the end of July events in the Italian war theatre seemed to indicate that France might soon be obliged to intervene in Italy to aid Sardinia, despite the Republic's antipathy for that state and her monarch. On 28 July the Provisional Government of Milan, a city hard pressed by Radetzky's army, sent an address to Paris requesting the Republic's 'alliance and intervention'.[1] The following day Reiset reported from Turin that the Sardinian army was 'badly beaten'. The French chargé d'affaires admonished his government to 'intervene if France had the desire to do so, for there is no longer any time to lose'. He added that he had sent a telegraphic dispatch to Paris to inquire on behalf of the Sardinian government as to what France's 'intentions' would be if she were to be requested officially to intervene in Italy.[2] On 30 July Reiset informed his government, again by telegraph, that a representative of the Sardinian government, Albert Ricci, was leaving for Paris:

. . . to come to an understanding with the Republic's government in case French intervention would become necessary.

It is possible that even before his arrival in Paris there would be a need in Lombardy for French troops.

Tomorrow, perhaps, I will be obliged to ask you, in the name of the Sardinian government, for the immediate entrance of the Army of the Alps into Italy.

Reiset stated that the military situation in Northern Italy had disintegrated to the point where 'France would have to start from the beginning again' militarily, but that French intervention seemed to be 'unfortunately inevitable'.[3]

Bastide's consternation was evident. On 31 July, when the false rumour of a major Sardinian victory reached Paris, he rejoiced despite his hatred for Charles Albert, for a Sardinian victory

[1] FAAE, Corr. pol., Turin 321 (28 July, Provisional Government of Milan to Bastide).   [2] Ibid. (29 July, Reiset to Bastide).
[3] Ibid (30 July, Reiset to Bastide).

would make French intervention unnecessary. Normanby reported to his government that Bastide was so preoccupied with avoiding French involvement in Italy that in view of Sardinia's victory he modified his previous position on Venice:

M. Bastide . . . informed me that General Cavaignac and his council had decided that they would not make any objection or raise any question, should even the whole of the Venetian States be added to the dominions of the King of Sardinia. Such a result was not certainly particularly agreeable to them, but they were anxious to show how much they desired an amicable settlement of these questions, and would not therefore raise any difficulties about points of this nature, on which they might be supposed to have a separate interest.[4]

When news later on in the day revealed that the supposed victory had actually been a disastrous Sardinian defeat, Custozza, which laid Milan open to Austrian invasion, Bastide was not dejected, for he reasoned that this might also lead to 'the pacification of Italy' by encouraging a victorious Austria to negotiate. Nevertheless, he now withdrew his categorical statement concerning Venice's incorporation into Sardinia; the war situation was fluid and France could not commit herself to any definite mediation terms.[5]

When word of Albert Ricci's proposed mission reached Paris it caused 'embarrassment' for the French government, which by now dreaded the sort of request that Ricci was prepared to make. General Cavaignac remarked to Normanby that 'he did not see why' his government 'should send an army there [to Italy] upon the mere demand of Charles Albert, and, as for the Italian people, all [his] information up to this time showed [him] that there was no desire for French intervention'.[6] It was evident that the French government, though concerned with the nature of an eventual Italian settlement, was even more interested in the rapid 'pacification' of Italy so that French military involvement in the Peninsula would not be necessary.

Fortunately for France, Sardinia was as reluctant to request French assistance as the Cavaignac regime was unwilling to grant it. Faced with the unpleasant alternative of accepting either military defeat at the hands of Austria or French intervention,

---

[4] Britain, PRO, F.O. 27/810 (31 July, Normanby to Palmerston).
[5] FAAE, Corr. pol., Angleterre 670 (31 July, Bastide to Tallenay).
[6] Britain, PRO, F.O. 27/811 (1 Aug., Normanby to Palmerston).

Charles Albert's government sent Ricci to Paris, but at the same time tried to use the good offices of the English minister in Turin to arrange for 'an honourable armistice' directly with Austria. In late July the diplomatic community in Turin was of the definite opinion that Sardinia 'would withhold any application for French intervention' as long as there was a possibility of agreeing to an armistice with Austria.[7] In fact, it seems that Charles Albert was so reluctant to request French intervention, believing that it would engender the growth of republicanism in Italy, that he reluctantly authorized Ricci's mission to Paris only because of extreme pressure from his cabinet to do so.[8] In the meantime, the Sardinian government, 'far from desiring French intervention', was fervently hoping that Great Britain would facilitate the conclusion of an acceptable armistice with Austria.[9] Upon his arrival in Paris Ricci spoke to Normanby and inquired whether England might be willing to work for an armistice between the belligerents in order to preclude the possibility of French intervention. When Normanby said that if England were to undertake such a mission it would be best not to have France committed to intervention before hand, Ricci willingly agreed to stall for time and to go no further than simply 'arranging with the French government the conditions of intervention in case the eventuality should arise'. Ricci admitted to Normanby that he believed French intervention to be a 'great danger' which should be averted.[10] If an armistice could not be arranged, Sardinia seemed anxious to see joint Anglo-French mediation agreed upon to make French intervention unnecessary. At the same time that Ricci was encouraging Great Britain to arrange for an armistice, Brignole was urging England to agree speedily upon joint mediation with France 'as the only means to avert intervention'.[11]

---

[7] *Parliamentary Papers*, lviii. 92 (30 July, Abercrombie to Palmerston); FAAE, Corr. pol., Turin 321 (1 Aug., Reiset to Bastide).

[8] Costa de Beauregard, op. cit., p. 305; Curato, *Le relazioni diplomatiche fra la Gran Bretagna e il Regno di Sardegna*, i. 288–9 (11 Aug., Abercrombie to Palmerston); Boyer, *La Seconde République, Charles-Albert et l'Italie du Nord en 1848*, pp. 194–7.

[9] Curato, *Le relazioni diplomatiche fra il Regno di Sardegna e la Gran Bretagna*, i. 189–90 (1 Aug., Pareto to Revel).

[10] Britain, PRO, F.O. 27/811 (2 Aug., Normanby to Palmerston).

[11] Ibid. (1 Aug., Normanby to Palmerston).

With both France and Sardinia hoping to avoid French military involvement in the Peninsula, both sides tended to temporize while they waited for the conclusion of either an armistice or a mediation agreement. Ricci, who had arrived in Paris on 1 August, had been sent to the French capital 'not to ask for armed intervention, but to find out what the attitude of the French government would be in case circumstances obliged [Sardinia] to request this intervention'.[12] It seems that Ricci had been empowered to work out with France a convention to regulate eventual French intervention, but that his instructions specifically forbade him to request such intervention without further orders from Turin.[13]

In his first brief conversation with Cavaignac on 2 August Ricci seemed to be intent on simply sounding out the French government about the possibility of French military assistance, for he spoke about French intervention in general. He remarked to Cavaignac that there were two ways in which France might intervene in Italy's favour, either 'morally' or 'materially', and suggested that the implementation of the first sort of assistance might obviate the need for resorting to the second. Cavaignac, for his part, assured Ricci that France was committed to hurrying to Italy's assistance upon Italy's request, but he displayed little desire to fulfil this commitment. He openly avowed to Ricci that France would dislike being obliged to intervene in Italy because such a move might occasion a European-wide war, and, more especially, because 'it could never be in France's interest to form a large state in Italy'.[14] Ricci's reluctance to request French armed assistance was definitely increased by the fact that Cavaignac 'had frankly admitted a jealousy of a large Kingdom of North Italy' in his first conversation with the Sardinian envoy.[15]

[12] Curato, *Le relazioni diplomatiche fra il Regno di Sardegna e la Gran Bretagna*, i. 189–90 (1 Aug., Pareto to Revel).
[13] Curato, *Le relazioni diplomatiche fra la Gran Bretagna e il Regno di Sardegna*, i. 264–6; *Parliamentary Papers*, lviii. 85–6 (29 July, Abercrombie to Palmerston).
[14] Sardinia, AST, Missioni diplomatiche speciali e temporanee (3 Aug., Ricci to Pareto). British diplomatic documents (Britain, PRO, F.O. 27/811, 2 Aug., Normanby to Palmerston) indicate that the first meeting between Ricci and Cavaignac occurred on the morning of 2 Aug. and not on the morning of 3 Aug. as other historians have surmised (Boyer, *La Seconde République, Charles-Albert et l'Italie du Nord en 1848*, p. 200).
[15] Britain, PRO, F.O. 27/811 (2 Aug., Normanby to Palmerston).

The brief meeting between Cavaignac and Ricci on 2 August set the stage for a much longer and detailed conference between the two men the following day. On the evening of 3 August an Italian delegation made up of Ricci, Brignole, and Guerrieri, the latter an unofficial representative of Milan, met with Cavaignac and Bastide for over two hours. The Italian delegation seemed to be somewhat divided, with Guerrieri favouring and Ricci opposing immediate French intervention in Italy.[16] The indecision among the Italian representatives seems to have given Cavaignac the opportunity to take the initiative and dominate the discussions. Cavaignac began by announcing that his government had given the order for a brigade to leave Paris and rejoin the Army of the Alps, an act which constituted a 'moral demonstration' on Sardinia's behalf. But, while the French were willing to assist Charles Albert's kingdom by a 'moral' gesture, Cavaignac soon made it clear that France had little desire to assist Sardinia materially. Cavaignac stated that if Austria were to cross the Tessin and invade Sardinia proper France would come to Sardinia's assistance. He quickly qualified this remark, though, by adding that Austria showed little inclination to do this, for she obviously intended to limit herself simply to reoccupying Lombardy. And, Cavaignac remarked, if Austria simply reoccupied Lombardy, France would not want to be drawn into a war which might degenerate into a general European conflagration. Moreover, Cavaignac repeated once again that 'the formation of a large state in Northern Italy was not compatible with France's interests'. While Cavaignac went on to speak about certain conditions which France would require for an eventual French intervention, Ricci had come to the conclusion that the Cavaignac government was opposed to any such move. The conversation ended when Cavaignac mentioned that his government could make no decision of any kind before consulting with the British; and both Bastide and Ricci agreed that it would be best to defer the question for the present and press for Anglo-French mediation.[17] As the participants left the room, Brignole was heard to mutter: 'I fear French intervention more

[16] Jules Bastide, *La République française et l'Italie en 1848: récits, notes et documents diplomatiques* (Leipzig, 1858), p. 60; Joseph Montanelli, *Mémoires sur l'Italie* (2 vols.; Paris, 1856), ii. 316–17; Costa de Beauregard, p. 310.

[17] Sardinia, AST, Missioni diplomatiche speciali e temporanee (4 Aug., Ricci to Pareto).

L

than I hope for it.'[18] Both France and Sardinia were looking to Great Britain, hoping that Britain's good offices would extricate them from a difficult, embarrassing situation.

In late July and early August the French government availed itself of every opportunity to impress upon Britain the necessity for an immediate agreement on the terms of mediation. On the last day of July Cavaignac told Normanby that the French people as a whole did not want to go to war and that he did not see why France should send an army to Italy to aid Charles Albert. However, Normanby related that: '. . . the General was pleased to appeal to my general knowledge of public opinion in France as assuring a report to Her Majesty's Government that [if Italy appealed for aid] no Government established here would long be able to resist the demand for armed intervention in Italy.' Cavaignac argued that Britain certainly did not want to see France obliged to intervene unilaterally in Italy, so mediation should be agreed on as soon as possible.[19]

The Assembly's resolution of 24 May, calling for the liberation of Italy, was still in effect and no republican government could afford to humiliate itself by refusing its long-promised assistance to Italy. After Cavaignac's discussions with Ricci, internal pressures on the French government increased. Normanby reported to his government that:

Upon every occasion on which I have seen General Cavaignac within the last few days, he has expressed the greatest anxiety for a prompt understanding upon the Italian question. Every day it is evident that he dreads some event which, by exciting the popular feeling here, may overpower his pacific resolves. I am bound to add that I have also received intimations in society and from most of the principal members of the Assembly of all the different parties amongst the friends of peace and order, impressing upon me the urgency of the case; the desire they have that the crisis should be averted by an immediate co-operation on our part; and saying that if something was not done within the next few days, a further reverse on the part of the Italians, or any great town taken, with the aggravating circumstances which would probably attend such an event in the present feeling of both parties, would create such an indignation throughout France as would for the time overbear all

[18] Montanelli, p. 318.
[19] Britain, PRO, F.O. 27/811 (1 Aug., Normanby to Palmerston).

prudential considerations, and would render it impossible for the Government to resist the demand for armed intervention.[20]

The Cavaignac government was using the pressure of French public opinion to impress Britain with the necessity of speedily agreeing to joint mediation.

On 6 August Milan, the 'great town' that the French feared might be taken, fell to Austrian troops. Already on 3 August Charles Albert had remarked to Reiset, who was visiting him on the battlefield, that he 'liked to see Frenchmen under fire'.[21] The Austrians were marching inexorably toward Milan and Charles Albert had probably already made the decision to withdraw rather than make a concerted effort to defend the Lombard capital. Moreover, by 3 August, it had become apparent that Abercrombie's attempts to effect an armistice between the belligerents was to no avail, despite the fact that Reiset had joined his efforts to those of Abercrombie in trying to persuade Radetzky to agree to a cease-fire. With Radetzky refusing to consider an armistice, the Sardinian government had little choice but to turn to France for some sort of assistance.[22] Early in the morning of 4 August the Sardinian king sent a dispatch to his representatives in Paris, ordering them to apply for 'not the intervention but only the co-operation of a French military army corps'.[23]

The dispatch did not reach Paris until the night of 6 August. The following morning Brignole presented to Bastide the official written request—a request which the French government had so long dreaded—for the 'co-operation' of a French 'army corps to assure the triumph of Italian independence'. This application for French assistance was made without any conditions attached. However, if France were to agree to grant this 'military co-operation', Brignole was prepared to present France with a politico-military convention to establish the conditions of

[20] Ibid. (5 Aug., Normanby to Palmerston).

[21] Comte de Reiset, *Mes Souvenirs* (3 vols.; Paris, 1901–2), i. 148.

[22] Curato, *Le relazioni diplomatiche fra il Regno di Sardegna e la Gran Bretagna*, i. 195–7 (4, 5 Aug., Pareto to Revel).

[23] Sardinia, AST, Lettere Ministri Francia (4 Aug., Vincent Ricci to Brignole); Planat de la Faye, i. 335–6. Vincent Ricci seems not to have been related to Albert Ricci, who had been sent on a special mission to Paris. As Sardinian Minister of the Interior, Vincent Ricci was writing to Brignole during the absence from Turin of Pareto, the Sardinian foreign minister.

French intervention.[24] The Sardinian government intended to call for the immediate entrance of some 40,000 French troops into Sardinia, along with the dispatch of some 10,000 additional men to Venice. Moreover, it seems that Sardinia planned to place several severe restrictions upon French military intervention. The Sardinian government had instructed Brignole to make clear in any politico-military convention which might be drawn up that 'the government of the King [of Sardinia] does not intend to accord any cessation of territory to France in the form of compensation. Savoy and the *comté* of Nice have given too much proof of their attachment to the King . . . for the government of His Sardinian Majesty to think in any way of abandoning them.' Moreover, Turin deemed it absolutely essential that France should agree to make no republican propaganda of any kind in Italy. Finally, the Sardinian government would have liked the Republic to agree not to send troops through Savoy on the way to Italy; it would be best, Charles Albert's government felt, if they were sent via Briançon and Suze, for if they were to pass through Savoy their presence could cause 'agitation' within that province.[25]

The Sardinian government stressed in its communications to

---

[24] FAAE, Mémoires et Documents, Italie 36 (7 Aug., Brignole to Bastide).

[25] Sardinia, AST, Lettere Ministri Francia (4 Aug., Vincent Ricci to Brignole). It is interesting to note that the French government conceived of rather different terms for any politico-military accord which might be drawn up to regulate the conditions of French intervention in Italy. As a contingency measure, the French had prepared a policy statement and military convention to be presented to Charles Albert when his government formally recognized the Republic and requested French military assistance. The policy statement bluntly proclaimed that it was not in France's interest to help Sardinia conquer all of Northern Italy. Consequently, the convention stated that joint Franco-Sardinian military operations in Northern Italy should be under the command of a French general, that neither peace nor an armistice should be established without the Republic's consent, that Sardinia should agree to allow Lombardy and Venice to decide whether or not they 'desired to be re-united with Sardinia' after the war ended, and that Sardinia should pledge herself to compromise in no way 'the absolute independence of other peoples of Italy, notably those of Modena, Tuscany, and the Papal States'. It seems that these undated documents, preserved among Cavaignac's personal papers (AD Sarthe, Documents des archives privées de M. Eugène Cavaignac, reel 25) were never presented to the Sardinian government, for France was able to avoid according Sardinia the assistance that she requested. In briefly discussing the eventual conditions of intervention with Ricci on 3 Aug. Cavaignac did stress, though, that any French expedition would have to be entirely under French command and that Turin would be required to pay for and supply the entire military operation.

both Paris and London that it had requested 'co-operation' and not 'intervention' from the Second Republic. This meant that French troops would be integrated into the Sardinian military establishment and would operate under Sardinian command.[26] Still, other Sardinian documents speak openly of French 'intervention' and clearly indicate that Charles Albert's government was quite aware that it had in effect asked for French intervention on 7 August.[27] Sardinia's reticence to use the actual word 'intervention' when applying to France, and Turin's open concern about the fate of Nice and Savoy, indicate that Sardinia was nearly as worried about France's military intervention in Italy as about Austria's military victories. Facing defeat on the battlefield and mounting criticism within Italy, Charles Albert's government had made only a half-hearted request for French assistance.

The French government, forwarned by Ricci on 6 August that a request for 'French armed assistance' was forthcoming from Turin, procrastinated when presented with Brignole's note and abstained from giving an immediate reply, referring to the fact that arrangements for joint mediation had been practically concluded between France and Great Britain.[28] Cavaignac then used the reception of Brignole's note to tell Normanby that:

... nothing could justify him [Cavaignac] at this moment ... in not at once working the telegraph to order a prompt compliance with the demand from Turin, but being able to say openly that there was such a certain prospect of a perfect understanding on the subject between France and England, as gave every chance of a pacific settlement.

The General said that he would do all he could to prevent the single action of France in this matter, which he thought would be a great misfortune, and also a great fault, if she could avoid it.[29]

Paris was making use of every opportunity to prod London into speedily approving the proposed joint mediation.

Pressure for mediation had been steadily building up on Great Britain. In early summer Palmerston had been disinclined to

---

[26] Curato, *Le relazioni diplomatiche fra il Regno di Sardegna e la Gran Bretagna*, i. 195–6 (4 Aug., Pareto to Revel).
[27] Sardinia, AST, Lettere Ministri Francia (9 Aug., Pareto to Ricci and Brignole).
[28] Ibid., Missioni diplomatiche speciali e temporanee (6 Aug., Ricci to Pareto).
[29] Britain, PRO, F.O. 27/811 (7 Aug., Normanby to Palmerston).

commit England to a proposal like the Hummelauer memorandum, calling for Venetia's retention by Austria, for the British government believed such terms would prove unacceptable to Italy. However, the rapidly changing military situation made Palmerston feel that perhaps such a settlement might be possible after all. Already on 7 July Charles Albert had seemed personally to be willing to forego possession of Venice if Sardinia could be guaranteed control of Lombardy, although at this time the Sardinian cabinet, parliament, and people still adamantly refused to consider abandoning Venice.[30] By early August Palmerston surmised that the badly defeated Sardinians would no longer demand possession of Venice, especially since Charles Albert was as adverse to French involvement in Italy as the French themselves. Therefore, on 2 August he informed Tallenay that the British cabinet had just agreed to accept as basis for mediation the so-called second Hummelauer proposal, that is, Vienna's proposal of 24 May calling for the liberation of Lombardy from Austrian control and the granting of liberal institutions to Venetia, which would remain under the suzerainty of an Austrian Archduke.[31] With a personal letter from Palmerston to this effect, Normanby took it upon himself on 5 August to discuss with Bastide and Cavaignac the terms which Palmerston had proposed. Normanby insisted, moreover, that once an Italian settlement was accomplished both Britain and France must agree to 'withdraw from any further interference in the internal affairs of that part of Italy'.[32] The British were still a somewhat reluctant and suspicious ally of the Second Republic.

Since July the French government had been prepared to accept the equivalent of the second Hummelauer proposal, a proposal which would limit Sardinia's control over Northern Italy. In their conversation on 5 August with Normanby about the mediation terms, both Bastide and Cavaignac displayed 'an apparent desire to overlook minor difficulties' in arriving at an agreement with Great Britain, but they did not conceal their 'great dislike of Charles Albert' and their 'unwillingness to concede anything to him that can possibly be avoided'. The French government seemed to feel that the Kingdom of Sardinia was basically 'an

---

[30] *Parliamentary Papers*, lviii, 62–3 (10 July, Abercrombie to Palmerston).
[31] FAAE, Corr. pol., Angleterre 671 (2 Aug., Tallenay to Bastide).
[32] Britain, PRO, F.O. 27/811 (5 Aug., Normanby to Palmerston).

unfriendly neighbour' which would always orient itself diplomatically toward Austria and against France. Cavaignac
expressed some misgivings about the mediators pledging themselves 'to secure to Charles Albert the accession of Lombardy'
because the Lombards might express a 'desire to be independent'
sometime in the future; he also 'felt another difficulty' about the
possibility that French acceptance of the Hummelauer proposal
might oblige France to support Austria in her efforts to reconquer
Venice. In reply to these reservations on the part of France,
reservations which Normanby attributed to the 'embarrassing
position of the French Government' rather than to personal
reticence on the part of Cavaignac and Bastide, the British ambassador replied by insisting that France must recognize the fact
that Lombardy had become a part of Sardinia. As for Venice,
Normanby dryly remarked that France would not be called
upon to back Austria in pacifying this territory, for if France
simply abstained from intervening on behalf of Venice, 'Austria
would want no assistance from anyone to restore her authority
there'.[33]

The French government finally accepted Normanby's terms,
assuring him that France had no designs whatsoever on Italian
territory. That France was not entirely satisfied with the mediation terms was evidenced by Cavaignac's remark on 7 August to
the effect that, now that Charles Albert had abandoned the
defence of Milan, he did not see why the Lombards should not
be able to dispose of their future as they themselves saw fit.[34]
Nevertheless, on 5 August the French government reluctantly
agreed to approve of Lombardy's incorporation into Sardinia as
a basis for an Italian settlement when it became apparent that
such an arrangement was *sine qua non* to British acceptance of
joint mediation.

On 7 August Palmerston approved of Normanby's initiative
on the 5th and proposed official adoption of joint mediation on
the basis of the Hummelauer memorandum of 24 May.[35] On
8 August, a day after receiving the official Sardinian request for
assistance, Bastide was delighted to be able to inform Sardinia
that, in accordance with the French Constituent Assembly's

---

[33] Ibid.
[34] Ibid. (7 Aug., Normanby to Palmerston).
[35] Ibid., F.O. 27/799 (7 Aug., Palmerston to Normanby).

resolution calling for the liberation of Italy, the French Republic was offering her joint mediation with England 'to assure peace and independence to your country without compromising the peace of the world'. Of course, Bastide also assured Sardinia that if the mediation were to fail France would resort to other means and would not hesitate to fulfil 'the debt of honour that she has voluntarily undertaken when she promised the liberation of Italy'.[36] In a similar manner, Cavaignac promised that France would have recourse to 'other means' if it were impossible to obtain the goal of an independent Italy by way of mediation.[37] Still, these half-hearted assurances had little value, for it was quite evident that the Cavaignac government was not at all anxious to intervene in Italy.[38]

The unwillingness of the Sardinian government to see French troops enter Italy is demonstrated by the fact that it signed the humiliating armistice of Salasco-Hess with Austria on 9 August. Even before knowing whether the French had agreed to offer the 'co-operation' that Turin had instructed Ricci to request, the Sardinians seem to have had second thoughts about the wisdom of carrying on the war with French armed assistance, and hastily signed a cease-fire agreement which called for the withdrawal of Sardinian forces behind the Tessin River into Sardinia proper,

[36] FAAE, Corr. pol., Turin 321 (8 Aug., Bastide to Brignole); Bastide, p. 63. The terms of the agreed joint mediation were as follows: (1) A cease-fire; (2) 'Austria should formally renounce all right of sovereignty over Lombardy'; (3) 'The present constitution of the Government of the North of Italy, being the result of the decision formally come to by the Lombards, is a fact which is taken as the basis of mediation, without its being understood that the two Powers guarantee anything subsequent to the conclusion of the Treaty of Peace, which is the object of the mediation'; (4) Lombardy should agree to take upon herself part of the Austrian debt; (5) 'Austria shall retain the Sovereignty of her Venetian Province, which shall be constituted, as Hungary is at the present day, with a separate government and administration'; (6) The future boundary between Venetia and Lombardy, to be decided upon definitely later, should be similar to the former boundary between the two provinces; (7) The future of the duchies of Parma and Modena would be decided upon in a 'separate arrangement'; (8) Private property should be respected and confiscated property restored in both Lombardy and Venetia (Britain, PRO, F.O. 27/811, 10 Aug., Normanby to Palmerston; FAAE, Corr. pol., Angleterre 671, 11 Aug., Normanby to Palmerston).

[37] Sardinia, AST, Missioni diplomatiche speciali e temporanee (8 Aug., Ricci to Pareto).

[38] Boyer has argued that France was prepared, and even willing, to grant Sardinia her military assistance in early August (*La Seconde République, Charles-Albert et l'Italie du Nord en 1848*).

thus permitting Austria to re-establish *de facto* control over all
of Lombardy. Then, on 15 August the Sardinian government
accepted the proferred Anglo-French mediation, a mediation
rendered more difficult from the outset because of Sardinia's
precipitous action in signing an armistice.[39]

The English and French governments both had reason to be
content with the announced mediation. All of Palmerston's
efforts had been directed toward maintaining the peace and preventing French intervention in Italy. Palmerston formally
announced to the British Parliament on 16 August that 'the
principle upon which we have acted is the principle of preserving
the peace of Europe'.[40] The British Foreign Secretary also bluntly
told Normanby that Great Britain's 'object in co-operating with
France in negotiation . . . would be thereby to dissuade the
French Government from armed interference in these Italian
affairs'.[41] Normanby himself avowed late in 1848 that 'ever since
the Revolution, the one great object which I have uniformly
kept in view is to prevent the appearance of a French soldier
beyond the French territory'.[42]

French objectives were also quite clear. Shortly after the question of mediation had been broached for the first time, Bastide
had assured Tallenay in London that if 'the English government
is greatly preoccupied with the possibility of a French military
intervention in Italy, I can tell you and only you confidentially
that, for our part, we have no desire to intervene'.[43] By the
summer of 1848 the French government sincerely regretted the
commitment made to Italy by the French Provisional Government, Executive Commission, and Constituent Assembly. The
Cavaignac government's aversion to military involvement in
Italy would become manifest throughout the autumn of 1848 as
it became increasingly evident that mediation would not bear
fruit.

Lamartine had been prepared to intervene in Italy for reasons
of territorial aggrandizement, but by the late summer of 1848

---

[39] FAAE, Corr. pol., Turin 321 (13, 16 Aug., Reiset to Bastide); *Parliamentary
Papers*, lviii. 205–8 (15 Aug., Abercrombie and Reiset to Revel; 15 Aug., Revel
to Abercrombie).

[40] Taylor, p. 91.

[41] Britain, PRO, F.O. 27/799 (28 July, Palmerston to Normaby).

[42] Ibid., F.O. 27/815 (30 Nov., Normanby to Palmerston).

[43] FAAE, Corr. pol., Angleterre 670 (23 July, Bastide to Tallenay).

France was unwilling to become militarily involved in the Peninsula under any conditions. The Cavaignac government's desire to avoid intervention in Italy is attributable to several factors. There is considerable evidence indicating that from late spring on the European diplomatic scene was no longer as favourable to French involvement in Italy as it had been in early April.[44] By late summer it seemed that French intervention in Italy might entail diplomatic complications of the first order with Germany. This development, along with Bastide's strong dislike of the Sardinian monarchy and the internal factors within France which were still diverting the Cavaignac government's attention from foreign affairs, best explain the French Republic's reluctance to become militarily involved in the Italian Peninsula by late summer.

In the late spring and the summer of 1848 French diplomats were distressed by the tendency of both Frankfurt and the individual German states to identify themselves with Austria's cause in Italy. As early as May the French agent in Baden, Lefebvre, reported that if France intervened in Italy, Austria would do everything in her power to try to obtain German support.[45] It seems that the German states were especially interested in seeing Austria retain the port of Venice, which was used as the primary German commercial outlet on the Mediterranean. Lefebvre reported from Baden, for example, that Germany would support Austria if Sardinia were to threaten the Emperor's hold on Venice.[46] In speaking to Lefebvre, Baron von Arnim of Baden had exclaimed that Germany would 'rather carry on eternal war with you' than see France aid Italy in liberating Venice.[47] It is necessary to note, however, that these reports came from Baden, a state which tended to be antagonistic to France ever since the springtime invasion of Baden by the German *corps franc* based in France.

As the summer advanced Germany seemed to be increasingly disposed to aid Austria in retaining not only Venice but Lombardy as well. By late July the Austrians claimed that Germany would probably support them if France were to attack Radetzky's

44 See above, pp. 125–6.
45 FAAE, Corr. pol., Bade 84 (5 May, Lefebvre to Lamartine).
46 Ibid. (21 June, Lefebvre to Bastide).
47 Ibid. (14 June, Lefebvre to Bastide).

forces in Northern Italy. A former Austrian ambassador to Turin, Buol, announced that if Sardinia called upon France for assistance, 'we also have allies whom we could call upon, and incalculable misfortunes will ensue'.[48] Then too, at this time, the Frankfurt Parliament was encouraging the strengthening of Germany's armed forces, possibly for use against Russia or to put down internal disorders, but possibly also for use in Italy. These developments led a French diplomat in Germany to believe that if France were to intervene in Italy Germany might 'regard the Italian question as a German question'.[49] Further-more, there is no doubt that certain coteries within the Frankfurt Assembly approved of and even hoped for war against France over Italy. Certain conservative groups in the Assembly seem to have believed that war with France would facilitate German unity. The Prussian party, among whose members there was a young junker named Otto von Bismark, was especially convinced of this, believing that German unity would be 'to the profit of the Prussian royal house'.[50]

There is some evidence to suggest that Germany was not over-anxious to become actively involved in the Italian question even if France were to afford Italy her military assistance. The French chargé d'affaires in Frankfurt, Savoye, reported at the beginning of August that the question of German involvement in Italy, if ever brought to a vote, would result in 'an open split in the heart of the Parliament' between conservative and liberal factions.[51] Furthermore, it is possible, as Savoye suggested, that the Frankfurt Parliament wished to settle the Schleswig-Holstein affair before becoming in any way involved in Italy.[52] Still, it seems that at the end of July and the beginning of August, after Archduke John of Austria had assumed the position of executive head of the German government in Frankfurt, an evolution was occurring in Germany's attitude toward Austria, rendering Germany more inclined to assist Austria if a Franco-Austrian war were to break out over Italy. In late July Bastide openly expressed his deep concern about the possibility that French

---

[48] Ibid. (30 July, Lefebvre to Bastide).
[49] Ibid., Corr. pol., Hesse-Cassel 34 (14 July, Rothan to Bastide).
[50] Ibid., Corr. pol., Allemagne 805 (21 July, Savoye to Bastide); Corr. pol., Bade 84 (6 Aug., Lefebvre to Bastide).
[51] Ibid., Corr. pol., Allemagne 805 (2 Aug., Savoye to Bastide).
[52] Ibid (4 Aug., Savoye to Bastide).

intervention in Italy might bring the Frankfurt Assembly to 'take up the question as a German interest' because of Germany's growing preoccupation with retaining the port of Venice and protecting the Tyrolean passes.[53] At the same time Paul Bourgoing, a French diplomatic agent, wrote his influential 'Memoir on the question of intervention in Italy and on the effect that the entrance into battle of a French army would have upon Germany'. Bourgoing argued that, now that Archduke John headed the German Central Government in Frankfurt, French intervention in Italy would 'without a doubt' occasion a 'war against all of Germany'. He concluded that it was not in France's 'true interest' to send troops into Italy.[54] That the French government placed considerable importance upon Bourgoing's 'Memoir' is evidenced by the fact that it is among the select diplomatic dispatches preserved in Cavaignac's personal archives.[55] Thom, the Austrian chargé d'affaires in Paris, was also of the opinion that France's fear of German involvement in Italy 'powerfully contributed' to the Republic's decision not to intervene in the Peninsula. And according to Thom, Thiers, who was often consulted by Bastide concerning foreign policy decisions, had done everything possible to convince Bastide of the danger which he felt France would face on the Rhine if a French army were to march into Italy.[56] The growing possibility of Germany assisting Austria in the case of French intervention beyond the Alps was certainly a factor influencing the Republic to avoid a course of action which was also distasteful to the Cavaignac government for other reasons.

It seems that the primary factor influencing the Cavaignac government not to intervene in Italy was the increasing distrust and animosity between France and Sardinia, a feeling which had grown into deep hatred by the summer.[57] Charles Albert, for his part, had ample reason to distrust France. Throughout the spring the Republic had obviously been interested in territorial aggrandizement at Italy's expense. In the summer the Sardinian king still feared France's ulterior motives. Bastide, being a true

[53] Britain, PRO, F.O. 27/810 (19 July, Normanby to Palmerston).

[54] FAAE, Mémoires et Documents, Autriche 52 (27 July).

[55] AD Sarthe, Documents des archives privées de M. Eugène Cavaignac, reel 25.

[56] Austria, HHS, Frankreich Korr. Kart. 337 (8 Aug., Thom to Wessenberg).

[57] See above, pp. 142–6.

republican with a deep respect for the self-determination of peoples, does not seem to have been animated by any real desire for territorial aggrandizement, as Lamartine had been. Still, the Sardinian government was not reassured by this. In late July Brignole wrote to the Sardinian foreign minister that to accept French intervention would be a 'calamity', for France would probably demand 'promises of compensation for her services'.[58] Then, too, the Sardinian government had become acutely aware that France did not favour the formation of a strong Kingdom of North Italy under Charles Albert's aegis.[59] Furthermore, the Sardinians still feared that if France were to intervene beyond the Alps she might encourage the establishment of a republic in Italy.[60] As Mazzini wrote in a letter to George Sand, the moderates who held power in the Peninsula seemed to be extremely fearful of the republican idea.[61]

Bastide was as antagonistic to the Sardinian monarchy as Charles Albert was suspicious of the Republic. Bastide, the staunch republican and one-time member of the secret societies, despised Charles Albert, who had once been the hope of Italian revolutionaries, but who had betrayed the liberal cause after coming to power. To Bastide, Charles Albert was a 'renegade Carbonari', as the French foreign minister referred to the Sardinian king in a letter to Bixio.[62] In a similar manner the Danish minister in Paris reported to his government after a discussion with the French foreign minister that Bastide spoke 'with very little consideration for the King of Sardinia'; he added that Bastide, remembering his association with Charles Albert when both he and the present king of Sardinia were fellow-members of the Carbonari, 'still thinks of this monarch as a traitor to the cause of liberty'.[63] Bastide evidently felt little enthusiasm for furthering in any way Charles Albert's cause.

Shortly after he was installed in the French Foreign Ministry, Bastide displayed his suspicion of Charles Albert when writing to the French minister in Switzerland. Bastide declared that, although France respected the principle of self-determination of

---

[58] Sardinia, AST, Lettere Ministri Francia (31 July, Brignole to Pareto).
[59] See above, pp. 150–1.
[60] FAAE, Corr. pol., Turin 321 (5 July, Reiset to Bastide); Corr. pol. des consuls, Turin 5, Gênes (23 July, Favre to Bastide).
[61] Sand, pp. 299–300. [62] Reiset, i. 177.
[63] Denmark, Rigsarkivet, Frankrig II (27 July, E. C. L. Moltke to Knuth).

peoples, 'we would have preferred, without any doubt, the triumph of a democracy like our own on the other side of the Alps; we would have liked the republican party, more numerous, skilful, and sympathetic to the people, to have been able to impose its principles; and we are far from overlooking the political consequences of such an aggrandizement' as the probable incorporation of Lombardy, Venice, Modena, and Parma into the Sardinian realm would constitute.[64]

The French government was seriously dismayed by the expansionist tendencies of the Sardinian monarchy. Bastide was rightly convinced that Charles Albert had actively aided Venice only when that city agreed to acknowledge his leadership.[65] Bastide was also aware, as Reiset remarked with considerable justification, that Lombardy had been forced to merge with Charles Albert's Kingdom by Sardinia's threats to remove its troops from Lombardy unless the Lombards recognized Charles Albert as sovereign.[66] French diplomats saw aggressive nationalism looming up in Italy similar to that which was developing in Germany. Immediately after the important Italian victory at Peschiera in late spring Reiset had noted that:

The Sardinians are so happy and proud today that they are already calling Charles Albert the future sovereign of *all* Italy. To listen to them, the states of Naples, Rome, and Florence will be in a very short time united under the *all powerful* sceptre of the *King of Sardinia*. . . .

It will soon be useful for French interests to counterbalance with talent and energy in Turin the far too ambitious views of Charles Albert, who already believes himself to be the absolute master of a population of 26 million people.[67] [Italics underlined in the original.]

As Reiset remarked on another occasion as well, France should 'seriously occupy herself from this time on with limiting Charles Albert's powers'.[68]

Bastide needed little encouragement to do just this. He readily admitted that France was not anxious to build an Italy united under the monarchy of Charles Albert.[69] In fact, he seemed prepared to discourage by discreet diplomatic means the spread of

---

[64] FAAE, Corr. pol., Suisse 561 (23 May, Bastide to Thiard).
[65] Bastide, p. 131.   [66] Reiset, i. 95–6.
[67] FAAE, Corr. pol., Turin 321 (2 June, Reiset to Bastide).
[68] Ibid. (5 June, Reiset to Bastide).   [69] Bastide, p. 30.

Sardinian influence within the Peninsula. In the late spring Bastide had spoken with Mazzini in Paris, asking him to inform the Provisional Government of Lombardy on his return to Italy that France would not permit Lombardy to be annexed by Sardinia without the approval by vote of the Lombard Chamber.[70] Then during June Bastide began to exert French influence in Sicily, favouring the candidacy of the Grand Duke of Tuscany against the Sardinian Duke of Genoa for the Sicilian crown.[71] In fact, throughout the early summer French agents in Tuscany tried to encourage the liberal Tuscan government to exert itself to counterbalance Sardinian influence in Italy.[72] In late July and early August, when France and England were discussing possible mediation terms, Bastide took every opportunity to try to separate Venice, and even Lombardy, from the Sardinian crown. In a similar manner, while France and Britain were discussing their mediation agreement, the French government attempted to convince England that the Duchies of Parma and Modena should not be joined to Sardinia. On 7 August Cavaignac had proposed to Normanby that if their inhabitants so desired the Duchies should be permitted to merge with Tuscany rather than with Sardinia.[73] The French government reiterated this the following day when it 'expressed a strong preference that they [the Duchies] should be united to Tuscany rather than [Sardinia]'.[74] Because of French concern about the Duchies, article seven of the mediation terms stated that a 'separate arrangement' would be made to determine the fate of Modena and Parma. The French evidently interpreted this as meaning that the Duchies would be 'free to join themselves to whomever they wished'; and as late as the end of August Bastide admitted that France 'would prefer' that the Duchies join 'Tuscany rather than Piedmont'.[75] In both the spring and summer the Cavaignac government had made every effort to check Sardinia's territorial expansion.

[70] FAAE, Mémoires et Documents, Italie 36 (6 June, Favre to Bastide).

[71] Ibid., Corr. pol., Naples 174 (17 June, Bastide to Admiral Baudin); Corr. pol., Naples 175 (19 June, Sain de Boislecomte to Bresson).

[72] See the concise, informative article by César Vidal, 'La Toscane et la France au lendemain de la chute de Louis-Philippe, mars–septembre 1848', *Bulletino senese di storia patria* (1951–2), 19–27.

[73] Britain, PRO, F.O. 27/811 (7 Aug., Normanby to Palmerston).

[74] Ibid. (8 Aug., Normanby to Palmerston).

[75] FAAE, Corr. pol., Toscane 182 (29 Aug., Bastide to Benoît-Champy).

Bastide was clearly antipathetic toward any movement for Italian unity under Sardinian leadership. In July he remarked in a dispatch to Rome that the Italians 'should appear a little less inclined to sacrifice themselves' to Charles Albert. 'Italian unity could be an excellent thing', but this unity should be 'based upon a system of federation between the states of the Peninsula, each conserving its independance and rights'.[76] In talks with Normanby he elaborated upon his ideas concerning Italian consolidation, remarking to the English ambassador that 'the nearest approach to unity which could be expected there was a confederation amongst the governing powers of the Peninsula, however separately constituted, and that Rome furnished on every account natural facilities as the centre of such a government'.[77] On the same day Bastide further clarified his position in writing to Sain de Boislecomte that, while France desired the liberation of Italy,

. . . we could not possibly allow it to be achieved to the profit of one Italian Power, thus establishing a domination perhaps more disquieting for Italy than that of Austria herself. That is to say that we could not remain passive and indifferent spectators to the projects of ambition and aggrandizement which King Charles Albert seems to be nourishing. The creation at the foot of the Alps of a monarchy of eleven to twelve million inhabitants, with outlets on two seas, thus constituting a formidable Power, would already be grave enough, without having this new state absorb the rest of Italy. We could allow Italian unity, but under the form and following the principle of a federation between independent states, each having their own sovereignty, balancing each other as much as possible, and not at all a unity which would place Italy beneath the domination and the government of one of these states, and the most powerful of all.[78]

Bastide admitted in his book on Italy that his government did not wish to encourage the formation of a strong, aggressive monarchy of twelve million people at France's very doorstep.[79] A united Italy, like a united Germany, could eventually prove to be a threat to France.

Animosity toward the Sardinian monarchy and concern about

[76] FAAE, Corr. pol., Rome 998 (25 July, Bastide to Harcourt).
[77] Britain, PRO, F.O. 27/810 (19 July, Normanby to Palmerston).
[78] FAAE, Corr. pol., Naples 176 (19 July, Bastide to Sain de Boislecomte).
[79] Bastide, p. 130.

complications with Germany were undoubtedly cardinal reasons why France chose not to intervene in Italy. However, domestic policy considerations also had a profound effect upon the French decision not to become involved in Italy at this time. The June Days had destroyed the hard-core radical formation within the French capital, but the frightened Parisians were not reassured that unrest was ended. In early July the British ambassador in Paris announced that 'the calm which has succeeded to the deadly struggle of last week does not on either side partake of the character of confidence in the future. Preparations are already making for a renewal of the fight.' Normanby admitted that on the side of the workers—he called them the 'anarchists'—'little has yet been actually done', but he argued that the activists were smarting for revenge. 'On the side of order', on the other hand, there was 'a very large increase in the garrison of Paris' and a 'continued search for arms'.[80] Rumours spread throughout the summer that another uprising was impending.[81] The search for arms among workers, artisans, and students continued throughout the summer in such popular areas as the Latin Quarter, Belleville, and Menilmontant. Insurgent suspects were still being arrested as late as 9 August; and on 8 August a convoy of from ten to twelve wagons of recently confiscated arms wound its way through the streets of Paris on the road to Vincennes.[82]

The government shared the popular fear of continued unrest in the French capital. Throughout the summer Cavaignac argued in the Assembly that the state of siege was absolutely necessary for internal security within Paris; and the state of siege was not lifted until 19 October. Owing to the fear of unrest in the capital, the Assembly passed a resolution on 11 July providing that as of 20 July 'at least fifty thousand men' of the regular army should be stationed in the Paris area.[83] Early in August some contingents of troops did depart for the Italian frontier to rejoin the Army of the Alps.[84] As a result, a shudder of fear arose in Paris. Word spread that the government was ready to close the army camp at St. Maur, and the government had to put the lie quickly to this rumour to restore confidence

[80] Britain, PRO, F.O. 27/810 (4 July, Normanby to Palmerston).
[81] De la Gorce, i. 402–3.
[82] *Le Constitutionnel*, 18 July, 9, 10 Aug.; *Le Moniteur universel*, 13 Aug.
[83] *Le Moniteur universel*, 12 July.
[84] FAAE, Corr. pol., Suisse 562 (4 Aug., Barmen to Funck).
8225148   M

among the shaky Parisians.[85] Despite some troop movements in early August, other army units were quickly dispatched to Paris and a Parisian newspaper could report that more than the 50,000 troops required by order of the Assembly were still stationed in Paris.[86] Moreover, besides the considerable concentration of troops within the French capital, throughout the summer some 48,000 French troops were also being deployed to keep order in the other revolutionary centres of France, such as Lyons, where army units were dispatched on three different occasions.[87] French troops were still committed in large numbers to internal peace-keeping duties, diverting strength from the units on the frontier which would have had to be called upon if France had intended to intervene in Italy.

Several contemporary observers were quick to notice that internal insecurity within France throughout the summer of 1848 was having a restraining effect on French foreign policy. At the very outset of the June Days Belgian diplomatic agents uttered a sigh of relief, for France was 'too occupied with her troubles to think of war and conquests'. The Belgian ambassador in London wrote to Brussels: 'I think that we can count upon the maintenance of peace for several more months.'[88] The Austrians, for their part, tended to be less fearful of French involvement in Italy after the June Days.[89] In a similar manner Palmerston, that astute analyst of French internal affairs, was convinced that the chances of France intervening in Italy had been greatly diminished by the June Days.[90] By the summer of 1848 *The Times* of London was also of the opinion that France would not intervene in Italy because of internal instability:

Nothing would be so fatal to the hope of tranquility on the other side of the Channel as a foreign war at the present moment. General Cavaignac has enemies enough from within to contend with, without seeking to complicate his situation by the chances of a collision

---

[85] *Le Constitutionnel*, 5 Aug.

[86] *Le Journal des débats*, 6 Aug.

[87] De Luna, p. 202. De Luna's work offers the most detailed discussion available on French internal developments between June and December, 1848, a period which has been relatively neglected by historians.

[88] Ridder, ii. 118 (22 June, Van der Weyer to King Leopold I).

[89] Austria, HHS, Frankreich Korr. Kart. 337 (1 July, Thom to Wessenberg); Greer, p. 238.

[90] Curato, *Le relazioni diplomatiche fra il Regno di Sardegna e la Gran Bretagna*, i. 161-2 (29 June, Revel to Pareto).

with any of the great Powers of Europe. . . . Even at the moment at which we write, a spark would be sufficient to light up again the furnace into which all that represents in France social order and the arts of peace may once again be cast. General Cavaignac is no doubt aware of the vast responsibility he would incur were he to commit a country so critically situated as is France just now, to the hazard of a contest with a Power [Austria] which even in its ruin has proved itself no contemptible opponent.[91]

A conservative French daily concurred in *The Times*'s analysis of the French internal situation. The *Journal des débats* remarked that 'there is only one party which war, a war without reason and necessity, could profit: the party which has been defeated in the streets'.[92]

Certain French statesmen also believed that internal policy problems had had a profound influence on the Cavaignac government's decision not to become involved in Italy. Lamartine asserted that when Italy finally called for French assistance in early August, the Cavaignac government 'no doubt no longer had the same liberty of movement, the same availability of military forces' because of 'the sinister June events'.[93] Reiset, when speaking about French intervention in Italy, intimated that 'the French government, especially after the June Days, was far from wanting to become involved in such an adventure'.[94] Bourgoing asserted in his 'Memoir' that French intervention in Italy, while it might entail the danger of war with Germany, would acquire 'an added perilous gravity from our interior situation and from the necessity to retain *at home* and *for our own use* a large portion of our military and financial resources'.[95] [Italics underlined in the original.] Bastide stated bluntly that 'the insurgents of June had come to the aid of Radetzky', for the French army was tied down in Paris by the threat of unrest there: 'we no longer had an army to send outside of France. . . . Our land forces were paralysed.'[96] Cavaignac himself supposedly argued in front of the Foreign Affairs Committee of the Constituent Assembly that French intervention in Italy would result in

---

[91] *The Times*, 3 Aug., quoted in *Le Constitutionnel*, 5 Aug.
[92] *Le Journal des débats*, 11 Aug.
[93] Lamartine, *Le Passé, le Présent et l'Avenir de la république*, p. 65.
[94] Reiset, i. 159.
[95] FAAE, Mémoires et Documents, Autriche 52.
[96] Bastide, p. 35.

'interior convulsions' as well as a general war.[97] A recent scholar has asserted that 'Cavaignac in particular, mindful of the results of revolutionary warfare during the first French Revolution, feared that war would result in a military dictatorship in France, and conquest rather than liberation abroad'.[98] It seems that the moderate republican fear of Jacobinism and Bonapartism following in the train of war, a fear which had pervaded France in the spring, was still prevalent after the June Days. The forty-eighters, who had learned their lesson from the First French Revolution only too well, were not inclined to venture into a path of conduct which could negate their June victory, enhance the position of their radical enemies, and possibly result in the demise of the moderate Republic. Internal policy considerations still weighed heavily upon the 'defenders of order' within France who were also responsible for formulating French foreign policy.

[97] Gaston Bouniols, *Histoire de la révolution de 1848* (Paris, 1918), p. 315.
[98] De Luna, pp. 340–1.

VIII

PACIFIC VERSUS ARMED MEDIATION

THE desire to avoid intervention in Italy remained the paramount foreign policy consideration of the Cavaignac government throughout the entire autumn of 1848. However, the French were willing to assist Italy as a whole, if not Sardinia in particular, as much as possible within the framework of the mediation. The Cavaignac government was bound by the Constituent Assembly's resolution of 24 May calling for 'the liberation of Italy'. Successful Anglo-French mediation of the Italian question was the only means the French government had of achieving some sort of 'liberation' for Northern Italy short of unilateral military intervention, intervention distasteful to Sardinia and repulsive to France. The French government realized that the best way to assure peace was to continue the mediation process. And the only way to justifying the role of mediator was to make the mediation meaningful. Thus, throughout the autumn of 1848 the French government made sincere efforts to bring the mediation to fruition.

The bases of mediation proposed by Palmerston were formally agreed to by Bastide in a note to Normanby dated 9 August.[1] Already at this time it was apparent that the English and French, although agreeing on the bases of joint mediation, envisaged two rather different means of implementing the mediation. Both England and France were primarily interested in preserving the peace, and both countries expressed confidence in the prospects for a successful outcome to the mediation in which the Italian cause would be peacefully advanced. Palmerston told the Sardinian representative in London that he believed the mediation would be acceptable to Austria and that it would be successful in its aims.[2] In a similar manner, the official French newspaper assured the French public that the joint mediation would

---

[1] FAAE, Corr. pol., Angleterre 671 (9 Aug., Bastide to Normanby).

[2] Curato, *Le relazioni diplomatiche fra il Regno di Sardegna e la Gran Bretagna*, i. 198–9 (8 Aug., Revel to Pareto).

achieve 'a prompt and honourable result', leading to 'the prompt re-establishment of peace in Italy'.[3] However, the French, unlike the English, were prepared from the outset to reinforce pacific mediation with armed Anglo-French mediation if this were necessary to realize an acceptable settlement to the Italian question.

On 7 August the French government suggested to the British ambassador in Paris that their two countries should engage in 'an armed mediation'. Cavaignac attested to the fact that 'his great desire was to avoid a war which would sooner or later involve all Europe'. The best way to do this, he argued, was for France and England to come to an agreement which would have the effect of imposing their will upon Europe. Furthermore, he suggested that 'by giving the mediation to a certain extent an armed character there would be an additional security to Europe against any aggression on the part of France as long as England was acting with her'.[4] The following day Cavaignac again proposed that 'if the mediation seemed likely to meet with any difficulties, it would be desirable that it should partake something of the character of a joint demonstration of an armed character'. He added that such an agreement would also constitute 'an effectual stop between France and that independent action which it was obvious would become a necessity for her if the mediation failed because Austria refused to surrender Lombardy'.[5] Then, in a detailed letter of secret instructions to Gustave de Beaumont, de Tocqueville's confidant and the newly appointed French minister to London, Cavaignac reiterated his belief that 'England's interest is to moderate and impede French action in the Italian solution' and that the two Powers should agree to 'an armed mediation', and perhaps eventually overt intervention, to be implemented if Austria insisted upon retaining Lombardy. Cavaignac stressed the point that France wished to end her isolation by forming a close alliance with England, an alliance which could 'impose peace upon Europe'. Finally, he intimated that France would take up arms if mediation failed, appealing to the 'masses' and 'peoples' of Europe and stirring up revolutionary support if necessary, a threat which French diplomats would use

---

[3] *Le Moniteur universel*, 12 Aug.
[4] Britain, PRO, F.O. 27/811 (7 Aug., Normanby to Palmerston).
[5] Ibid. (8 Aug., Normanby to Palmerston).

continually against both Austria and England in their desire to ensure the success of mediation.[6] At a time when mediation had just been proposed, the French were actually inviting England to restrain France's actions by acceding to a programme of joint armed mediation which the Powers could use to pressure Austria into accepting the mediation. France was trying to convince the British of the need to act together in joint armed mediation so that she would not be obliged to act alone if the mediation failed.

The English viewed joint mediation in a somewhat different light from the French. Before the terms of mediation had been agreed upon, Palmerston had written to Normanby that 'Her Majesty's Government, though they might consent to mediate, would not be parties to any forcible interference in these matters'. Moreover, the British Foreign Secretary had avowed that the very reason Britain was engaging in mediation was 'to dissuade the French Government from armed interference in these Italian affairs'.[7] London, therefore, could not be expected to accede to the course of action now proposed by Paris.

When the French made their first suggestion that joint mediation might be transformed into joint armed mediation, in which both France and England would intervene in Italy on a minor scale to facilitate the negotiating process, Normanby told Ricci that England 'could never take the least part in an intervention, not wanting to strip Austria's Italian possessions from her by brute force'. At the same time he warned Cavaignac 'that the formal declaration of an intervention could be harmful to the success of mediation, for Austria would find it incompatible with her dignity to treat under the weight of an intervention, realized before friendly negotiations had begun'.[8] Great Britain had accepted joint mediation only to preclude the possibility of French intervention in Italy, and from the outset made it clear that she would have no part in intervention of any kind, even if it were in the form of a small joint expedition with the sole

---

[6] AD Sarthe, Documents des archives privées de M. Eugène Cavaignac, reel 25 (8 Aug., Cavaignac to Beaumont). Beaumont was sent to London to replace Tallenay, who in turn was appointed French minister to Frankfurt, replacing Savoye.

[7] Britain, PRO, F.O. 27/799 (28 July, Palmerston to Normanby).

[8] Sardinia, AST, Missioni diplomatiche speciali e temporanee (8 Aug., Ricci to Pareto).

purpose of strengthening the position of the mediating Powers. As for the French, their desire to implement joint armed mediation would increase as it became progressively more apparent that Austria had no intention of making any concessions whatsoever to the mediating Powers unless she were forced to do so.

In early August the mediating Powers had some reason to believe that Austria might prove amenable to a settlement similar to the one outlined in the mediation proposal which they had submitted to Sardinia and Austria for their acceptance.[9] As late as 7 August the diplomatic world believed that Austria wished an Italian settlement, wanted to extract herself from much of Northern Italy, and might be willing to grant Lombardy her independence.[10] Under these circumstances Bastide decided to try to cajole Austria into accepting Anglo-French mediation. In his first approach to Austria he seems to have purposely refrained from mentioning his government's attempts to complement the mediation with provisions for armed mediation, adopting instead an unusually friendly tone in addressing the Austrian minister in Paris. Bastide assured Thom that:

We have at this time only two interests in Italy, one to re-establish peace there, the other not to see created on our southern borders a powerful state, which would be displeasing to us. The offer of mediation, which we in concert with England have addressed to you, is purely friendly; it is not an armed mediation, which, as well as intervention, has not and will not enter into our minds, and still less into our wishes, as long as we do not know the result of the proposals [of joint mediation] sent yesterday to the courts of Vienna and Turin. To think at this time of an intervention would be to depart from our role of unofficial mediator, and we wish to persevere in this to the very end. . . . As for the . . . proposals, we have taken for a basis—for one was necessary—the overtures made by the cabinet in Vienna to London in the month of May last [the second Hummelauer proposal]. They do not prejudice in any way the final settlement and we understand very well that after the battlefield developments of the last two weeks you do not wish to be held to the terms which you offered under entirely different conditions three months ago. . . .[11]

In a discussion with Thom four days later Bastide repeated his

9 For the terms of this proposal, see above, p. 158.
10 *Parliamentary Papers*, lviii. 139 (7 Aug., Ponsonby to Palmerston).
11 Austria, HHS, Frankreich Korr. Kart. 337 (10 Aug., Thom to Wessenberg).

government's awareness of the fact that a victorious Austria might no longer be willing to accept the Hummelauer proposals as such, and expressed France's willingness to accede to a settlement in which Vienna would simply grant autonomy and liberal institutions to her Italian holdings.[12] At the same time he attempted to gain Thom's confidence by expressing France's interest in Austria's well-being and suggesting that this well-being could best be advanced by the establishment of peace in Italy.[12] Then, less than ten days later Bastide displayed satisfaction with news from Italy indicating that the Lombards were so disenchanted with Sardinia that they were no longer interested in merging with Charles Albert's kingdom, preferring instead to retain connections with Venice, which would remain attached to Austria.[13] By these intimations Bastide was obviously trying to influence Austria to readily accept the proferred mediation, suggesting that the proposed terms were flexible and not binding. Thom, for his part, could rightly conclude from Bastide's language that France was willing to let Austria retain Lombardy provided that some 'concessions' were made to allow France to save face; some concessions made to Northern Italy would furnish the Republic 'with the means to say that she was freed from her commitments' toward Italy.[14]

Bastide was trying to play both sides against the middle by appealing to Britain and Austria simultaneously and in contradictory terms in an effort to advance the mediation cause. However, while the French foreign minister was attempting to intimidate England and charm Austria, disquieting news arrived from Italy. After driving Charles Albert from Milan, the Austrian army had entered the Papal Legations and was marching on Bologna, a move which suggested that the Austrians intended to entrench themselves militarily in Northern Italy. This development determined the French government to exert further pressure on both England and Austria to bring the mediation to fruition. Cavaignac told Normanby that 'the whole character of the question was changed, as Austria had no more right to Bologna than to Lyons'. Cavaignac's statement made Normanby reflect that 'one cannot help fearing that, in consequence of

---

[12] Ibid. (14 Aug., Thom to Wessenberg).
[13] Ibid. (23 Aug., Thom to Wessenberg).
[14] Ibid. (16, 23 Aug., Thom to Wessenberg).

this entirely unexpected turn of events, the French army may feel themselves obliged to take a step in advance to cross the frontier they have been invited to pass'.[15] Two days later Bastide informed Normanby that 'it was impossible that France could submit to such an invasion of the Papal territory'. He added that indeed 'the Pope had already applied to [France] for assistance'.[16]

The Pope had requested that a French general and fleet be placed at his disposal, supposedly for protection against Austria, but probably for use against possible internal disorders.[17] Faced with another Italian request for assistance and a seemingly aggressive act by Austria, Bastide promised a general and a French ship to the Pope and protested to Austria about the advance of Imperial troops.[18] At the same time he pressed Britain to reconsider the concept of armed mediation, for it was no longer an academic question and it might have to be invoked in light of Austria's menacing attitude toward Papal territory.

Bastide wrote to Beaumont to inform him of the Austrian advance into the Legations and instruct him 'to apply pressure upon Palmerston for the armed mediation which becomes more urgent every day'.[19] Accordingly, Beaumont visited the British Foreign Secretary and stressed the need for armed mediation, trying to convince Palmerston that because 'the success of purely friendly mediation was becoming improbable, it was becoming necessary to foresee already at the present time the need for armed mediation and to regulate its conditions'. Beaumont described his conversation with Palmerston in the following manner:

I was profoundly disappointed to see him opposed to the only means which appeared to me able to render efficacious the present mediation . . . I assured him that . . . the Republic [would be] inevitably drawn into a war if the Austrians remained in Milan . . . but that even if she decided to act alone in case of necessity, she felt the sincere desire to act only in common accord with England; that this

---

[15] Britain, PRO, F.O. 27/811 (9 Aug., Normanby to Palmerston).
[16] Ibid. (11 Aug., Normanby to Palmerston).
[17] FAAE, Corr. pol., Rome 988 (4, 14 Aug., Harcourt to Bastide).
[18] Ibid. (14 Aug., Bastide to Harcourt); Corr. pol., Autriche 436 (12 Aug., Bastide to Delacour); Austria, HHS, Frankreich Korr. Kart. 337 (23 Aug., Thom to Wessenberg).
[19] FAAE, Corr. pol., Angleterre 671 (11 Aug., Beaumont to Bastide).

common action was in the interest of everyone, [that if] friendly mediation failed, France would find it necessary to recommence alone a war which once begun could not be limited, while if prepared and conducted jointly could naturally be contained in a pattern prescribed in advance.

As Beaumont suggested, Palmerston would not hear of the French proposal to go beyond friendly mediation. The British Foreign Secretary repeated his faith in the mediation being eventually successful and added that Austria would be more inclined to negotiate if she were not threatened. Beaumont concluded the report of his conversation in London by stating that he was convinced that Britain's policy, unless she were obliged to change it by French threats of unilateral intervention in Italy, 'was to hold to pacific friendly mediation . . . and once this phase of the mediation was outdated, no matter what happened, to leave us with our feet in the air in Europe while she remained tranquilly on her rock'.[20]

After receiving Beaumont's discouraging report, Cavaignac tried to appeal personally to Normanby, arguing that French public opinion would oblige his government to intervene unilaterally in Italy if Austrian troops remained in Bologna or advanced on Tuscany or the Papal States; the only way to avoid this was by agreeing to make 'a strong joint remonstrance' which would induce Austria immediately to withdraw from the Legations.[21] But this too was to no avail. The British were as unresponsive as ever to French pleas for implementing armed mediation if the necessity for it arose.

The Cavaignac government increasingly felt the need to supplement friendly mediation with provisions for armed mediation because of both the progressive hardening of Austria's attitude toward Italy and the political developments within the Peninsula itself. By the middle of August it became apparent that Austria believed herself entitled to some 'territorial indemnity' for her victories and that she intended to retain all of her Italian provinces.[22] This amounted to a *de facto* refusal by Austria of the proposed mediation. Then, too, Venice had broken away from Sardinia when Charles Albert signed the armistice of Salasco–Hess

[20] Ibid. (12 Aug., Beaumont to Bastide).
[21] Britain, PRO, F.O. 27/812 (14 Aug., Normanby to Palmerston).
[22] *Parliamentary Papers*, lviii. 171 (13 Aug., Cowley to Palmerston).

with Austria and had established itself as an independent republic, headed by the Italian patriot Daniel Manin. The Venetian Republic announced that it would not submit to Austrian hegemony, that it would resist by force of arms any Austrian attempt to reconquer Venetia. This decision on the part of Venice was to have important repercussions upon French policy toward Italy.

While the new Venetian Republic bravely prepared to resist Austrian attempts to overrun Venetia, the Sardinian fleet, which had been cruising off Venice, was preparing to withdraw from the Adriatic in conformity with the armistice terms.[23] With the Austrian fleet advancing on Venice, it seemed that the city would certainly fall unless the mediating Powers came to its aid. In such dire straits the Venetian Provisional Government turned to the French Republic for succour. On 9 August the French consul in Venice, Vasseur, was handed a note officially requesting French armed assistance.[24] Manin followed this up with impassioned personal pleas to Bastide, 'invoking the aid of the free people of France' and reminding the French foreign minister that this had been promised by the 24 May resolution of the French Constituent Assembly. Manin announced that Venice's 'peril was extreme', that her 'independence rested upon the prompt assistance' which he felt certain France would accord a fellow Republic.[25] French armed assistance had once again been requested by Italy. In light of France's firm commitment to grant Italian states French assistance upon their request, it seemed that the Republic might be obliged to become militarily involved in Italy after all.

Bastide seems to have been genuinely moved by Venice's plight. He had great respect for Venice's republican form of government and for the heroic defence that the beleaguered city was putting up against Austria. In reply to the Venetian appeal for assistance, he tried to persuade Austria to extend the armistice of Salasco–Hess which had been signed on 9 August to cover

[23] FAAE, Corr. pol., Autriche 436 (15 Aug., Delacour to Bastide); Austria, HHS, Frankreich Korr. Kart. 337 (14 Aug., Thom to Wessenberg).
[24] FAAE, Corr. pol. des consuls, Autriche 8, Venise (4 Aug., Provisional Government of Venice to Bastide). Document dated 4 Aug., but first handed to the French consul on 9 Aug.
[25] Planat de la Faye, i. 343, 376–7 (11 Aug., Manin to Bastide; 14 Aug., Provisional Government of Venice to Bastide).

Venice, and thereby terminate the immediate threat to the city. He also strove to persuade Austria to grant Venice the most liberal institutions possible under Austrian tutelege. However, Bastide would try to attain all of these goals through mediation or the threat of armed mediation and not through the use of French troops. Venetian independence might have been dear to France, but it was not worth war. Throughout the autumn the Cavaignac government would prove as reluctant to go to war for Venice as for Sardinia, persevering in its role of mediator even when it became evident that mediation alone had little chance of success.

On 12 August Venice made a formal request for a shipment of French guns.[26] On 20 August a Venetian representative, Tommaseo, arrived in Paris carrying a request for French armed intervention.[27] Already on 19 August Bastide had made clear what his reply would be. In a letter to the Provisional Government of Venice he declared that:

France does not repudiate her solicitude for the Italian cause or the declarations emanating from her [Constituent Assembly] in favour of this noble cause. Our dispositions have not changed; but on the other hand, Gentlemen, France has the right, and at the same time the duty toward herself, also to consult her own interests and to take equally into consideration the interests of peace in general. Therefore, she has found it appropriate and necessary to consecrate her efforts, before anything else, to preparing a peaceful solution, and it is in this sense and toward this end that, in concert with England, she has proposed to the Emperor of Austria and the King of Sardinia a friendly mediation. The negotiations have commenced: it is advisable to await the result.[28]

Bastide ended his letter with assurances that the Republic would take up the sword if mediation failed. Nevertheless, his declaration smacked too much of Lamartine's speech of 26 March, refusing aid to the Poles, to be reassuring to the Venetians.

When Tommaseo visited the Foreign Ministry to deliver his note, Bastide informed him that even before the Venetian request

---

[26] FAAE, Corr. pol. des consuls, Autriche 8, Venise (12 Aug., Vasseur to Bastide).   [27] Planat de la Faye, i. 401.
[28] FAAE, Corr. pol. des consuls, Autriche 8, Venise (19 Aug., Bastide to Provisional Government of Venice).

arrived two French ships had been ordered to cruise in the Adriatic near Venice. France would not send troops, though, because this could lead to a European conflict.[29] The French Republic regretted that it could not accord Venice the armed assistance that she requested, but France could not 'intervene with arms in Italy at the moment when she was proposing a pacific mediation to Austria'. Bastide announced that he had sent a stern note to Austria demanding a 'categorical reply' as to whether or not Vienna would accept the mediation and consequently suspend military operations against Venice; if Austria refused to do so France would act to assist Venice.[30] But for the present time France would go no further. Both Bastide's letter to the Provisional Government of Venice and his reply to Tommaseo indicated quite clearly that, despite her sympathy for the Venitian cause, France was first and foremost a mediator.

Bastide seems to have made no immediate effort to send off the shipment of guns which Venice requested. This does not, however, constitute a sign of French disinterest in the Venetian cause. Throughout the year 1848 the French Republic readily sold arms to not only Venice, but also Milan, Sicily, and Sardinia.[31] The French Provisional Government had authorized the sale of up to 100,000 guns to Italy in April and many of these weapons were being delivered to Sardinia and Venice by the autumn.[32] Lamartine had been somewhat reluctant to deliver arms to Venice in the spring when he was offering his good offices to Austria; and the Venetians had accused him of duplicity.[33] Nevertheless, Bastide had shown his sympathy for Venice as soon as he assumed his portfolio, for he offered 20,000 weapons to that city on 17 May.[34] During the summer, when Venice voted for incorporation into Sardinia, weapons destined originally for Venice were offered to Sardinia. In fact, most

---

[29] Planat de la Faye, i. 400–2 (23 Aug., Tommaseo to Provisional Government of Venice).   [30] Ibid.

[31] A detailed study of this is presented by Ferdinand Boyer: 'Les fournitures d'armes faites par le gouvernement français aux patriotes italiens en 1848 et en 1849', *Rassegna storica del Risorgimento*, xxxvii (1948), 95–102; 'Comment la France arma le Piémont en 1848', ibid. xlix (1960), 485–90. Boyer interprets the sale of arms by France to Italy in 1848 as indisputable evidence that France was devoted to the Italian cause and actively assisting Italy.

[32] Boyer, *Rassegna storica del Risorgimento*, xxxvii. 97.

[33] Planat de la Faye, i. 213–14 (7 May, Zanardini to Provisional Government of Venice).   [34] Garnier-Pagès, x. 5–6; Bastide, p. 137.

French arms shipments in August were being made to Sardinia. By October, though, arms shipments were being made directly to Venice once again.[35] The French Republic in 1848 seems to have been quite willing to sell arms to any of the Italian states, even to Sardinia for which Bastide felt aversion. The Republic had promised to assist Italy, and shipments of arms were a token of assistance.

When the Venetian Republic asked France for armed assistance, Bastide decided to apply increased pressure on both London and Vienna to revive the mediation and obviate the need for intervention. Since the inception of the mediation, the French government had assured Italy that it was prepared to resort to arms if peaceful negotiations failed.[36] Now France made a concerted effort to convince Europe, and especially England and Austria, that the Republic was sincere in its proclaimed willingness to declare war if mediation proved unsuccessful.

In London Beaumont launched a campaign to pressure the British government into accepting closer ties with France and agreeing to armed mediation. Beaumont believed that only one thing could oblige England to act in joint armed mediation with France: the fear that France would act alone, precipitating a general European war. Beaumont assured his government that he would 'neglect nothing to give England this conviction'.[37] As Beaumont wrote on another occasion, this time to his confidant de Tocqueville, 'the only way to prevent war is to convince Europe that if the Italian affair does not receive a solution which saves our honour we will be forced to cross the Alps'.[38] The French minister in London was convinced that 'all of France's diplomatic powers' lie in holding the sword so that 'although not drawn from its sheath, it appears always suspended and ready to act'.[39] In line with this strategy, on 22 August Beaumont informed Lord Russell that France would not hesitate to intervene alone in Italy if England would not co-operate in armed mediation with her. Beaumont also suggested to Russell that perhaps

---

[35] Boyer, *Rassegna storica del Risorgimento*, xlix. 487; xxxvii. 98; FAAE, Corr. pol. des consuls, Autriche 9, Venise (3 Oct., Vasseur to Bastide).

[36] See above, p. 158.

[37] FAAE, Corr. pol., Angleterre 671 (12 Aug., Beaumont to Bastide).

[38] De Tocqueville, *Œuvres complètes*, vol. viii, part 2, p. 19 (15 Aug., Beaumont to de Tocqueville).

[39] FAAE, Corr. pol., Angleterre 671 (6 Sept., Beaumont to Bastide).

a European Congress could meet to settle many of the problems facing Europe, especially those of Italy.[40]

The British government testified to its partnership with France in the mediation by officially recognizing the French Republic on 19 August, contributing to the process whereby all of the European Powers with the exception of Russia would officially recognize the Republic by the end of September. Still, the English were not willing to go beyond this to strengthen their ties with France and turn the mediation *entente* into an armed mediation alliance. Nevertheless, the French persisted in their efforts. Normanby reported from Paris that General Cavaignac was 'very impatient' that Austria had not accepted the mediation and was still threatening Venice and the Legations.[41] Bastide informed London that France had sent a note to Austria urging that Power to accept the mediation and suspend hostilities against Venice. He added that his government would appreciate Great Britain making a similar move, for if Austria did not accept the mediation France would have to answer Venice's appeal. He admonished Beaumont

. . . to try, Sir, to bring Lord Palmerston to recognize that common action by France and England is alone efficacious. As this moment all the Great Powers of Europe are in a state of isolation. Such a state of affairs is essentially compromising to the peace. The first two Powers that unite and declare vigorously that the only aim of their alliance is the keeping of the peace, so necessary to all, will lay down the law to Europe and will have rendered her an immense service. . . . Now there is only one important thing to do: conserve the peace and allow the peoples to provide for what they believe to be their own individual well-being without being condemned to throw themselves once more against each other. If England wishes this as we do, success is assured. When we will have placed Europe back on its feet, then will be the time to return to such questions as preponderance and rivalry.[42]

The French foreign minister was obviously attempting to allay any fears which Britain might have of France and to draw the two countries into a common alliance.

Haunted with the fear of war, France pressed on for common,

[40] FAAE, Corr. pol., Angleterre 671 (22 Aug., Beaumont to Cavaignac).
[41] Britain, PRO, F.O. 27/812 (24 Aug., Normanby to Palmerston).
[42] FAAE, Corr. pol., Angleterre 671 (24 Aug., Bastide to Beaumont).

armed mediation with England to preclude the possibility of being drawn alone into a war in the Peninsula. On 25 August Beaumont submitted a memorandum proposing close co-operation and armed mediation to Palmerston, who had requested such a document, for consideration by the British cabinet.[43] This document reminded the English government that, although France desired peace, she had definite commitments to Italy. Poland had been too distant for France to go to her rescue; but Italy was at France's doorstep and the French Republic would act unless Austria agreed to the mediation. In this memorandum the Cavaignac government argued that

The only means of preventing war, or if war broke out to contain it within limits set up and determined in advance, is for France and England to come together as of today [and agree] upon the conduct that they will take if the pacific mediation agreed upon in common does not succeed. . . . There are two great nations which can assure to the world the maintenance of this very precious [peace]; to do so all they have to do is unite. The accord of a united England and France can impose order and peace everywhere.[44]

While the British cabinet was considering the French proposals, word came from Vienna to the effect that Austria could not accept the bases of mediation offered to her by London and Paris, that she preferred instead to try negotiating directly with Sardinia.[45] This was tantamount to a rejection of the mediation, for it was well known that Sardinia, which had agreed to joint mediation on 15 August, had no intention of treating directly with Vienna. That Austria was now simply attempting to prolong the mediation process was evident to both the English and French governments.[46] Normanby could report to his government that Cavaignac and Bastide were 'both much annoyed at the unfavourable reception which had been given on the joint mediation by the Austrian Minister'.[47] Although the French government promised to refrain from precipitate action and await the word from London concerning joint mediation, General Cavaignac did argue 'that the time was now come when

[43] De Tocqueville, *Œuvres complètes*, vol. viii, part 2, p. 26 (26 Aug., Beaumont to de Tocqueville); Taylor, p. 153.

[44] FAAE, Corr. pol., Angleterre 671 (25 Aug., Beaumont to Palmerston).

[45] Ibid., Autriche 436 (23 Aug., Delacour to Bastide).

[46] Sardinia, AST, Lettre Ministri Francia (2 Sept., Brignole to Perrone).

[47] Britain, PRO, F.O. 27/812 (29 Aug., Normanby to Palmerston).

it became absolutely necessary to ascertain whether England would take another step in common', for 'it was obvious Austria was acting upon the supposition that [England] would not act and it only required a demonstration on [England's] part to bring her to reason'.[48] If England would not co-operate with France the French government would be obliged to go to war, break the European peace, and, if necessary, carry on a 'war of propaganda' by appealing to all peoples to once again rise up in revolution— as if France had it in her power to do so in the autumn of 1848.

As Vienna showed signs of becoming less conciliatory, Paris made every effort to persuade London to agree to armed mediation. Beaumont asked Palmerston at least to join France in sending a stern note to Vienna, for, he argued, the French government must be able to inform the National Assembly either that hostilities had ceased and the mediation had been accepted or that the rejection of the mediation by Austria had forced France to take whatever actions her interests might dictate.[49] At the same time Bastide decided to spell out clearly to Great Britain the sort of joint armed mediation which France envisaged. He informed Beaumont in London that France could not in any way agree to alter the bases of mediation in favour of Austria:

Consequently, having decided neither to modify the bases nor to wait for future events which would determine Austria to accept them, we should regard our first steps taken in common toward Austria as rejected by her. Nevertheless, we wish to make a last effort to give the Italian events a pacific solution; we should think that if Austria rejects the mediation which is offered to her it is because she is persuaded that the part played by England in this mediation has no other importance than that of a simple advisor. Therefore, if the Cabinet in London desires as completely as we do to prevent a European war, it must resolve to take a more decisive attitude.

This is what we propose: Venice is still holding out against the Austrians. . . . Our appearance in this place would indubitably awaken all the Italian fervour. . . . It is necessary for us to occupy this city without delay; we propose to England to come with us, either by an Anglo-French garrison or a French garrison and an English naval division, as England might wish [sic]. At the same time our Army of the Alps would move closer to the border and a joint declaration of the two Powers would invite Austria once again to accept the media-

---

[48] Britain, PRO, F.O. 27/812 (29 Aug., Normanby to Palmerston).
[49] Ibid., F.O. 27/825 (29 Aug., Beaumont to Palmerston).

tion as it is offered to her. . . . Insist with all of your power in approaching the English government to encourage her to adopt this resolution; if unfortunately she does not enter into these views nothing will remain but to request the National Assembly to authorize us to recall our minister in Vienna and hurl our army into Lombardy.[50]

If Austria still remained adamant in rejecting the mediation after this joint demonstration, Cavaignac stressed the fact that he was prepared to go to war against her.[51]

The English government now understood exactly what the French meant by the term 'joint armed mediation'. But the clarity and bluntness of the French proposals seem to have made them even more repugnant to a government which valued its neutrality above everything else and wanted under no circumstances to become militarily involved on the Continent. It seems that Palmerston, for his part, did personally support the French proposal during the meeting in council of the English cabinet. The British Foreign Secretary felt that it was best to co-operate with France and restrain her rather than risk letting her act on her own.[52] In a conversation on 31 August he told Beaumont that if it depended on him alone, 'you and I could establish within one half hour the bases of a good treaty', which, faithfully 'and loyally executed, would guarantee the peace of Europe'.[53] Despite Palmerston's personal feelings, though, Beaumont admitted that there was 'very little chance that England would ally herself so closely to us in this affair'.[54] Beaumont had pressed Palmerston for an intimate *entente* with France, but he realized that the British government was exceedingly wary of committing itself militarily in any way, especially to a new and unstable Power like France.[55]

[50] FAAE, Corr. pol., Turin 321 (29 Aug., Bastide to Beaumont).

[51] Britain, PRO, F.O. 27/812 (29 Aug., Normanby to Palmerston).

[52] Russell, i. 340–1 (30 Aug., Palmerston to Russell); Britain, PRO, F.O. 27/800 (1 Sept., Palmerston to Normanby).

[53] De Tocqueville, *Œuvres complètes*, vol. viii, part 2, p. 36 (31 Aug., Beaumont to de Tocqueville, letter 'begun on 31 August and finished on 2 September'); AD Sarthe, documents des archives privées de M. Eugène Cavaignac, reel 24 (1 Sept., Beaumont to Cavaignac).

[54] De Tocqueville, *Œuvres complètes*, vol. viii, part 2, p. 34.

[55] AD Sarthe, Documents des archives privées de M. Eugène Cavaignac, reel 24 (1 Sept., Beaumont to Cavaignac).

On the last day of August the British cabinet voted against both strengthening ties with France and adopting armed mediation.[56] Even before Beaumont's pessimistic reports had arrived in Paris, the French government had few illusions about Britain's stand. In a private note to Beaumont Cavaignac confided that, while he deplored the prospect of such a refusal on the part of England, 'he thought it possible'.[57]

Palmerston partially complied with France's wishes by writing to Vienna, entreating Austria to include Venice in the cease-fire; he also instructed Ponsonby, Britain's ambassador in Vienna, to advise Austria

... to consider the very difficult position in which the French Government is placed in regard to these Italian affairs. That Government is, Her Majesty's Government are firmly convinced, sincerely desirous of maintaining peace, and disinclined to interfere in the affairs of Italy by force of arms. But it would be a most fatal mistake for the Austrian Government to imagine that France is unable to interfere if she were resolved to do so.[58]

In early September, moreover, Palmerston instructed Ponsonby to join Delacour in demanding that Austria give a definite reply to the offer of pacific mediation.[59] But this is all that England was willing to do for France. Instead of coming to a closer agreement with the Republic, both Palmerston and Normanby applied themselves to restraining France by advising her 'to wait, and not to act with precipitation' so that Austria would have more time to consider accepting the mediation.[60] French efforts to provide for joint armed mediation with England had been largely unsuccessful, but it could be hoped that Austria would reply favourably to the Anglo-French notes to Vienna. Everything now depended upon Vienna's willingness to accept the mediation —and on Paris's willingness to make war.

The French applied as much pressure on Austria to agree to the mediation as they did on England to accept armed mediation.

[56] De Tocqueville, *Œuvres complètes*, vol. viii, part 2, pp. 36–7; Taylor, p. 155.

[57] De Tocqueville, *Œuvres complètes*, vol. viii, part 2, p. 37.

[58] *Parliamentary Papers*, lviii. 241–2 (31 Aug., Palmerston to Ponsonby).

[59] FAAE, Corr. pol., Angleterre 671 (6 Sept., Beaumont to Bastide).

[60] Britain, PRO, F.O. 27/800 (1 Sept., Palmerston to Normanby); F.O. 27/813 (3 Sept., Normanby to Palmerston).

After receiving the Venetian appeal for assistance, Bastide renewed his efforts to persuade Vienna to evacuate the Legations and include Venice in the armistice.[61] By late August Austria's uncompromising attitude seems to have decided Bastide to substitute a more threatening attitude, and on 23 August he informed Delacour that a continued Austrian occupation of the Legations would be considered as a *casus belli* by France; furthermore, because of the new developments in Venice, Austria should decide whether or not she would accept the mediation and cease operations against Venice, 'for we can refuse our assistance to Venice only if the accepted mediation permits us to foresee a peaceful solution to the Italian question'.[62] The French foreign minister repeated these demands in notes of 27 and 28 August, attesting to France's desire for peace, but claiming that the Republic would resort to arms if Austria remained implacable.[63] France had submitted what amounted to an ultimatum to the Austrian government.

At the same time the French government took other threatening diplomatic and military gestures. During the last week of August Bastide sent notes to the French agents in Prussia, Baden, Sardinia, Rome, Tuscany, and Genoa, informing them in almost identical statements that France desired a pacific settlement to the Italian question, but that she would resort to arms if necessary.[64] This was undoubtedly intended to forewarn Europe that France was seriously considering armed mediation and to serve to intimidate Austrian diplomats in these capitals. The French foreign minister frankly admonished the French consul in Milan to show great reserve toward Austrian officials in order to make it clear that France did not consider the Italian question as 'consumed and ended'; without being provocative France should demonstrate that the Republic did not consider 'the peaceful solution of Italian affairs as the only possible one'.[65]

To complement their diplomatic menaces the French government took measures to form in Marseilles a naval expedition, which, according to Bastide, would consist of three steamships

[61] FAAE, Corr. pol., Autriche 436 (20 Aug., Bastide to Delacour).
[62] Ibid. (23 Aug., Bastide to Delacour).
[63] Ibid. (27, 28 Aug., Bastide to Delacour).
[64] Ibid., Corr. pol. des consuls, Turin 5, Gênes (29 Aug., Bastide to Favre).
[65] Ibid., Autriche 10B, Milan (27 Aug., Bastide to Denois).

and 3,000 men.[66] A brigade of troops was made ready in Marseilles and frigates from the Mediterranean fleet were loaded with three months' supplies in Toulon. The order was given to make ready to depart for Venice to implement armed mediation; but the final order to sail was not issued in the hope that Austria would accept peaceful mediation after all.[67] Bastide did use the fact that the expedition was standing ready to sail to inform Austria that, because friendly mediation had not been accepted, France 'was substituting armed mediation for friendly mediation in the Italian question'. Thom was 'stupefied' to hear that France, with the blessing if not the concurrence of Great Britain, was sending troops to Venice to protect French citizens there 'and to co-operate with the inhabitants for the defence of this city'. Bastide suggested that French occupation of Venice could be prevented only by Austria applying the armistice of 9 August to Venice and ceasing all hostilities against that city.[68]

The French effort at intimidation was beginning to have some effect upon Austria, Thom, for example, suddenly revised his opinion at the beginning of September concerning the possibility of France intervening in Italy. On 29 August he still believed that the Cavaignac government would somehow manage to preserve the peace, and even as late as 30 August reported that 'they fear war here more than anything else, and I am told by everyone that there is nothing that the government will not do to avoid it'.[69] On the same day Bastide spoke to Thom about the 'extremely unfortunate consequences' which could result from Austria's refusal to accept the mediation, and the following day Normanby told Thom that Austria's attitude made 'a general war seem inevitable'. Then, on 1 September, while the Austrian chargé d'affaires was taking note of the fact that reinforcements were being sent to the Army of the Alps, Bastide informed him of the intended French naval expedition to Venice.[70] As a result of these events, Thom's confidence in France's peaceful inten-

---

[66] FAAE, Corr. pol. des consuls, Autriche 8, Venise (27 Aug., Bastide to Vasseur).

[67] Stern, ii. 522–3. An examination of the Marseilles press indicates that five ships and up to 5,000 men were prepared to leave on the expedition (*Gazette du Midi*, 4, 5, 9 Sept.; *Le Semaphore de Marseille*, 10 Sept.).

[68] Austria, HHS, Frankreich Korr. Kart. 337 (1 Sept., Thom to Wessenberg).

[69] Ibid. (29, 30 Aug., Thom to Wessenberg).

[70] Ibid. (30, 31 Aug., 1 Sept., Thom to Wessenberg).

tions seemed to have been badly shaken, and he immediately asked his government what dispositions to take concerning the embassy in Paris if an Austro-French war were to break out. By 3 September Thom could remark that 'many people here believe that the French government only wants to intimidate us and will not push things to the last extremity. This opinion appears very hazardous to me.'[71]

A similar reappraisal of French intentions made the Austrian ministry in Vienna more apprehensive about French involvement in Italy. At the end of August the Austrian government still declared that its occupation of the Legations was only a temporary military measure and that mediation was unacceptable in its present form. All that Wessenberg was willing to do was to promise England and France that Austria would grant Lombardy and Venice liberal institutions.[72] However, on 2 September Delacour presented Bastide's letter of 23 August to Wessenberg. The Austrian foreign minister at first replied with a reiteration of the official Austrian position. Delacour then demanded 'a categorical and definite reply' to the proferred mediation, putting this in the form of a written ultimatum. Later that day Delacour learned from Wessenberg that Austria would accept the joint mediation.[73] Delacour's 'insistence' upon a 'definitive reply' had been the factor which had determined the Austrian cabinet to make its rapid about-face.[74]

A formal note from Wessenberg to Delacour on 3 September made the Austrian acceptance of the Anglo-French mediation official. However, the same note also clearly indicated that, while Austria was prepared to accept the good offices of the mediating Powers, she was willing to concede little at the bargaining table. The Austrian foreign minister proclaimed that 'the Imperial Government welcomes the mediation' with 'its aim of bringing an end to the war. . . . Nevertheless, it must make it known in advance . . . that the mediation which will take place cannot possibly be based on the state of affairs which existed' at the time when the Hummelauer memorandum was first issued in late May.[75] Then too, on the very day on which Wessenberg notified

[71] Ibid. (1, 3 Sept., Thom to Wessenberg).
[72] FAAE, Corr. pol., Autriche 436 (29, 30 Aug., Delacour to Bastide).
[73] Ibid. (2 Sept., Delacour to Bastide).
[74] Austria, HHS, Frankreich Korr. Kart. 338 (3 Sept., Wessenberg to Thom).
[75] FAAE, Corr. pol., Autriche 436 (3 Sept., Wessenberg to Bastide).

Delacour of Austria's acceptance of the joint mediation the Austrian foreign minister instructed his representative in Paris to inform France that his government was determined to maintain the territorial bases of the existing treaties.[76] The Austrian government demanded the right to enjoy the fruits of battle and retain its reconquered Italian provinces. In other words, Austria agreed to Anglo-French mediation, but she refused its bases. Wessenberg had wisely decided to accept a French demand in order to placate the Republic, but to do so only with reservations which rendered the accepted mediation meaningless.

Both Bastide and Cavaignac, it seems, were 'extremely joyous' when word arrived in Paris on 7 September to the effect that Austria had accepted the mediation.[77] Bastide, for his part, exclaimed to the French agent in Turin that 'this news has caused a happy impression here. As a result one has reason to envisage the maintenance of peace.'[78] It seems that maintaining the peace had been France's main concern in pressing Austria to accept the mediation. When informed that Austria had attached certain important reservations to her acceptance, Bastide displayed little emotion or disappointment. He remarked to the Austrian chargé d'affaires that the French government was quite aware that Austria was no longer willing to acknowledge the Hummelauer proposal as the basis for mediation. France did not expect Austria to do so. The French government was simply pleased that Austria had agreed to the proferred mediation. Bastide did not conceal from Thom his 'happiness with the prospect . . . of arriving by pacific means at an arrangement of Italian affairs'.[79]

Austria's decision to accept the mediation had served to extricate France from a delicate situation in which armed action seemed imminent and inevitable. Throughout the remainder of the autumn the Cavaignac government would continue to exert pressure on London and Vienna to bring about an Italian settlement, but never again would the French manœuvre themselves into a position where they were as close to taking up arms as they had been at the beginning of September.

[76] Austria, HHS, Frankreich Korr. Kart. 338 (3 Sept., Wessenberg to Thom).

[77] Sardinia, AST, Lettere Ministri Francia (8 Sept., Brignole to Perrone).

[78] FAAE, Corr. pol., Turin 322 (7 Sept., Bastide to Sain de Boislecomte). In late August Sain de Boislecomte moved from Naples to Turin, replacing Reiset in the French ministry there.

[79] Austria, HHS, Frankreich Korr. Kart. 337 (9 Sept., Thom to Wessenberg).

IX

PEACE AT ALL COSTS

FRANCE might have been anxious to implement joint armed mediation with Great Britain in order to advance the mediation process, but once the British government refused to adopt such a policy the French government showed little inclination to act unilaterally and intervene in Italy. France, after all, had actively sought joint Anglo-French mediation in order to avoid becoming militarily involved in Italy. A letter dated 29 August from Bastide to the French minister in Florence, Benoît-Champy, indicates that even in late August French participation in mediation was still motivated by the desire to avoid military action at any price. Benoît-Champy had encouraged his government to intervene in Italy and had questioned the wisdom of an *entente* with England, a Power which he believed had her own designs on the Peninsula and was more of an enemy to France than Austria.[1] In reply to Benoît-Champy Bastide sternly reprimanded him for suggesting that the Republic should immediately take up the sword to come to the aid of Italy. He stated that France would intervene if it became absolutely necessary to do so, but added that Benoît-Champy's point of view

. . . gives reason to believe that you are not sufficiently aware either of the situation or of the thought of the government of the Republic concerning the Italian question. The means of preliminary mediation were too evidently indicated by the circumstances in Italy itself, by the interests of France, and by the necessity of general peace for them not to be able to explain and justify themselves. As for the co-operation of England in the mediation, do I need to say that England concurred with us only with the view of preventing a military intervention and that we have no illusions about this subject? We also have weighty motives for preferring a pacific solution. Therefore, if joint mediation succeeds, our aims and those of the English Cabinet will have been achieved in the most desirable manner.[2]

[1] FAAE, Corr. pol., Toscane 182 (12, 21 Aug., Benoît-Champy to Bastide).
[2] Ibid. (29 Aug., Bastide to Benoît-Champy).

Both France and England clung tenaciously to mediation throughout the autumn because of their common desire to avoid French military involvement in Italy.

There is considerable evidence to suggest that France would not have gone so far as to implement armed mediation by sending a small expedition to occupy Venice without the concurrence of Great Britain even if Austria had not agreed to negotiate on 2 September. Word of Austria's acceptance of the mediation did not reach Paris until 7 September. However, the Cavaignac government was aware of the British cabinet's refusal to join France in joint armed mediation by 1 September. Shortly after this the Cavaignac ministry decided not to send the force of three steamships and 3,000 men to implement armed mediation by occupying Venice. The decision was taken some time between 1 and 4 September, for on the 4th Cavaignac informed Normanby that he had 'given up' the idea of sending troops to Venice.[3]

In a secret meeting of the French council of ministers, which probably took place on 3 or 4 September, Bastide favoured sending the expedition, but Cavaignac opposed it. Bastide was supported by Lamorcière, the Minister of the Army who seemed to be the one firm advocate of armed intervention in the government, believing that France's honour called upon her to go to war for Italy. Cavaignac's position was supported by a majority of one when the issue was put to a vote and orders were immediately sent to Marseilles to cancel plans for sending the expedition.[4] The French government, of course, did not inform Austria of its decision, for on 1 September Bastide had notified Thom that the Republic was resolved to act. Still, from 2 September on the French government began to adopt a considerably different attitude toward Austria. The French had menaced Austria as much as was possible. They now began to appeal to Austria to compromise with the Republic concerning Italy.

On 2 September Bastide informed Thom that a division of the Army of the Alps was embarked at Marseilles but that his government had decided not to act immediately. France would give the Viennese government more time to reply to the mediation offer.[5] Three days later Bastide told Thom that he had

---

[3] Britain, PRO, F.O. 27/813 (4 Sept., Normanby to Palmerston).
[4] Stern, ii. 522–3; Planat de la Faye, i. 412; Bell, i. 434.
[5] Austria, HHS, Frankreich Korr. Kart. 337 (1 Sept., Thom to Wessenberg).

'more confidence today' in Austria's assurances to grant Northern Italy liberal institutions 'than [he] had a few days ago'. In an attempt to entice Austria both to accept the mediation and treat Northern Italy liberally he reminded Thom that 'although the request that Austria should abandon Lombardy figures among the propositions that we have put forward as the basis for our offer of mediation, we do not insist upon this, and we limit ourselves instead to asking that you accord this province, and Venetia as well, the most liberal institutions possible'.[6] Then, on 7 September, the day when word of Austria's acceptance of the mediation reached Paris, Bastide took Thom completely into his confidence and made an almost fraternal appeal for Austria to make minor concessions which would satisfy France and preclude the possibility of a Franco-Austrian war over Italy. Bastide attested that

... we firmly wish to arrive at a pacific arrangement of the affairs of Italy. We find ourselves placed, or to speak more accurately, we have placed ourselves, rather imprudently, in an embarrassing position; we only ask to get out of it honourably, and we hope that you will help us a little in this; the promise which the Viennese cabinet has made to accord national institutions to the Italian provinces of the Austrian Empire largely satisfies our wishes in this regard; if the Imperial cabinet holds this promise, and if it takes into consideration our request [that Venice be spared from attack] ..., I am fully confident that what has given us so much concern will end to our common satisfaction.[7]

Faced with the alternative of unilateral armed mediation or accepting a compromise settlement of the Italian question, the Cavaignac government decided in favour of the latter. The French government was in an 'embarrassing position', for it had sacrificed its publically stated principles in its desire to maintain the peace and had acquiesced to Austrian control of Northern Italy. Bastide was beseeching Austria to make a firm commitment to refrain from attacking Venice and to grant liberal institutions to her Italian provinces because he realized that the French public demanded at least this from its government.

One of the arguments which Bastide and Cavaignac had employed throughout the late summer to encourage England

6 Ibid. (4 Sept., Thom to Wessenberg).
7 Ibid. (7 Sept., Thom to Wessenberg).

to support France in armed mediation was that French public opinion would oblige the Cavaignac government to go to war if joint mediation did not succeed. This argument had proved successful in late July and early August, and the French government continued to resort to using it throughout August. Normanby reported from Paris on 24 August that:

The General assured me, and in this he was confirmed by M. Bastide, that they had forced public opinion upon these subjects as far as it would go, anxious as all were to preserve the peace; and if they permitted the Austrians to remain in the Legations, and at the same time refused the assistance asked by the Venetians, their power for good would soon be at an end. . . .

The General reverted with evident uneasiness to the possibility of Venice being taken by the Austrians after this appeal for assistance, and whilst his hands were tied by the proposal of mediation, and deprecated the effect this would have on public opinion in France.[8]

Ten days later, when it seemed that Austria would not accept the proposed mediation, Normanby again wrote to his government:

I had an interview this afternoon with General Cavaignac and M. Bastide. I found the General much impressed with the difficulties of his position toward the Assembly, arising from the delay of the Austrian Government in returning any answer to the communications that have been made at Vienna on the subject of Italy. . . . The General assured me I must recollect that the Assembly had passed a vote with respect to the enfranchisement of Italy and had left it in charge of the Executive Government to carry out their intentions. They would, one of these days, demand a severe account from him of what he had done. He had wished the expedition to Venice, as an indication, not as a cause of war.[9]

It seems that Cavaignac feared being called to account by French public opinion if an honourable settlement of the Italian question were not realized.

There is conflicting evidence as to just what French public opinion at this time expected from its government's Italian policy. It seems that by late summer and early autumn a majority of Frenchmen both within the French National Constituent Assembly and the country at large wanted above all the preservation of peace and felt no compelling desire to intervene militarily

[8] Britain, PRO, F.O. 27/812 (24 Aug., Normanby to Palmerston).
[9] Ibid., F.O. 27/813 (4 Sept., Normanby to Palmerston).

in favour of the Italians. Alexis de Tocqueville, that keen analyst
of the French political scene, was of the impression that by
September a large segment of the French public was willing to
support an Italian settlement in which Austria's Northern
Italian provinces received something less than independence.
De Tocqueville wrote to his friend Beaumont that:

. . . not only France, but the Assembly as well, are very willing to be
content with a settlement such as the following: 'preservation of
the former territorial possessions in Italy, actual and considerable
alterations in the institutions.' Peace established on such bases
would seem to be not only acceptable but honourable (in light of the
present state of affairs); it would be approved by the Assembly and
defended by all of our friends. . . . Basically, there is little interest
here for the Italians, who have proven themselves to be so little
worthy of liberty. The only wish here is to save the honour of France
and, above all, to preserve peace.[10]

In an earlier letter to Beaumont de Tocqueville had also noted
the pacific sentiment which he believed prevailed in the French
Assembly. He had observed in early August that, with the exception of the Mountain, 'the vast majority of the Assembly' wished
to preserve the peace. De Tocqueville was persuaded that within
the Assembly 'the passion for peace grows increasingly as war
seems to be more imminent', and in August as in September he
believed that 'the Assembly is disposed to approve of everything
that the government will do to avoid war' and was prepared 'to
be content with anything that could cover our honour to a certain
degree'.[11] If de Tocqueville's assessment of the situation was
correct, it seems that the majority of both the Assembly and the
general public was willing to support the government's pacific
Italian policy.

   Foreign observers tended to concur in de Tocqueville's general
analysis. The Austrian chargé d'affaires in Paris reported in mid-
August that 'the Italian cause is not very popular today in
France'. By the middle of September he was convinced that 'the
majority' of the members of the French Assembly 'dread war,
and only aspire to maintaining order and peace'.[12] In a similar

---

[10] De Tocqueville, Œuvres complètes, vol. viii, part 2, pp. 43–4 (14 Sept.,
de Tocqueville to Beaumont).
   [11] Ibid., pp. 17–18 (10 Aug., de Tocqueville to Beaumont).
   [12] Austria, HHS, Frankreich Korr. Kart. 337 (16 Aug., 4 Sept., Thom to
Wessenberg).

manner the Sardinian ambassador in Paris noted that both the French government and Assembly were 'hardly favourably' disposed toward the 'Italian cause'. He added: 'It is evident that for the moment the principal wish of the country and its representatives is above all the preservation of peace.'[13] Still, contrary to these assessments, in early September Bastide confided to his friend Emmanuel Arago that 'public opinion in France has pronounced itself in such a manner in favour of Italian independence that it will be hardly satisfied unless Austria is completely driven back beyond the Alps'.[14] It is likely that Bastide, acutely aware of France's public commitment to the Italian cause, was most sensitive to those elements within France which were favourable to the Italians. And while the majority of Frenchmen seem to have become disenchanted with the Italian cause by late summer, there was, nevertheless, a very vocal element of French public opinion which at this time was becoming increasingly critical of the Cavaignac government's cautious Italian policy.

In late summer elements of the Parisian press continually prodded the administration to live up to its commitments to Italy. The leftist, Bonapartist, Parisian daily, *La Liberté*, reminded the Cavaignac government that it was a matter of French honour to assure independence to Italy. The same paper denounced the mediation as an English ruse which would never serve to liberate Lombardy.[15] The radical *La Réforme* proclaimed that France should not fail Italy. Austria was obviously procrastinating by refusing to give a definite answer to the mediation offer: '. . . it is time that our armies take the place of our unsuccessful diplomats. Because our words have been able to obtain nothing, it will be by the voice of our cannon that Italy will be freed.'[16] Criticism of the government's Italian policy does not seem to have been limited to the press. A poem was circulated, appealing to Cavaignac to save Italy before it was too late.[17] Furthermore, a pamphlet, written by a member of the Paris *garde mobile*, denounced mediation as 'a trap' and asked the government to resort to armed action to save Italy, even if this

---

[13] Sardinia, AST, Lettere Ministri Francia (22 Sept., Brignole to Perrone).
[14] FAAE, Corr. pol., Prusse 302 (9 Sept., Bastide to Arago).
[15] *La Liberté*, 14, 12 Aug. [16] *La Réforme*, 30 Aug., 1 Sept.
[17] Auguste Thorel Saint-Martin, 'Au Général Cavaignac sur la guerre d'Italie', Bibliothèque nationale, Ye 52892.

were to result in a European war. France could not allow Italy
to fall, as Poland had, to the forces of reaction: 'Italy is calling,
fly to her aid.'[18]

At times the Parisian press became quite caustic in its remarks
and openly criticized the Cavaignac government for its inaction.
Even the editor of the conservative *Le Constitutionnel* insinuated
that, diplomatically, France was as impotent as during the
Spanish marriages affair, 'because France was placed . . . between
a possible general war and an almost impossible negotiation'. *La
Réforme*, when it first heard rumours of the proposed Anglo-
French mediation, quipped: 'What will Europe say when it hears
that instead of an army we are sending a diplomat to assist the
Italians; Louis Philippe never did otherwise.' At the end of
August this same sheet admonished the government to accept
war instead of following 'the shameful policies of Louis Philippe'.
L'Evénement, a daily inspired by Victor Hugo, also made scath-
ing remarks about the affinity between the Republic's and Louis
Philippe's foreign policies.[19] Moreover, it seems that the Parisian
press was not alone in inveighing against the government's
Italian policy. On 26 August the Procureur Général of Lyons
seized an issue of *Le Peuple souverain* of that city for its vitu-
perative charge that French troops in the Lyons area, as in the
time of Louis Philippe, would be used to oppress the people of
Lyons rather than to liberate Italy from Austria.[20]

It remained for the small, monarchist Parisian sheet, *Le
Lampion*, to deliver one of the most bitter indictments of the
Cavaignac government's foreign policy. On 10 August in an
article entitled 'Peace at all costs' *Le Lampion* criticized *Le
National* for duplicity in its foreign policy statements. It pointed
out that *Le National* would have denounced Louis Philippe for
carrying on a foreign policy like the one now implemented by
the Republic, but now *Le National* argued that 'things have
changed'. *Le Lampion* suggested that all that had changed was
the fact that men of the *National* faction were now at the helm.
Mediation in which Italy would not be liberated was not 'worthy
of France'. The men of the *National* (Bastide and Cavaignac)

---

[18] Joseph Martin, 'Sauvons l'Italie! Appel d'un garde mobile au secours de
l'Italie opprimée', Bibliothèque nationale, Lb 54. 1140.

[19] *Le Constitutionnel*, 8 Aug.; *La Réforme*, 8, 31 Aug.; *L'Evénement*,
5, 15 Oct.   [20] France, Archives nationales, BB[18], 1467A, pièce 6307.

should be frank and admit that now that they were in power they too wanted 'peace at all costs'.[21]

During August leftist members of the National Constituent Assembly also began to question the government's foreign policy. When Bastide informed the Assembly of his ministry's decision to undertake joint mediation with England, his announcement was met with severe criticism from the Montagnard representative Baune. When speaking of mediation the French foreign minister had spoken of its leading to the 'pacification' of Italy. Baune was quick to question Bastide's use of this word when referring to the goals of the mediation, reminding him that the Assembly had called for not the 'pacification' but the 'liberation' of Italy. France had promised, Baune declared, to march to Italy's assistance if the Peninsula were ever threatened by Austrian hegemony. He suggested that the time had now come to do just this. Baune ended his impassioned speech by reminding his colleagues that 'we owe Italy the assistance of France; it is a debt which we have contracted, and it would be a cowardly act not to pay it'.[22]

Critical interpellations of the government's foreign policy continued on 21 August. Puységur proclaimed that France had not overcome the policy of isolation which had marked the July Monarchy's foreign policy. Jules Favre was more pointed in his criticism. He asserted that Cavaignac's policy 'resembled in no way' the policy enunciated by the Provisional Government or spelt out by the Assembly on 24 May. Certainly France wanted peace, Favre remarked, but at the same time the Republic had 'told all nationalities, and especially the Italian nationality, that . . . if they called upon her that call would be heard'. Favre, for his part, was convinced that the French government did not want to go to Italy's aid.

Cavaignac's policies had come under severe attack in both the Assembly and the press and he felt obliged to mount the rostrum to defend himself. Recognizing the fact that on 24 May the Assembly had called for 'the liberation of Italy', he declared, however, that

in light of the sentiment manifested by the Assembly, I have always remained convinced that the first thought of the nation was to

[21] *Le Lampion*, 10 Aug.   [22] *Le Moniteur universel*, 11 Aug.

conserve an honourable peace, to satisfy the interest of her honour and her policies without troubling, if it were possible, the peace of the world. . . . In a country like ours it takes more courage to defend the party of peace in certain circumstances than to push toward war: this courage, I assure you, is not lacking in me.[23]

Two weeks later Bastide mounted the rostrum to announce Austria's acceptance of the mediation in these words:

The Assembly will hear, with satisfaction I believe, the conclusion of this first period of the negotiations, which assure more and more to the Republic that high rank which she must occupy in the council of sovereigns, and which, in assuring more and more the maintenance of the general peace, will permit France, I hope, soon to lower taxes.[24]

In defending its Italian policy, the Cavaignac government prided itself on preserving peace for France without really answering the charges of its foreign policy critics.

The Cavaignac government's concern for criticism of its foreign policy is shown by the fact that it was extremely reluctant to release information to either the public or the National Assembly about its diplomatic procedures. Throughout the autumn of 1848 the government justified its pacific stance by claiming that no established European Power had officially requested French intervention and that had this occurred France would have immediately responded to that request. At least two major Parisian newspapers correctly reported that Ricci had officially requested intervention of a sort from France on 7 August.[25] Unruffled by this, however, Cavaignac solemnly proclaimed to the Assembly on 21 August that France had offered her armed assistance to Italy in early August only to have Italy reject the offer.[26] Neither Sardinia's nor Venice's official request for armed assistance was ever disclosed publicly, or in the Assembly, by the Cavaignac government. In fact, Normanby claimed to be making an important disclosure when he stated in the prologue of the 1858 French edition of his work that Sardinia had made a request for intervention on 7 August 1848.[27]

[23] Ibid., 22 Aug. [24] Ibid., 9 Sept.
[25] *Le Siècle*, 9 Aug.; *La Presse*, 9 Aug. [26] *Le Moniteur universel*, 22 Aug.
[27] Constantine Henry, Lord Normanby, *Une Année de révolution, d'après un journal tenu à Paris en 1848, par le marquis de Normanby* (2 vols.; Paris, 1858), ii. 455–7.

Furthermore, throughout the autumn the French government strove to avoid detailed discussion of any kind of its Italian policy by the Assembly. The proposed terms of the mediation were never disclosed by the government; and Cavaignac even refused to give the Foreign Affairs Committee of the Assembly any details about the joint mediation.[28] In a similar manner, the General asked the Assembly to refrain from requesting the communication of recent diplomatic documents, arguing that absolute secrecy was necessary for the success of the mediation.[29] It seems that the Assembly's discussion of the Italian problem was unwelcome to a government which realized that it was deviating from that body's directive of 24 May and which wanted to avoid public censure of its policy.

The government was highly concerned about increased public discussion of its Italian policy both because it feared that public opinion would oblige it to go to war and because such discussion threatened to reveal the duplicity of its policies. To be sure, the radical republicans within the Assembly were not numerous or influential enough to force the government to adopt a more bellicose Italian policy. As de Tocqueville had stated, most members of the Assembly seem to have concurred in the government's desire to avoid armed intervention; and an examination of the Assembly's debates shows that during discussion of questions relating to foreign affairs the government's spokesmen were resolutely applauded, while the regime's critics received little open support. Still, the Assembly's discussion of the Italian problem had the effect of continually reminding France of her pledges to Italy, something which was quite embarrassing to a government which remained extremely aware of its commitments to Italy.[30]

From the very inception of the joint mediation Bastide had realized that its success was somewhat dubious.[31] Cavaignac seems to have been of the same opinion. In September Palmerston disclosed that he had had a long conversation with Beaumont, who insisted that negotiations with Austria should get under way as soon as possible. The French agent in London argued that mediation was absolutely necessary, for 'even if we

---

[28] *Le Journal des débats*, 12 Aug.   [29] *Le Moniteur universal*, 22 Aug.
[30] Général Pierre-E.-M. Ibos, *Le Général Cavaignac: un dictateur républicain* (Paris, 1930), p. 206.   [31] Bastide, pp. 65, 95.

should fail in accomplishing all we wish, which Cavaignac thinks likely, everybody in France would at least be satisfied that every possible effort had been made'.[32] The French government was quite aware of both the limitations and advantages of continued mediation. Though it harboured few illusions as to the eventual success, it realized that mediation could serve to preserve the government's honour and to obviate the need of military intervention in the Peninsula, something which the government was determined to avoid.

In the autumn of 1848, as in the summer, the French government had good reasons for wanting to avoid military involvement in Italy. For one thing, internal difficulties still plagued France in the late summer and early autumn just as they had earlier in the year. On 21 August rumours circulated that Paris 'was on the eve of another day' because of popular discontent with the Assembly's attempts to indict Louis Blanc and Caussidière for inciting revolt on 15 May and during the June Days.[33] At this time the Danish minister in Paris informed Copenhagen that tension was building up within the French capital to the point where many were comparing the atmosphere to that which had prevailed just before the June Days.[34] In a similar vein the Austrian chargé d'affaires in Paris noted that anxiety and uneasiness were increasing within the French capital. He reported that 'the state of seige and the presence of an army of 55,000 men have become a *conditio sine qua non* of public tranquillity within Paris, and the day when one or the other shall be in default this tranquillity shall be found compromised in the most grave manner'.[35] Then, too, at this time *Le National* was highly concerned about monarchists 'provoking disorders' in several departments by their demonstrations in favour of the Legitimist pretender, Henry V; during the entire month of September *Le National* gave almost daily reports of 'legitimist intrigues' occurring all over France.[36] Then, in the by-elections of September Louis Napoleon Bonaparte was re-elected to the Assembly— he had been elected in the June by-elections but had resigned,

[32] Russell, i. 340–1 (26 Sept., Palmerston to Russell).
[33] *Le National*, 21 Aug.
[34] Denmark, Rigsarkivet, Frankrig II (23 Aug., E. C. L. Moltke to Knuth).
[35] Austria, HHS, Frankreich Korr. Kart. 337 (16 Aug., Thom to Wessenberg).
[36] *Le National*, 24 Aug., 8 Sept.

refusing to accept a seat in the Assembly—and Bonapartist demonstrations also began to occur. On 23 September strict security measures were taken in Paris after rumours circulated of a Bonapartist *coup*.[37] Workers also continued to agitate. At Elbeuf and Lyons workers demonstrated against the increase of the number of hours in the working day from eleven to twelve, clashing with the national guard. In Paris arms were still being collected in the working class quarter of Belleville as late as the end of August. The government deemed the situation within Paris to be so unstable that it did not lift the state of siege in effect since the June Days until 19 October. Moreover, even at the end of October there were still some 50,000 troops stationed in Paris.[38]

In the late summer and early autumn of 1848 several foreign observers still attributed France's pursuance of a cautious foreign policy to the difficulties and instability facing the Cavaignac government on the internal front. Lefebvre reported from Baden that the feeling persisted in Germany that it was impossible for France to wage war because of both her financial state and the internal difficulties which continued to plague her after the June Days.[39] The French consul in Milan informed Bastide that Austrian diplomats were convinced 'that France, because of the difficulties which have agitated and continue to agitate her internally, is not prepared to send 50,000 men into Italy, that she has too many of her own problems to try to concern herself with those of others'.[40] A Venetian diplomat, Tommaseo, reported from Paris that the French would not act because 'they are frightened of internal dangers'.[41] Sardinian diplomatic agents in France seem to have concurred in these analyses. A brother of Albert Ricci, General Joseph Ricci, who had been sent to France in late August on a military mission, believed that the strength which radical elements within France were still showing after the June Days, as well as 'the misery which is ever increasing in the manufacturing cities', made the French government 'fear another armed uprising'. He added: 'This is the principal reason

[37] *Le National*, 24 Sept.
[38] *Le Constitutionnel*, 30 Aug., 21 Sept., 24, 31 Oct.
[39] FAAE, Corr. pol., Bade 34 (2 Sept., Lefebvre to Bastide).
[40] Ibid., Corr. pol. des consuls, Autriche 10B (5 Sept., Denois to Bastide).
[41] Planat de la Faye, i. 402 (23 Aug., Tommaseo to Provisional Government of Venice).

it dreads foreign complications.'[42] In a similar manner Count Henri Martini, who replaced General Ricci as a Sardinian military representative in France during the autumn, argued that internal instability did not permit the French government 'to preoccupy itself with anything besides internal questions. . . . France today is paralysed by the fear of socialism. . . . Foreign questions, even those of utmost interest for France, follow their course almost unperceived.'[43]

Foreign observers were not the only ones to stress internal difficulties in explaining France's reluctance to adopt a bold foreign policy in the late summer of 1848. Bastide himself referred at this time to the French internal situation as having a restraining effect upon his government's foreign policy. In writing to Sain de Boislecomte in Turin Bastide assured him that, although France was prepared to go to war at any time, 'our dispositions for war will be even more certain if we succeed in putting off the scourge until next spring. We are certain that our army will be larger and better organized, and even more available because then we will no longer need to employ a considerable part of it on the interior.'[44] By Bastide's own admission the French army was still being deployed against the radicals within France rather than against the Austrians in Italy.

The unfavourable European diplomatic scene also remained a major factor discouraging the French government from going to war on Italy's behalf. When Sardinia first requested French intervention, Germany seemed to be moving progressively closer to upholding the Austrian position in Italy.[45] By the middle of August indications were that the Frankfurt Assembly was definitely prepared to give her unqualified support to Austria's Italian policy. Throughout the autumn there was a very distinct possibility that the German Confederation would become involved if France intervened in Italy. With Franco-German relations strained and Germany seemingly siding with Austria, French statesmen were undoubtedly convinced that limiting Austrian influence in Northern Italy was not worth a major European war.

[42] Sardinia, AST, Missioni diplomatiche speciali e temporanee (21 Aug., Joseph Ricci to Sardinian foreign minister).
[43] Ibid., Lettere Ministri Francia (Count Martini to Perrone).
[44] FAAE, Cor. pol., Turin 322 (6 Sept., Bastide to Sain de Boislecomte).
[45] See above, pp. 160–2.

The increased support which Germany seemed prepared to afford Austria by mid August did not go unnoticed in either the French press or the diplomatic community. On 13 August an influential Parisian daily proclaimed with much vituperation that the German princes had duped their people into supporting Austria in Italy.[46] French diplomats also noted that by the middle of August the German governments, and the Frankfurt Assembly especially, were beginning fully to support Austria's position in the Peninsula instead of simply sympathizing with it. The French chargé d'affaires in Frankfurt reported to Paris on 12 August that up until a week earlier Germany was not seriously considering intervention in Italy even if France aided Sardinia. But he added that 'today . . . Austrian interests are declared synonymous with German interests'; Germany would feel obliged to aid Austria if the occasion arose. He added that if 'democracy had been victorious in Germany' relations between France and her neighbour to the East would have been cordial; 'but on this side of the Rhine democracy and liberty are far from being triumphant, and the old monarchical system feels the need to encourage nationalist sentiments'.[47] It seems that Austrian victories in Italy had flattered German pride and had made German statesmen identify themselves with the Austrian cause.[48] Rothan, the French attaché in Kassel, made a succinct analysis of the situation when he remarked that:

The Austrian army's successes have given Germany confidence in her own powers unknown to her before. People who were ordinarily the most pacific . . . now say that war alone can achieve and consolidate the work of [German] unity. Besides these very liberal men there also remains the party of reaction which particularly places its hopes in a war against France. . . . The day that the French army crosses the Alps I would not be astonished to see even certain liberal newspapers discuss the advantages of a Russian alliance.[49]

In the latter part of August Raumer, the Frankfurt Assembly's envoy who had been sent to Paris to establish diplomatic relations with the Republic, bluntly told Bastide that 'French armed intervention in Italy would undoubtedly lead to the most regret-

---

[46] *Le National*, 13 Aug.
[47] FAAE, Corr. pol., Allemagne 805 (12 Aug., Savoye to Bastide).
[48] Ibid., Bade 34 (15 Aug., Lefebvre to Bastide).
[49] Ibid., Hesse-Cassel 34 (10 Aug., Rothan to Bastide).

table complications'.[50] In a similar manner Frankfurt's envoy in London was announcing publicly that 'Germany would certainly come to Austria's assistance in case of French intervention' in Italy.[51] Germany was adamant in insisting that Austria must retain Venice, which complemented Trieste as a Mediterranean port for Germany's products.[52] By early September Austria seemed to be confident of German assistance if France intervened in Italy. By late autumn Germany seemed ready to assist Austria to retain both Lombardy and Venice.[53]

The change in the German attitude toward Italy made the French government realize that war with Germany was a distinct possibility. Speaking hypothetically, Bastide remarked that if France unfortunately did have to go to war with Germany, France could attack simultaneously from the Tyrol, through Holstein, and in the Rhineland, where republican sentiment could be exploited.[54] A Parisian newspaper, which was usually quite reliable in its reports on foreign affairs, related that France intended to strengthen her forces in the Rhineland at the same time that she planned to implement armed mediation in Venice.[55]

The Frankfurt Assembly, for its part, seems to have taken no exceptional military moves in the Rhineland as a result of the Italian crisis. However, in late October German newspapers reported that some 50,000 troops were being assembled in Bavaria to go to the aid of Austria which was experiencing an uprising in Vienna.[56] The rumour soon proved to be false, for Frankfurt, it seems, had 'neither the means nor the disposition' to form a 50,000 man army. Still, it remained possible that the Frankfurt government would make every effort to concentrate forces in the Tyrol if France should intervene in Italy.[57] Bastide

[50] Robert John Hahn, 'The Attitude of the French Revolutionary Government toward German Unification in 1848' (Ph.D. dissertation, Ohio State University, 1955), p. 216; Austria, HHS, Frankreich Korr. Kart. 337 (6 Sept., Thom to Wessenberg).
[51] Curato, *Le relazioni diplomatiche fra il Regno di Sardegna e la Gran Bretagna*, i. 243–4 (7 Sept., Revel to Perrone).
[52] FAAE, Corr. pol., Bade 34 (21 Aug., Lefebvre to Bastide).
[53] *Parliamentary Papers*, lviii. 360–1 (11 Sept., Ponsonby to Palmerston); *Le National*, 2 Sept.; FAAE, Corr. pol., Bade 34 (17 Nov., Lefebvre to Bastide).
[54] FAAE, Corr. pol., Prusse 302 (9 Sept., Bastide to Arago).
[55] *La Presse*, 29 Aug.
[56] FAAE, Corr. pol., Angleterre 672 (25 Oct., Beaumont to Bastide).
[57] *Parliamentary Papers*, lviii. 548, 565 (30 Oct., 4 Nov., Cowley to Palmerston); FAAE, Corr. pol., Allemagne 806 (30 Oct., Tallenay to Bastide).

was convinced that 'Austria would be supported by Germany' if war broke out.[58] And, as the French foreign minister avowed, France did not wish to engage herself

... in a war where we would be without auxiliaries and would have all of Europe against us. I say without auxiliaries, for the supposed German democrats, the Frankfurt democrats, have begun by choosing an Emperor [Archduke John], and would be the last to want to lose the position which Austria occupies between the Alps and the Po and which Germany regards as her territory. If there were a war, the German democrats would only see in it an occasion to found and solidify German unity in giving their contingents the fraternity of [fighting together under] the same flag.[59]

Germany's involvement in Italy in support of Austria remained a definite eventuality which France had to take into consideration.

There is no doubt that Germany's stance on the Italian question was a factor adversely affecting Franco-German relations in the late summer and autumn of 1848. In the spring of 1848, while Germany was in the throes of revolution, the French had been enthusiastic about the emergence of a liberal and republican Germany friendly to France. At this time France seemed to have abandoned her traditional aversion to a strong, unified Germany. Certain elements of the French press, in fact, had actively endorsed the German unification movement. *Le National* had applauded Germany's efforts to unify herself, believing that a united Germany would act to liberate Poland. The *Journal des débats* and *La Démocratie pacifique* had been encouraged by the possibility of German unity because they hoped a strong Germany would prove a barrier against Russia.[60] However, as the year advanced France became progressively disillusioned with her neighbour across the Rhine whose republicanism failed and liberalism wanted, while her aggressive nationalism became increasingly apparent. By autumn the French attitude toward Germany had evolved to the point where springtime enthusiasm had given way to suspicion and dismay.[68] In a similar manner

[58] FAAE, Corr. pol., Toscane 192 (23 Oct., Bastide to Benoît-Champy).
[59] Ibid., Turin 322 (10 Oct., Bastide to Sain de Boislecomte).
[60] *Le National*, 15 Mar.; *Le Journal des débats*, 15 May; *La Démocratie pacifique*, 19 Mar.
[61] This metamorphosis in France's attitude toward Germany has been analysed by two students of Franco-German relations in 1848, by Robert Hahn in his doctoral dissertation and by Rudolf Buchner in his recent book (*Die*

the French attitude toward German unity also underwent a profound change. Germany's bellicose attitude toward Denmark, Poland, and Italy made the French government reconsider Richelieu's policy of favouring German disunity.[62]

It could be argued that the Cavaignac government struck a neutral and disinterested pose concerning the question of German unity. Bastide had instructed the French agent in Hanover to assume an 'attitude of reserve and expectation' toward the German unity movement, a movement which was still far from achieving its aims.[63] Cavaignac's instructions to Le Flô indicate that France informed the Tsar that, while the Republic was 'waiting to pronounce itself' until German unity was a 'fait accompli', still the Republic had 'no intention of in any way hindering or contesting this unity in its accomplishment'.[64] Finally, Bastide again denied that France was opposing German unity in writing to the French agent in Hanover; she was, he declared, simply waiting to see whether the independent German states would surrender their sovereignty to Frankfurt before acting to recognize the new Germany.[65] Nevertheless, indications are that these notes did not truly represent the Cavaignac government's position on German unity. The instructions to Hanover were written in reply to Hanoverian charges that France was attempting to obstruct German unity, charges which France was bound to deny. And France could not be expected to divulge her true feelings about German unity to the Russian Tsar. A detailed analysis of the diplomatic record indicates that the Second Republic in the late summer and autumn of 1848, far from encouraging German unity in any form or even remaining neutral on this issue, strove to discourage by diplomatic means a movement which it felt to be detrimental to French interests.

By the summer of 1848 the thought of a strong, united Germany seemed to inspire fear and anxiety among French

deutsch-französische Tragödie, 1848–1864 (Würzburg, 1965). While Buchner merely outlines this profound transformation of French attitudes in a few pages of his book, Hahn studies it in great detail in his very competent dissertation.

[62] See above, chapters III, VI, VII, for background material on France's policies toward Germany, Poland, and Denmark.

[63] FAAE, Corr. pol., Hanovre 68 (14 Aug., Bastide to Petetin).

[64] AD Sarthe, Documents des archives privées de M. Eugène Cavaignac, reels 24 and 26 (9 Sept., Cavaignac to Le Flô).

[65] FAAE, Corr. pol., Hanovre 68 (2 Oct., Bastide to Fontenilliaf).

statesmen. Such traditionalistic diplomats as de Tocqueville and Albert de Broglie clearly perceived the danger which a strong united Germany posed for France.[66] As de Tocqueville remarked to Senior, 'France cannot see with pleasure the new growth of a great military Power right next to her borders'.[67] Already in June Thiers and other members of the Constituent Assembly's Financial Committee had suggested that funds from the hard-pressed French Treasury be allocated to strengthening French armaments because they perceived the potential threat which a unified German nation could pose to French interests.[68] Bastide, for his part, concurred in the belief that the formation of a unified Germany was not in France's interests. In a dispatch to Emmanuel Arago, who was favourable to German unity and believed that unity would result in the democratization of Germany, Bastide replied that Arago might be correct in his assumptions, but added that 'unity will also make this people of forty million souls a redoubtable Power for Germany's neighbours, which is not the case today; and, therefore, I do not see it as being in our interest to desire this unity and even less to encourage it. The invading spirit of Germany is already not too reassuring.'[69] Similarly, the French foreign minister told Thom that he was completely disabused about 'the principle of nationalities', which was now being employed to bring about the unification of states such as Germany, 'something which', Bastide believed, 'was not and could not be in France's interest'.[70]

Since May Bastide had supported Denmark against Germany because of the parallel which he so perspicaciously drew between Germany's coveting Schleswig-Holstein and the possibility of her coveting Alsace-Lorraine. By the summer Bastide was fully convinced that a strong, united Germany could pose a most serious threat to France's border provinces. Bastide avowed to Delacour that he was disturbed by the fact that the feeling of German nationality which promoted German unity also encroached upon

---

[66] Albert de Broglie, 'De la politique étrangère de la France depuis la révolution de février', *Revue des deux mondes*, xxxiii (1848), 293–321.

[67] Eugène de Eichtal, *Alexis de Tocqueville et la démocratie libérale: étude suivie de fragments des entretiens de Tocqueville avec Nassau William Senior, 1848–1858* (Paris, 1897), p. 230.

[68] Austria, HHS, Frankreich Korr. Kart. 337 (19, 23 June, Thom to Wessenberg).

[69] FAAE, Corr. pol., Prusse 302 (31 July, Bastide to Arago).

[70] Austria, HHS, Frankreich Korr. Kart. 337 (23 Aug., Thom to Wessenberg).

the rights of France's allies and 'menaced' France herself 'in a part of her territory'.[71] The reference to Alsace-Lorraine was obvious. As the Danish minister in Paris remarked in a dispatch to Copenhagen, the French government was most 'concerned by the invading spirit of the new German Empire [Frankfurt], with which France wishes to remain on good terms, but not at all costs; Alsace-Lorraine would be too heavy a loss for France to permit Germany to indulge herself in such absorptions'.[72] On other occasions Bastide drew a clear parallel between Schleswig-Holstein and Alsace-Lorraine. In writing to Lefebvre in Baden he admitted that he had 'very little sympathy for German unity', because the German pretension that any land inhabited by Germans belongs to Germany, a pretension which had already led to German aggression against Denmark and Poland, 'menaces us [France] concerning Alsace-Lorraine'.[73] In a similar manner Bastide informed another French diplomat stationed in Germany that he was wary 'of a single state of forty-five million people at the very doorstep of France'. This was especially true because the Frankfurt Assembly seemed to him to be motivated by 'this spirit of ambition which, taking unity of race and language for the basis of German unity, claims the right to unite to the German Empire territories such as that portion of the Duchy of Poznań where German is spoken [as well as] a part at least of Schleswig and Limbourg, and menaces us in the possession of Alsace'.[74] The French government was ever aware that 'the German principle of assimilation' could 'one day lead the unitarians of Frankfurt to demand Alsace-Lorraine from us [France]'.[75] In light of what was to happen in 1871, Bastide's words seem almost prophetic. Although French diplomats, such as Lamartine, had been favourable to Germany and not unfavourable to the movement for German national unity in the spring of 1848, by the autumn of that year the formulators of French foreign policy were as apprehensive about German unity as they were about Italian unity.[76] They realized quite well that neither movement was in France's national interests.

---

[71] FAAE, Corr. pol., Autriche 436 (27 Aug., Bastide to Delacour).
[72] Denmark, Rigsarkivet, Frankrig II (27 July, E. C. L. Moltke to Knuth).
[73] FAAE, Corr. pol., Bade 34 (31 Aug., Bastide to Lefebvre).
[74] Ibid., Allemagne 806 (9 Sept., Bastide to Tallenay).
[75] Ibid., Prusse 302 (7 Sept., Bastide to Arago).
[76] It is interesting to note that by the summer of 1848 even Lamartine seems

The French knew that they could not openly oppose German unity. To do so would only strengthen and encourage the movement. Therefore, the Republic expressed its willingness to accept German unity if the people of Germany desired and were able to realize such a development.[77] Still, German aggressiveness, coupled with Germany's increasing support for Austria, made Bastide decide to do everything in his power to discourage German unity surreptitiously by diplomatic means. The French foreign minister made this clear in a secret letter to Arago in which he stated that

German unity is an excellent principle as long as it remains within the limits of democratic fraternity among the different peoples who compose the great Germanic family. However, if under the pretext of unity and fraternity, they wish to absorb Schleswig, which is Danish, Limbourg, which is Dutch, Lombardy and Venice, which are Italian, Poznań, which is Polish, and perhaps Alsace and Lorraine, German unity becomes a thing which must be combatted. Therefore, since this tendency is manifest, it is necessary, from now on, to encourage Prussia, Bavaria, and the other states to conserve their independence and their nationality.[78]

At a time when it was becoming apparent that the important German states, like Prussia, Hanover, and Bavaria, seemed determined not to surrender their sovereignty to Frankfurt, the French government was prepared to revert to its traditional policy of promoting German disunity.[79]

Already by late July French diplomats were reporting a definite 'reaction' by Prussia against German unity under Frankfurt's aegis.[80] Arago reported on 29 July that a Prussian official, Griesheim, had published a brochure in which 'the idea of the centralization of the Germanic power' was 'rejected' with 'energy' and 'vigour' as not being in Prussia's interest. Upon receiving

to have altered his attitude toward Germany. As an influential member of the National Constituent Assembly's Foreign Affairs Committee, Lamartine appears to have become aware of Germany's aggressive attitude, for he was now drawing parallels between Germany's stance on Schleswig-Holstein and the attitude that she might adopt toward 'Alsace, Lorraine, and the three bishoprics' (Austria, HHS, Frankreich Korr. Kart. 337, 8 Aug., Thom to Wessenberg).

[77] FAAE, Corr. pol., Allemagne 806 (2 Nov., Bastide to Tallenay).
[78] Bastide, pp. 50–1 (5 Aug., Bastide to Arago).
[79] FAAE, Corr. pol., Allemagne 805 (2 Aug., Savoye to Bastide); Corr. pol., Prusse 302 (20 July, Arago to Bastide).
[80] Ibid., Prusse 302 (24 July, Arago to Bastide).

Arago's report, Bastide wrote in the margin: 'It is necessary to encourage opinion in the same sense as the brochure.' He elaborated on this remark in the next dispatch that he sent to Arago, noting that the ideas put forth in Griesheim's brochure 'already justified the presentiments expressed' in his dispatch of 31 July—in which Bastide had spoken about the 'invading spirit' of Germany and had stated that it was not in France's interest to 'encourage' German unity—and adding that he entirely concurred with Griesheim's conclusion that German unity was not in Prussia's interest. Bastide concluded by stressing that it was necessary 'to encourage this opinion, within the limits of what is appropriate'.[81] When the opportunity arose, Bastide would act to discourage German unity by enticing Prussia to challenge Frankfurt over the question of participation in the Italian mediation.

Frankfurt's desire to support Austria's Italian policy and at the same time to enhance the Central Government's (the Frankfurt Assembly's) prestige as a Power led her to issue requests both for recognition by Paris and for the right to play a role in mediating the Italian problem. The French government procrastinated in recognizing the new German Central Government, arguing that it could not do so until the other German states had surrendered their own sovereignty and had completely merged with the Central Power. While the Cavaignac government simply temporized and put off its decision to recognize Frankfurt, French opposition to Frankfurt's inclusion in the mediation was apparent immediately. De Tocqueville remarked, after a confidential discussion with General Cavaignac around the end of August, that 'the General appeared to be far distant from the idea of a *rapprochement* with the unitary authority of Frankfurt, and strongly inclined to keep it definitely away from the questions that are being discussed at the moment'.[82] Despite the fact that both England and France were inclined to discourage other Powers from joining the mediation, Bastide now approached Prussia about her inclusion in the mediation to counter the presence of Frankfurt.[83] Throughout 1848 the French believed

[81] Ibid. (29 July, Arago to Bastide; 1 Aug., Bastide to Arago).
[82] De Tocqueville, *Œuvres complètes*, vol. viii, part 2, pp. 37–8 (3 Sept., de Tocqueville to Beaumont).
[83] Ibid., pp. 57–8 (10 Oct., Beaumont to de Tocqueville); FAAE, Corr. pol., Prusse 302 (24 Aug., Bastide to Arago; 25 Aug., Arago to Bastide).

Frankfurt to be the aggressive culprit in Germany, while tending to exaggerate Prussia's liberalism and friendship for France.[84] Furthermore, the Cavaignac government felt that Prussia would probably support France and England if she were admitted to the mediation; and Prussia might be able 'to act in Frankfurt to make her pacific and moderate ideas concerning Italy prevail'.[85] Bastide exhorted Prussia to exert her independence from Frankfurt and to play her role as a great Power by entering the mediation.[86] France now hoped that Prussia, 'France's natural ally', could challenge Frankfurt for the leadership of the German Confederation.[87]

Frankfurt, for her part, obviously intended to uphold the Austrian position in the mediation. Gagern, President of the Frankfurt Assembly, conceived of Germany's presence at the mediation as a means of limiting Anglo-French influence in the Peninsula and guaranteeing to Austria the retention of a 'strong defensive boundary' in Italy.[88] Then, too, the Frankfurt Assembly's election of Archduke John to head the German Confederation brought Bastide to remark caustically that the Austrians had been right in calculating that Germany would eventually swing over to support the Austrian cause in Italy, for now 'German democracy' had 'taken care to inaugurate its advent by endowing itself with an Austrian emperor'.[89] In view of Frankfurt's commitment to the Austrian cause, both England and France were inalterably opposed to her participation in the mediation.[90] But while the French were advancing Prussia's candidacy to counter Frankfurt's, Palmerston took the position that no other Powers besides France, England, and the belligerents should partake in the negotiations. The British point of view prevailed, and the two German Powers were refused admittance to the mediation, although they were permitted to send observers.[91]

---

[84] Arago argued, for example, that Prussia showed more sympathy for the Polish cause and more moderation toward the Schleswig-Holstein question than Frankfurt (FAAE, Corr. pol., Prusse 302, 2 Aug., Arago to Bastide).

[85] Ibid. (16 Aug., Bastide to Arago; 17 Aug., Arago to Bastide).

[86] Ibid. (24 Aug., Bastide to Arago; 25 Aug., Arago to Bastide).

[87] Ibid., Prusse 303 (7 Oct., Bastide to Arago).

[88] Ibid., Saxe 108 (17 Aug., Reinhard to Bastide).

[89] Ibid., Prusse 302 (6 Sept., Bastide to Arago).

[90] *Parliamentary Papers*, lviii. 241 (31 Aug., Palmerston to Cowley).

[91] Britain, PRO, F.O. 27/800 (26, 28 Sept., Palmerston to Normanby).

In explaining France's reasons for supporting Prussian admission to the mediation process, Bastide openly avowed to Palmerston that he hoped Prussia's inclusion would have the advantage of enabling Prussia, 'finally acting like a great Power, to hinder Frankfurt from setting itself up as the Imperial Power over all Germany'.[92] Bastide hoped that Prussia's inclusion in the mediation would serve to 'detach Prussia from Germany'.[93] Moreover, Bastide confided to Tallenay that it was in France's interest to 'tighten' France's 'traditional ties' with Prussia 'in the spirit of that policy of division and counterpoise that France has always followed to her advantage toward Germany'.[94] France had definitely intended to use Prussia's participation in the mediation process as a means of encouraging Prussia and the other decentralist forces within Germany to continue their opposition to Frankfurt's efforts to achieve German unity. By the autumn of 1848 France's foreign minister was once again following Richelieu's policy of sponsoring a disunited Germany.[95]

During the summer and autumn of 1848 Prussia had assumed the leadership of those German states which preferred a federated to a united Germany. Therefore, even after England aborted the French attempt to include Prussia in the mediation, France still favoured Prussia over Frankfurt and tended to hope that Prussia would supplant Frankfurt as the dominant Power

---

[92] Ibid., F.O. 27/825 (14 Sept., Bastide to Beaumont). A copy of this dispatch was communicated to Palmerston.

[93] Bastide, p. 117 (20 Sept., Bastide to Beaumont).

[94] FAAE, Corr. pol., Allemagne 806 (9 Sept., Bastide to Tallenay).

[95] James Garvin Chastain in his recent doctoral dissertation has tried to establish a revisionist interpretation of Franco-German relations in 1848, asserting that the French Republic pursued a *kleindeutsch* policy in the summer and autumn of that year, favouring a unified Germany under Prussian leadership. This interpretation is based upon the gratuitous assumption that French statesmen in 1848 were romantic idealists, 'dreamers', and not adherents of *Realpolitik*, men who did not foresee the implications the German unity would have for France. It is documented largely by select quotations from Emmanuel Arago, the French envoy in Berlin who favoured both German unity and Prussia, but who seems to have had no real influence upon policy-making decisions. On the other hand, Chastain systematically neglected the numerous policy statements which show the formulators of French foreign policy in the autumn of 1848 to be quite aware of the threat which a united Germany constituted for France and to be unfavourable to German unity in any form. Chastain has committed the grave error of misrepresenting France's support of Prussia within the context of the German Confederation as French support of German unity under Prussia.

within the German Confederation. Viewing Prussia as both a decentralizing agent and a liberal Power friendly to France, the French foreign minister expressed the desire that Prussia 'could march at the head of a liberal Germany and aid us to terminate the difficulties that the ambition of Vienna and Frankfurt tend to perpetuate in Italy'. This sentiment led Bastide to instruct Arago 'to cultivate the friendship of Prussia', for Prussia in the future could be 'France's best and most reliable ally'.[96] Officially, the Cavaignac government struck a posture of complete neutrality toward internal developments within Germany, but there is no doubt that France felt a certain affinity toward Prussia, the country which seemed to provide the most effective means of frustrating Frankfurt's pretensions to leadership of a united Germany.

The French were not unhappy with the movement which brought about the decline of Frankfurt's authority and the ascendancy of the federative over the unitary idea in Germany during the autumn of 1848. The Danish minister in Paris, reporting in early September to his government on France's reaction to the dispute between Prussia and Frankfurt over the ratification of the Malmoe armistice, a dispute which served to increase the dissension between the two German Powers, remarked that Bastide 'seemed to rejoice over the excesses of the Germans, which [he believed] augur well for the future and for the downfall of German unity'.[97] By the middle of September it became quite clear to French diplomats that the individual German states would not willingly surrender their sovereign powers to the Central Government in Frankfurt.[98] On 29 September Tallenay could report from Frankfurt that Germany now seemed to favour a federated rather than a united state. He added: 'I do not hesitate to say that a united democratic Germany is more dangerous to the Republic than a federated Germany', for a 'united democratic Germany will necessarily become, by the force of things, ambitious, invading, tending to absorb in its circle all the provinces of German origin and especially those where the German tradition and language is maintained.'[99] In

---

[96] FAAE, Corr. pol., Prusse 303 (17, 20 Oct., Bastide to Arago).
[97] Denmark, Rigsarkivet, Frankrig II (9 Sept., E. C. L. Moltke to Knuth).
[98] FAAE, Corr. pol., Prusse 302 (13 Sept., Bastide to Arago).
[99] Ibid., Allemagne 806 (29 Sept., Tallenay to Bastide).

late September Bastide could rejoice that France's actions to
encourage Prussia to assert her independence from Frankfurt
had been successful, for 'this Germanic Empire, which was
threatening us with the weight of its 45 million people, henceforth finds itself reduced to the dimension of an ill-unified confederation, without serious danger for France'.[100]

By late autumn Tallenay was reporting that Frankfurt's effort
to unify Germany was being paralysed by the opposition of the
independent German states; Frankfurt was becoming increasingly dependent upon Prussia and Austria, a development which
'would bring Germany back to the federative unity' principle
which had been on the ascendancy in Germany before 1848.[101]
Tallenay was convinced that these events 'were of the nature to
reassure us, at least for the time being, against the dangers which
could have resulted for both Germany and us from a strong
democratic unity within this country'. Germany seemed to 'contain within herself enough discordant elements' to block unity
and therefore to 'protect us for a long time yet from a pre-
ponderant and menacing homogeneity [within Germany]'.[102] At
the same time Bastide remarked that, in light of the internal
difficulties facing all three aspirants for German leadership, it
seemed improbable that Germany would be united under Frankfurt, Berlin, or Vienna and unlikely that Germany could
materially assist Austria in Italy. He seems to have displayed
his true sentiments concerning these developments when he
observed that, 'from these different points of view that I have
indicated, it appears to me that the present situation is favourable to the policies of France'.[103] The movement for German
unity now seemed to be disintegrating from within, while a
federative Germany under Prussian and Austrian tutelage was
emerging. By December Tallenay could remark that France had
been wise in having observed strict official neutrality toward
German internal developments, for Frankfurt's ambitions had
been stifled by the Germans themselves.[104]

In the summer and autumn of 1848 the Cavaignac government
also tried to parry the German menace by establishing an *entente*

[100] Bastide, p. 117 (20 Sept., Bastide to Beaumont).
[101] FAAE, Corr. pol., Allemagne 806 (8, 16 Nov., Tallenay to Bastide).
[102] Ibid. (5 Nov., Tallenay to Bastide).
[103] Ibid. (2 Nov., Bastide to Tallenay).
[104] Ibid. (16 Dec., Tallenay to Bastide).

with Russia. A *rapprochement* between the bastion of reaction and the centre of revolution had been possible after the middle of March when the Tsar proclaimed his intention not to interfere in the internal affairs of other European states.[105] In April Lamartine assured the Russian chargé d'affaires in Paris, Kisselef, that France was supporting the Polish cause only because of the pressure of French public opinion; he added that it was regrettable that Poland had erected a barrier between France and Russia for the previous twenty years, for he personally believed that 'the most natural alliance for France is an alliance with Russia'.[106] Because of the potentially explosive situation in both Poland and Germany, the Tsarist government, encouraged by Lamartine's terse reply to the Polish delegation in Paris, began considering the possibility of a Franco-Russian *entente*.[107] Lamartine, for his part, continued to make overtures to St. Petersburg in an attempt to improve relations with Russia and to persuade the Tsar to recognize the Republic.[108] Nevertheless, these efforts came to naught and Franco-Russian relations took a turn for the worse, for the Tsar was profoundly alienated by the French Assembly's pronouncement of 24 May in favour of the liberation of oppressed nationalities.[109] Any possibility of a Franco-Russian *rapprochement* disappeared, and relations between Paris and St. Petersburg languished until Cavaignac's advent to power.

After the June Days relations between the Republic and the Russian Empire improved appreciably. The Tsar took the initiative by sending a letter to Cavaignac, congratulating him on his 'magnificent conduct' in defeating the 'party of anarchy' in Paris.[110] The Austrian chargé d'affaires in Paris, for one, felt that the Tsar's letter to Cavaignac marked a turning point in Franco-Russian relations.[111] Then, too, by the summer the Polish insur-

[105] See above, p. 29.

[106] M. N. Pokrovski, *Pages d'histoire: la méthode du matérialisme historique appliquée à quelques problèmes d'histoire concrets* (Paris, 1929), pp. 61–3.

[107] Ibid., pp. 66–7; Eugène, le vicomte de Guichen, *Les Grandes Questions européennes et la diplomatie des puissances sous la Seconde République française* (2 vols.; Paris, 1925–7), i. 108 (19 Apr., Bloomfield to Palmerston).

[108] Pokrovski, pp. 51, 65–6; Karl Robert, comte de Nesselrode, *Lettres et Papiers du chancelier comte de Nesselrode* (11 vols.; Paris, 1904–12), ix. 93.

[109] Bapst, *Les Origines de la guerre de Crimée*, pp. 10–11.

[110] Pokrovski, p. 69.

[111] Austria, HHS, Frankreich Korr. Kart. 337 (18 Aug., Thom to Wessenberg).

rections had been crushed by Prussian troops, thus removing a possible source of friction between Paris and St. Petersburg. Moreover, Germany's aggressive proclivities, especially *vis-à-vis* Denmark, were of growing concern to both France and Russia. Thom observed that the Franco-Russian *rapprochement* which occurred during the summer 'had primarily been brought about by the events in Frankfurt, events which the two Powers [France and Russia] view with extreme displeasure'.[112] By the summer of 1848 sources of disagreement between the Republic and the Russian Empire were on the wane, while the interests of the two countries were beginning to coincide.

As the two Powers moved closer together, the influential Count Chreptovitch, the Russian minister in Naples and the son-in-law of Nesselrode, suggested the possibility of a Franco-Russian alliance in speaking to the French agent in Naples. At the same time Chreptovitch offered the Republic a free hand in Italy if Paris would cease to champion the Polish cause.[113] Then, in the middle of August Kisselef had a long conversation with Cavaignac in which he mentioned that their two nations had numerous interests in common and suggested that France might send an unofficial representative to St. Petersburg.[114] Shortly thereafter Nesselrode, the Russian Chancellor, elaborated upon what he conceived of as being these mutual interests in a detailed letter to Kisselef; the Russian Chancellor warned France 'of the appearance in the middle of Europe of a compact and solid Power . . . of 45 million men' which could result in the 'violation of all equilibrium' in Europe.[115] Cavaignac, for his part, was most receptive to the Tsar's admonition, for the French government was also quite aware of Germany's aggressive attitude. Furthermore, France feared a collision with Germany over Italy, and a Russian alliance could prove most valuable in such an eventuality.[116] The French sent Le Flô, a general and a friend

---

[112] Ibid. (28 Aug., Thom to Wessenberg).

[113] FAAE, Corr. pol., Naples 176 (22 July, Sain de Boislecomte to Bastide).

[114] Bapst, *L'Empereur Nicolas Ier et la Deuxième République*, p. 16.

[115] Pokrovski, pp. 70–1 (30 Aug., Nesselrode to Kisselef).

[116] De Luna is incorrect in attributing a Franco-Russian alliance proposal to Cavaignac's initiative (pp. 347–8), for the Tsarist government had suggested such an alliance already in July. Moreover, Cavaignac did not wish to conclude an alliance with Russia simply to end French isolation, as de Luna suggests, but because of the possible threat from Germany.

of Cavaignac, to St. Petersburg in September to work for closer relations with Russia.

In late summer it seemed that France and Russia were on the verge of forming an *entente*.[117] Yet a *rapprochement* of the two Powers failed to develop in the autumn. For one thing, already in July the French had displayed considerable concern about the Russian invasion of Moldavia, which occurred shortly after disorders had broken out in Bucharest on 23 June.[118] Bastide saw the Russian invasion of the Danubian Principalities as a manifestation of traditional Russian expansionism in Eastern Europe, as well as a latent threat to the Straits. This Russian action undoubtedly led Bastide to suggest to Normanby that France and Britain should 'support Austria in the East', for Austria could constitute a barrier to Russian expansion in Eastern Europe. At a time when the Austrian stronghold in Italy seemed to be crumbling, Bastide argued that the Viennese government should be encouraged to turn her attentions elsewhere. The French foreign minister believed that 'it was for her [Austria's] dignity, perhaps for her preservation that, receiving whatever might be a fair compensation for her sacrifice of her Italian interests, she should, as soon as possible, concentrate her strength in that portion of her dominions, where she might, ere long, be so seriously threatened'.[119]

Even in the spring, when France was inalterably opposed to Austria's Italian policy, Lamartine had intimated to Thom that 'the Viennese Court should find a compensation for the loss of her Italian states in the Danubian provinces; the French government wants Austria to be strong on that front'.[120] In the summer, when the French government was trying both to convince Austria to accept the joint mediation and to blunt the German unification movement, Bastide spoke to Thom in a similar manner. The French foreign minister declared that France wished to see Austria remain strong in Germany and in the 'East, where the development of her riches and power call her; it is in this area that we wish her to move back her frontiers, rendering herself mistress of all the Lower Danube, stretching

---

[117] FAAE, Corr. pol., Wurtemberg 72 (10 Aug., Fontenay to Bastide).

[118] The Tsar had ordered the invasion of Moldavia in conjunction with the Porte, who simultaneously sent Turkish troops into Walachia.

[119] Britain, PRO, F.O. 27/810 (14 July, Normanby to Palmerston).

[120] Austria, HHS, Frankreich Korr. Kart. 337 (1 May, Thom to Ficquelmont).

out her possessions as far as the Black Sea; and if ever the cabinet
of Vienna wished to give this tendency to its policies, it could
count upon the sincere and energetic support of France'.[121] Then,
in the autumn, during the October uprising in Vienna, Bastide
again suggested to Thom that Austria was wrong in trying to
preserve her Italian provinces, 'a source of abundant embarrassment and weakness' for her, and that her 'true and most permanent interests were in the countries washed by the lower course
of the Danube', where Austria was 'in rivalry with a Power whose
ambitious views there are only too notorious'.[122] To be sure,
throughout 1848 it was in France's interest to divert Austria
away from the Italian Peninsula, where a collision of Austrian
and French interests was only too evident. Undoubtedly it was
this desire to influence Austria to turn away from Italy which
explains a large part of France's purpose in encouraging Austria
to expand eastward. Moreover, it seems likely that France would
have liked to set her two potential arch enemies, Austria and
Russia, at loggerheads over the Balkans. Still, it seems that
throughout 1848, and especially from the summer on when
Russia invaded Moldavia, the Cavaignac government was apprehensive about the 'notorious ambitions' of Tsarist Russia along
the Danube.

Worried by Russian expansion into Moldavia, Bastide approached Great Britain about a possible joint Anglo-French
diplomatic protestation. On 13 July he suggested that Russia's
invasion of Moldavia made it imperative for France and England
to come to an accord on the Eastern Question.[123] Throughout the
autumn the French government saw the Russian advance into
the Principalities as an 'expansionist policy', as a move threatening Turkey and the Straits while also foreshadowing the expansion of Russian influence among the Slavs in the Balkans.[124]
Palmerston, it seems, took a much less alarmist view of the
Russian move, arguing that it was only 'temporary' and not
serious.[125] Still, French insistence did eventually induce England

[121] Ibid. (23 Aug., Thom to Wessenberg).
[122] Ibid. (19 Oct., Thom to Wessenberg).
[123] FAAE, Corr. pol., Angleterre 670 (13 July, Bastide to Tallenay).
[124] Ibid., Corr. pol., Angleterre 671 (4 Sept., 20 Oct., Bastide to Beaumont).
[125] Ibid. (2 Aug., Tallenay to Bastide). It is interesting to note that Palmerston was largely unperturbed by the Russian advance, correctly analysing
it as foreshadowing simply a Russian move against revolutionary Hungary

to agree to issuing a joint protest to Russia in January 1849.[126] In the summer of 1848 when a common concern for the consequences of German unity seemed to be drawing France and Russia together, other developments, such as the Russian advance into the Balkans, seemed to be dividing them.

Then, too, it seems probable that France's attitude toward the Polish question in the autumn of 1848 also hurt relations between the French Republic and the Russian Empire. In a confidential letter of instructions to Le Flô, who was leaving for St. Petersburg, Cavaignac stated his desire for friendly relations with Russia, but also expressed continued sympathy for Poland.[127] Although in the summer of 1848 France had temporarily abandoned the Polish cause and relegated it to a secondary position in her diplomatic priorities because of her efforts to improve relations with Germany and Russia, the Republic had not entirely forgotten the Poles.[128] In fact, in late October the Berlin Assembly passed a measure assuring Poznań a separate and independent existence. This brought Arago, the French minister to Berlin, to rejoice, for it seemed that a semi-independent Grand Duchy of Poznań might be re-established after all.[129] Arago was optimistic about Poznań's fate as late as 28 December, when he sent his last dispatch before being replaced in Berlin by de Lurde. The quixotic French diplomat was convinced that the partition of Poland was being undone and a new Poland established.[130] Any such development, of course, would have been anathema to the Tsar. France's continued sympathy for the Poles could only have contributed to the general Franco-Russian estrangement which was occurring by late 1848.

Finally, the uncertain political situation in France adversely

---

(de Tocqueville, *Œuvres complètes*, vol. viii, part 2, pp. 107, 111–12, 2 Dec., Beaumont to de Tocqueville).

[126] FAAE, Corr. pol., Russie 202 (3 Jan. 1849, Drouyn de Lhuys to Le Flô; 25 Jan. 1849, Vayer to Drouyn de Lhuys).

[127] AD Sarthe, Documents des archives privées de M. Eugène Cavaignac, reels 24 and 26 (9 Sept., Cavaignac to Le Flô).   [128] See above, pp. 133–4.

[129] FAAE, Corr. pol., Prusse 303 (23 Oct., Arago to Bastide).

[130] Ibid. (28 Dec., Arago to Drouyn de Lhuys). Arago's visions of a rejuvenated Grand Duchy of Poland were soon shattered. In February 1849 the Frankfurt Parliament decreed that the so-called German part of the Grand Duchy be incorporated into the German Empire. Despite its previous vote of October 1848, the Berlin Assembly adopted and confirmed Frankfurt's decree in November 1849.

affected relations between Paris and St. Petersburg in the autumn
of 1848. Le Flô received a friendly reception upon his arrival in
St. Petersburg and he immediately requested official recognition
for the French Republic. The Tsar replied by declaring his desire
for cordial relations with France; but he also displayed concern
about the sort of constitution that the Republic was drawing up
and, more especially, about the outcome of the French presidential elections. It seemed that the Tsar's government had decided
to recognize the Republic, but only when its form of government
was duly constituted.[131] As autumn wore on and it became
apparent that Louis Napoleon would become a candidate for the
French presidency, Nesselrode announced that Russia would
refrain from recognizing the Republic until after the presidential
elections. Le Flô protested, but Nicholas insisted that he did not
want to send an ambassador to France only to withdraw him a
month or two later if Louis Napoleon, whom the Tsar viewed
as a threat to the established European order, were elected president.[132] Le Flô succinctly summarized Russia's position in the
following manner: 'The point is this: they fear Louis Napoleon
Bonaparte, they dread his election, they feel that this will bring
war, so they abstain' from recognizing the Republic.[133]

Another factor which contributed to the progressive estrangement between France and Russia in the autumn of 1848 was the
attitude that the Tsar assumed toward Austria and the Italian
question. Bastide had hoped that Le Flô's mission to St. Petersburg, even if it did not lay the basis for a full-fledged *entente*,
would at least afford the Republic the opportunity 'to enlighten
sufficiently the Emperor so that he would not throw himself,
head down' into supporting the Austrians.[134] By autumn, however, Russia was becoming increasingly sympathetic to Austria's
position in Italy. Already in early September the Tsar made it
known that he opposed any mediation settlement in which
Austria lost territory guaranteed to her by treaty.[135] The Emperor
seemed to dread Russian involvement in Europe; yet at the same
time he suggested that he would interfere in Europe if France

[131] FAAE, Corr. pol., Russie 202 (21, 26 Sept., Le Flô to Bastide).
[132] Bapst, *L'Empereur Nicolas Ier et la Deuxième République*, pp. 20, 22–5.
[133] FAAE, Corr. pol., Russie 202 (11 Nov., Le Flô to Bastide).
[134] Ibid., Prusse 302 (6 Sept., Bastide to Arago).
[135] Ibid., Autriche 436 (4 Sept., Delacour to Bastide).

acted to alter territorially the existing treaties.[136] By early November Franco-Russian relations had cooled to the point where Le Flô reported that Russia was moving closer to Austria and would probably aid her if France crossed the Alps. The Tsar was at least committed to giving Austria moral if not material support.[137] By December the Tsar's government made it known that Russia would support Austria if France were to intervene militarily in Italy.[138] The Austrian chargé d'affaires in Paris was convinced that Russia's decision 'to support Austria with all the weight of its power in the eventuality of a conflict' in Italy was a primary factor determining France not to become involved under any circumstances in an Italian war.[139]

France had sought Russian support to counter possible German assistance to Austria; now the situation had evolved to the point where it seemed likely that Russia too might assist Austria if the occasion arose. France had failed entirely in her diplomatic efforts to discourage German involvement in Italy. There remained a definite possibility that French intervention in Italy would bring war with Austria, Germany, and even Russia. The possibility of a European coalition forming against France was certainly an important factor encouraging the French not to go to war in Italy.

The threat of internal disorders combined with the fear of a European conflict were in themselves reason enough to motivate the Cavaignac government to work for peace. Throughout the summer and autumn of 1848, though, the cardinal factor determining the French not to become involved militarily in Italy was the hostility which the Cavaignac government felt toward the Sardinian monarchy. During the autumn of 1848 Cavaignac, and especially Bastide, remained as inalterably opposed to the expansion of Sardinia and the establishment of a strong Kingdom of North Italy as they had been in the summer. The Republic's leaders, favourable to a federated republican Italy, were as convinced as ever in the autumn of 1848 that an Italy united under the Sardinian monarchy would pose a direct threat to French security.

[136] FAAE, Corr. pol., Allemagne 806 (30 Oct., Tallenay to Bastide); Corr. pol., Turin 322 (31 Oct., Bastide to Sain de Boislecomte).
[137] Ibid., Russie 202 (2, 11 Nov., Le Flô to Bastide).   [138] Nesselrode, ix. 205.
[139] Austria, HHS, Politisches Archiv IX, Frankreich Kart. 29 (6 Dec., Thom to Schwarzenberg).

By the autumn of 1848 Sardinian diplomats had become extremely aware of the latent hostility which the Cavaignac government felt for Charles Albert's realm. From one point of view, Sardinia was reassured by the fact that Bastide and Cavaignac did not seem to be following in the footsteps of Lamartine in coveting Nice and Savoy. Ricci had come away from his discussion with the French leaders on 3 August with the definite impression that, unlike Lamartine, they had 'no intention of demanding territorial compensation for French intervention'. On 6 August Ricci reported that in a subsequent conversation Bastide had reaffirmed France's intentions concerning this matter.[140] Then, on 11 August, Cavaignac had sworn before the French Assembly's Foreign Affairs Committee that his government had no desire for 'territorial aggrandizement' at Sardinia's expense, that 'even if he were offered Savoy, he would not want it'.[141] Still, men such as Brignole and Ricci, Sardinia's agents in Paris, had few illusions about the Cavaignac government's attitude toward their country.

In late September Brignole stated his belief

. . . that the present head of the French Republic [Cavaignac] has little sympathy for us. . . . From time to time he makes a display of his alleged affection for the cause of Italian independence, he promises the moon and stars; but, in reality, I believe him to be rather indifferent to the success of this cause, and if he desires to see it triumph, it is on the condition that Italy, rid of the Austrians, should remain as weak and divided, or even more so, than it was previously, and especially that Sardinia should not become too powerful.[142]

Brignole was fully cognizant of Cavaignac's 'prejudices' against 'the aggrandizement of the King's states'.[143] Ricci concurred in his colleague's belief in French hostility to Sardinia. In November Bastide had supposedly told a group of Italians residing in Paris that the real reason for France's sending a fleet to the Adriatic was to make certain that Sardinia did nothing 'to compromise the liberty of the Republic of St. Mark [Venice]'. This

[140] Sardinia, AST, Missioni diplomatiche speciali e temporanee (4 6 Aug., Ricci to Pareto).

[141] Ibid., Lettere Ministri Francia (12 Aug., Brignole to Pareto).

[142] Ibid. (22 Sept., Brignole to Perrone).

[143] Nicomede Bianchi, Storia documentata della diplomazia in Italia dell'anno 1814 all'anno 1861 (8 vols.; Turin, 1865–72), v 498–9 (31 Aug., Brignole to Perrone).

made Ricci exclaim that the French foreign minister was displaying 'always the same double faced policy, the same antipathy
toward us', being 'secretly hostile to everything that could be
advantageous to us in Italy'.[144] Already in late October Ricci
had remarked that 'M. Bastide is secretly hostile to us, that is to
say, that he is working either for the formation of a republic or
an independent state in Lombardy'. Ricci was convinced that
Bastide 'is at the bottom of his heart a bitter enemy of our
government and of King Charles Albert, and . . . is quite far
from being favourable to the consolidation of a large state in
upper Italy. His political plan consists of substituting [for it]
either a Lombardo-Venetian republic or one or two monarchical
states independent of Piedmont.'[145] Ricci's suspicions seemed to
be confirmed by Normanby's disclosure that France, 'while
desiring the weakening of Austrian power in the Peninsula, does
not want this to profit the King of Sardinia'.[146] As in the spring
and summer of 1848, Sardinian diplomats realized that their
supposed ally, republican France, had little sympathy for King
Charles Albert's realm. Many of Sardinia's suspicions concerning
France's desire to block the aggrandizement of the House of
Savoy proved to be well founded. Throughout the late summer
and autumn the Cavaignac government showed its antagonism
toward Sardinia by its willingness to alter the bases of mediation
to frustrate Sardinian expansion.

In July and early August, when the two mediating Powers
were negotiating a mediation agreement, France had proved
reluctant in acquiescing to Sardinia's domination of Northern
Italy.[147] Still, once the mediation had been accepted by both
England and Sardinia, France was bound to supporting the
agreed-upon bases of mediation. This meant, in effect, that
France had committed herself to working for an Italian settlement in which Lombardy would be attached to Charles Albert's
Kingdom. To be sure, the mediation only called upon Austria
to renounce her claims to Lombardy without mentioning
explicitly that Lombardy would join Sardinia. But Lombardy
had voted to incorporate herself into Sardinia and this had become a *fait accompli* in July.

---

144 Sardinia, AST, Legazione in Parigi (21 Nov., Ricci to Perrone).
145 Ibid. (25, 26 Oct., Ricci to Perrone).
146 Ibid. (25 Oct., Ricci to Perrone).   147 See above, pp. 142–5, 157, 164–5.

Immediately after formally agreeing to mediation with Great Britain in early August the French government seemed prepared to accept a situation in which Lombardy would be attached to Sardinia. Then, in the middle of August, the French consul in Milan, Denois, reported that it might be difficult to consummate the fusion between Lombardy and Sardinia because the Lombards now detested Charles Albert as a result of his failure to defend Milan.[148] As a result of this dispatch, Bastide now began seriously to reconsider the possibility of permanently separating Lombardy from Sardinia. He admitted his profound interest in the reports of Lombardy's 'animosity' toward Charles Albert, and noted that the bases of mediation called for a unity between the two Northern Italian states, 'but nothing prevented the negotiations from taking into consideration the manifestation of a desire to the contrary and the conditions arising from new circumstances'.[149] A week later, when France believed that Austria still might not accept the profered mediation, Bastide suggested in a letter to Arago in Berlin that Prussia might propose a European conference on the Italian question, in which all the European Powers, including Russia, would take part. Bastide went on to explain that:

... in this conference new bases of negotiation could be arrived at, such as Lombardy and Venetia brought together in a single state, on the model of something like Hungary, with constitutions, a national army and an archduke, with the city of Venice constituted as a free city like Hamburg or Lubeck, and with the Austrian debt shared by Italy. I have every reason to believe that these bases will be accepted by M. Wessenberg. I do not propose them officially in the name of my government, but the sincere desire that we have in maintaining the peace of the world obliges us, I believe, to accept them.[150]

At the same time the French foreign minister was confiding to the Austrian chargé d'affaires in Paris that France would agree to a settlement in which Austria's Northern Italian provinces were simply given autonomy and liberal institutions.[151]

By October Bastide admitted that if Lombardy alone were liberated from Austria 'she would have to be forcibly reunited

---

[148] FAAE, Corr. pol. des consuls, Autriche 10B, Milan (16 Aug., Denois to Bastide).   [149] Ibid. (27, 30 Aug., Bastide to Denois).
[150] Ibid., Corr pol., Prusse 302 (6 Sept., Bastide to Arago).
[151] See above, pp. 175, 193.

with Sardinia', while if a united Lombardo-Venetian state were to be autonomous under an enlightened Austrian rule 'the people of North Italy could form themselves progressively into a veritable nation. . . . In a word, it would be better for Italy, and for us, to have a limited independence, but equal in both parts, rather than a complete emancipation in only one of the two halves'.[152] Bastide's concept of 'Italian independence' had been justly criticized by Baune in the French National Assembly; as far as the French foreign minister was concerned, a 'liberated Italy' meant first and foremost a Northern Italy free from Sardinian control. Bastide was ready to acknowledge continued Austrian control over Northern Italy because of his fear of war and his profound hostility toward Charles Albert's Kingdom.[153]

The Sardinian government, for its part, suspicious of France's intentions concerning the fate of Northern Italy, pressed the Cavaignac government in the autumn of 1848 to abide by the original mediation terms based on the second Hummelauer proposal. Brignole asked Bastide point-blank to commit France to maintaining the agreed-upon bases of mediation in which Lombardy would merge with Sardinia. Bastide refused, however, arguing that the bases of mediation must remain flexible, for if they were posed as an ultimatum there would no longer be reason for negotiation.[154] He maintained this position throughout October and November. Although he conceded the fact that France was bound at least to propose to Austria a settlement based upon the terms of mediation, he would not consider these bases as an ultimatum; and if Austria refused to admit them—as she most evidently did—Bastide avowed that it would probably be necessary to alter them. Bastide admitted that France was 'no more engaged than before to give Lombardy to Sardinia'.[155]

The French seem to have been quite frank about their objectives when discussing the Italian situation with Austrian diplomats. In August and early September Bastide had informed the

[152] Bastide, pp. 124–5 (11 Oct., Bastide to Beaumont).

[153] Ferdinand Boyer, true to his thesis that France had only the best of intentions towards Italy throughout 1848, argues that as late as the autumn of that year France was still sympathetic toward the Sardinian cause, that France still remained Sardinia's 'disinterested' and 'loyal friend' (*La Seconde République, Charles-Albert et l'Italie du Nord en 1848*, pp. 178, 234, 335–6).

[154] FAAE, Corr. pol., Turin 322 (2 Sept., Bastide to Brignole).

[155] Ibid. (18, 26, 27 Oct., 12 Nov., Bastide to Sain de Boislecomte).

Austrians that France was not anxious to see Sardinia aggrandized and that France simply wished Lombardy-Venetia to
obtain liberal governments under Austrian rule. In the autumn
Bastide repeated to Thom his willingness to accept the established territorial settlement in Northern Italy as long as Austria
abided by her pledge to grant liberal, national institutions to
these areas.[156] At the same time Koller, the Austrian chargé
d'affaires in London, reported that Beaumont had assured him
that 'it is not we who want to enrich Sardinia with Lombardy.
Lord Palmerston is in this respect much further engaged, but the
liberal institutions which Baron Wessenberg has promised satisfy
us.'[157] Moreover, Bastide repeated to Thom his contention that
'France too wished the maintenance of the treaties concerning
the state of possession in Italy, that she did not and could not
desire the aggrandizement of Sardinia', that if Charles Albert
ever became 'King of Italy' France would have to ask for Savoy
as compensation. Bastide also made it quite clear to the Austrian
chargé d'affaires that the Cavaignac government wished above
all 'to extract itself with honour from certain engagements more
or less imprudently contracted by previous administrations toward public opinion'.[158] While the Cavaignac government had
assured Sardinia that it had no designs upon Savoy, Bastide had
suggested to Thom that the French were still interested in territorial indemnity for the expansion of the Sardinian realm. Above
all, it seems that by the autumn of 1848 the French were
primarily concerned with saving face and preserving the peace.

French opposition to Sardinian expansion was an extremely
important factor in determining the Cavaignac government not
to become militarily involved in Italy. The Cavaignac government would not abet the process of Italian unity any more than
it would encourage the move for German unity. Bastide might
have been sympathetic to the Italian cause, but he clearly perceived the implications which a unified Italy presented for
France. The Cavaignac government believed that it was simply
not in France's interest to go to war to assist Italy, especially
when France might be faced with internal disorders and war with
Germany if she became militarily involved in the Peninsula.

---

[156] Austria, HHS, Frankreich Korr. Kart. 337 (12, 16 Oct., Thom to Wessenberg). [157] Taylor, p. 160 (21 Sept., Koller to Wessenberg).
[158] Austria, HHS, Frankreich Korr. Kart. 337 (24 Sept., Thom to Wessenberg).

X

DIPLOMATIC TEMPORIZATION

FRANCE wanted peace at all costs. Great Britain was primarily interested in restraining France and preserving the peace. Austria was resolved not to surrender her hold on Northern Italy unless obliged to do so by force of arms. Sardinia was impotent to act by herself. From September on it seemed inevitable that the drawn-out mediation would have no positive results. Still, for all the parties involved mediation could serve to temporize, save face, and preserve the peace. In many ways the intricacies of mediation from September to December were simply a prolongation of the state of affairs which existed already in September and which predestined the mediation to futility.

Austria's acceptance of the joint mediation on 2 September had solved nothing, for she had rejected its bases. The Austrian government had attempted to avoid mediation entirely, for after Custozza it was convinced that the Imperial armies were strong enough to hold Lombardy.[1] After accepting the mediation Vienna made it clear that it desired the mediation to have the existing treaties as its basis. As a British diplomat remarked, Austria wanted the mediation simply to guarantee her the *status quo ante bellum*.[2] Moreover, Austria soon made it known that she was not even willing to extend the cease-fire to include Venice, despite pleas by Ponsonby and Delacour for her to do so.[3] Wessenberg curtly informed the mediating Powers that their good offices would be employed only to facilitate negotiations between Vienna and Turin. Austria held that there was a distinct 'difference between a belligerent Power, such as Sardinia, and an insurgent city [Venice]; one concludes an armistice with a belligerent Power, one pacifies an insurgent city'.[4] Delacour, for his

[1] *Parliamentary Papers*, lviii. 351 (11 Sept., Cowley to Palmerston).
[2] Ibid., lviii. 331 (8 Sept., Cowley to Palmerston).
[3] FAAE, Corr. pol., Autriche 436 (6 Sept., Delacour to Bastide); *Parliamentary Papers*, lviii. 336 (6 Sept., Ponsonby to Palmerston).
[4] Austria, HHS, Frankreich Korr. Kart. 338; FAAE, Mémoires et Documents, Autriche 71 (6 Sept., Wessenberg to Delacour).

part, was convinced that Austria's attitude toward Italy had stiffened after her acceptance of the mediation.[5] Vienna now seemed ready to reduce Venice by force of arms, pressing to the utmost her rights over her Northern Italian provinces.

While the French government was no longer interested in realizing a settlement similar to the second Hummelauer proposal and gaining independence for either Lombardy or Venice, it did hope to influence Austria to grant a certain amount of autonomy and liberal institutions to her Italian provinces. Above all, France did not want to see Austria reduce Venice by force of arms, because such a development could oblige the French government to intervene in Italy. Fearing that Austria was no longer willing to compromise and bring about an Italian settlement concomitant with French interests, the Cavaignac government decided to once again apply pressure on Great Britain in order to arrive at a united front *vis-à-vis* Vienna.

On 15 September Beaumont informed Palmerston that the mediation seemed to have failed and that France might have to resort to arms after all.[6] Beaumont realized that Palmerston would never agree to armed mediation, but he hoped that by threatening unilateral French action Britain would press Austria to open negotiations immediately and possibly demand more from Austria than a simple promise of liberal institutions for Northern Italy. Four days later Beaumont had a long discussion with Palmerston in which he told the British foreign minister that France could not countenance an Austrian attack upon Venice, and suggested that an Anglo-French fleet sail in front of Venice to prevent the renewal of hostilities; he added that France was continuing her role of mediator only in deference to Great Britain's wishes.[7]

Reports were now circulating to the effect that the Austrian fleet once again was moving to blockade Venice. It seemed as though Austria was about to implement her threats to 'pacify' the insurgent city of Venice.[8] Bastide was extremely concerned

[5] FAAE, Corr. pol., Autriche 436 (9 Sept., Delacour to Bastide).

[6] Ibid., Corr. pol., Angleterre 671 (15 Sept., Beaumont to Bastide); de Tocqueville, *Œuvres complètes*, vol. viii, part 2, pp. 49–50 (16 Sept., Beaumont to de Tocqueville).

[7] FAAE, Corr. pol., Angleterre 671 (19 Sept., Beaumont to Bastide).

[8] Ibid., Corr. pol. des consuls, Autriche 8, Venise (20, 23 Sept., Vasseur to Bastide).

about these reports, for the dramatic fall of the Venetian Republic would flout the mediation, enrage French public opinion, and
oblige the Cavaignac government to champion the Italian cause
to the point where France's armed intervention in favour of
Venice might be required. Bastide expressed his consternation
when Thom informed him that the Austrian fleet was now planning to attack Venice, remarking that 'despite the French
government's desire to maintain the peace, this aim could not
be attained' if Venice were to fall to Austrian arms.[9] If Venice
were attacked the French government 'could not remain passive
in face of this act of hostility without raising against it the
justified indignation of public opinion'. Bastide informed Britain
that negotiations must commence immediately or France might
have to resort after all to a war in which it would be necessary
to stir up the people of Europe by revolutionary propaganda.[10]
An Austrian attack on Venice would cause France 'the
greatest embarrassment', so France pressed Britain once again
to approve of the sending of an expedition to occupy Venice
and forestall Austria's actions.[11] The French were again employing their time-tested device of threatening to go to war and
stir up revolution in Europe in order to enlist British diplomatic
support.

The French threats of war evoked a stern response from the
British government. Palmerston told Beaumont that mediation
could not be imposed upon Austria: 'We must weigh upon
Austria with our advice and not compel her with our arms.'[12]
Normanby warned Bastide that 'propagandism' was 'abhorent'
to the English and that any French attempt to appeal to the
revolutionary principle would 'lead to an immediate and complete separation from England'.[13] Palmerston summed up the
British attitude when he informed Beaumont that the British
wished to co-operate with France in negotiations, 'but if the
French Government should push matters to the extremity of
war, we must at once stop and no longer bear them company'.[14]

[9] Austria, HHS, Frankreich Korr. Kart. 337 (14 Sept., Thom to Wessenberg).
[10] FAAE, Corr. pol., Angleterre 671 (26 Sept., Bastide to Beaumont).
[11] Britain, PRO, F.O. 27/813 (30 Sept., Palmerston to Normanby); F.O.
27/800 (3 Oct., Palmerston to Normanby).
[12] FAAE, Corr. pol., Angleterre 671 (19 Sept., Beaumont to Bastide).
[13] Britain, PRO, F.O. 27/813 (28 Sept., Normanby to Palmerston).
[14] Ibid., F.O. 27/800 (3 Oct., Palmerston to Normanby).

In the face of this adamant opposition to the use of force, the French backed down from their threatening attitude.

Though Palmerston absolutely refused to consider the French proposal to threaten Austria with the use of force, he did send off notes to Vienna encouraging Austria to desist from military action against Venice and to withdraw entirely from the Peninsula, for her presence there would inevitably lead to renewed uprisings and eventual French intervention in Italy.[15] Austria should at least dissolve her blockade against Venice, because such action was 'not consistent' with the mediation. He added, moreover, that Austria should demonstrate 'a little patience', for she would eventually receive Venice anyhow by the very terms of the mediation.[16] Palmerston assured Beaumont that he was certain his admonitions to Vienna would suffice to preserve Venice from an Austrian attack.[17] Nevertheless, the French had the impression even at the end of September that although England still supported Lombardy's union with Sardinia, she was ready to abandon Venice completely to Austria. Beaumont remarked that Venice's plight was 'heart-rending', but he 'feared that all [France's] diplomatic efforts' in Britain on Venice's behalf were 'futile'. Palmerston, it seems, had decided that Venice must be sacrificed to Austria.[18] This decision became manifest on 16 October when Palmerston informed Manin and the Venetian government that it would be best for the Venetians to come to an amicable agreement with Austria for the surrender of their city.[19]

Despite the failure of their diplomatic efforts to enlist concrete support for Venice from England, the French did not seriously consider resorting to arms to save Venice. Instead, France opened up a diplomatic offensive toward Vienna, trying to persuade the Austrians to refrain from attacking Venice. In a note to Vienna Bastide requested Austria not to assault Venice, for such an act would 'openly injure France' without being necessary for Austria 'to maintain what she regards as her rights' over Venice. He warned that if French public opinion were disaffected, then

[15] *Parliamentary Papers*, lviii. 439, 472–3 (29 Sept., 9 Oct., Palmerston to Ponsonby).

[16] Ibid., lviii. 456, 386–7 (2 Oct., 20 Sept., Palmerston to Ponsonby).

[17] FAAE, Corr. pol., Angleterre 671 (9 Oct., Beaumont to Bastide).

[18] Ibid. (30 Sept., Beaumont to Bastide).

[19] Planat de la Faye, i. 469 (16 Oct., Palmerston to Manin).

France would be forced to start a conflict which would degenerate into a 'war of peoples, who are just awaiting a signal from France, against all thrones'.[20] At the same time Bastide told Thom that if Venice were to fall France's honour 'would be profoundly offended and public opinion in France would arrive at a degree of excitement which was threatening for the peace'.[21] Not only might the fall of Venice provoke war, but, as Bastide pointed out to Thom on several different occasions, such an event would cause his government 'immense embarrassment' in the face of French public opinion and would 'unfailingly' bring about his government's fall.[22] On one occasion Bastide assured Thom that personally, 'as far as I am concerned, speaking frankly to you, I regret that you have not already occupied Venice'.[23] Still, both the French foreign minister and Cavaignac consistently argued that their government could not allow Venice to fall at this time.[24]

By the end of September France's entreaties seemed to have had some effect. Wessenberg let it be known that Austria could not formally extend the armistice of 9 August to include Venice, but that Austrian forces would not at this time attempt to retake Venice by force of arms. Bastide was most pleased when informed that 'the Austrian fleet was blockading Venice only with the view of upholding [Austria's] rights over this city' and that Austria would abstain from using 'all overt hostile acts' against Venice.[25] Then, on 20 September the Austrian Emperor published a 'Manifesto to the inhabitants of the Lombard-Venetian Kingdom' in which he solemnly committed himself to granting constitutional governments to his Northern Italian provinces.[26] The French had few illusions as to the value of such a pledge, but, as Ponsonby remarked to Wessenberg, such a promise 'should give to the French Government an argument in support of [its] pacific policy'.[27] The French government could deem itself satisfied with

[20] FAAE, Corr. pol., Autriche 436 (26 Sept., Bastide to Delacour).
[21] Ibid. (25 Sept., Bastide to Delacour).
[22] Austria, HHS, Frankreich Korr. Kart. 337 (17, 18, 24, 26, 28 Sept., Thom to Wessenberg).   [23] Ibid. (17 Sept., Thom to Wessenberg).
[24] Ibid. (27 Sept., Thom to Wessenberg).
[25] Ibid., Frankreich Korr. Kart. 338 (28 Sept., Wessenberg to Thom); Frankreich Korr. Kart. 337 (3 Oct., Thom to Wessenberg).
[26] *Parliamentary Papers*, lviii. 466.
[27] Ibid. 393–4 (15 Sept., Ponsonby to Palmerston).

these apparent concessions by Austria. The mediating Powers and Austria now began an exchange of notes proposing different mediation sites. Britain and France proposed Milan, Switzerland, and Rome, while Austria countered with Innsbruck, Padua, and Verona. For the next two months they continued to exchange notes without being able to agree upon the site for negotiations.

France seemed willing to accept Austrian assurances of autonomy for Northern Italy, but Sardinia was not. One of the most difficult tasks that France faced in the late autumn of 1848 was restraining Sardinia from reopening hostilities. The Sardinians had protested against Austria's rejection of the bases of joint mediation as soon as they received word of this development.[28] As September wore on, Charles Albert's government began to manifest its discontent with Vienna's position by complaining to the mediating Powers that Austria was breaking the terms of the armistice by not delivering certain Sardinian war stores detained by the Austrians at Peschiera. Finally, the Sardinians announced their intention to send their fleet back to Venice until Austria conformed to the mediation terms.[29] Throughout the autumn Britain and France expended much diplomatic energy on trying to persuade Sardinia to withdraw her fleet and Austria to deliver the war material. Of much greater significance for the maintenance of peace, however, were suggestions from Turin that Sardinia was determined to resort to arms once again to settle the Italian problem. Sardinia, it seems, had little hope of defeating the Austrians alone, but she felt that renewing hostilities might oblige France to intervene in Italy on her behalf.

Charles Albert's government was experiencing acute internal pressure from the Sardinian Chambers and Sardinian public opinion in general to go to war to obtain Lombardy. Already in late September tension had built up within Sardinia to the point where the Kingdom seemed to be faced with internal disorders or at least the advent to power of the party which favoured an immediate resumption of the war. At this time the Sardinians officially requested the Powers to open negotiations as soon as possible in order to relieve popular pressure on their

[28] Ibid. 382–3 (12 Sept., Perrone to Revel).
[29] Ibid. 398 (21 Sept., Palmerston to Ponsonby); FAAE, Corr. pol., Turin 322 (6 Oct., Sain de Boislecomte to Bastide).

government.[30] By early October rumours spread that Charles Albert was determined to renew hostilities.[31] It seems, moreover, that the difficult position in which Charles Albert's government was placed made Turin consider more seriously than ever the possibility of having recourse to French armed assistance after all.

It was already evident that Austria, re-entrenched in Lombardy and nearly victorious in Venetia, was intending to retain her Northern Italian possessions. Then, in mid October an Austrian diplomat, Count Gozzo, secretary to the Austrian legation in Dresden and a personal friend of Albert Ricci, frankly informed the Sardinian envoy to Paris that Vienna was determined to hold all of the Italian territories accorded her by the 1815 settlement. At the same time he suggested that Vienna was no longer apprehensive about the possibility of French intervention: 'Two months ago Vienna was so frightened of the red trousers of the French infantry that Italian affairs could have been settled by the mere insertion of a simple article in the French *Moniteur* [*universel*], but now that we know that French public opinion has pronounced itself against intervention in Italy, you have nothing more to hope for from the opening of negotiations even when they do commence.'[32] The Cavaignac government's desire for a peaceful settlement to the Italian question, as well as France's poorly disguised hostility for Charles Albert's government, was already convincing certain Sardinian diplomats that the mediation would come to naught.[33] As Sain de Boislecomte remarked in writing from Turin on 2 October to his friend Hetzel, *chef du cabinet* in the French foreign ministry under both Lamartine and Bastide, 'hope in France diminishes every day' among the Sardinians.[34] Now an open avowal of Austrian intentions from a high-placed Austrian official must have convinced the Sardinians that mediation alone would not advance the Italian cause. Facing increased internal pressure

---

[30] *Parliamentary Papers*, lviii. 411 (19 Sept., Abercrombie to Palmerston); ibid. 445–6 (22 Sept., Perrone to Abercrombie and Sain de Boislecomte).

[31] Ibid. 485 (5 Oct., Ponsonby to Palmerston).

[32] Sardinia, AST, Legazione in Parigi (12 Oct., Ricci to Perrone).

[33] Curato, *Le relazioni diplomatiche fra il Regno di Sardegna e la Gran Bretagna*, i. 280, 284–5 (29 Sept., 3 Oct., Revel to Perrone).

[34] A Parménie and C. Bonnier de la Chapelle, *Histoire d'un éditeur et de ses auteurs, J.-P. Hetzel* (Paris, 1953), p. 109.

from the 'war party', Charles Albert's government began in desperation to consider renewing hostilities. Such an action could perhaps prod the French into assisting Sardinia militarily, or at least have the effect of obliging the mediating Powers to take a firmer stand on Italy's behalf.

The news that Sardinia might resort to arms once again was most disquieting to the two mediating Powers. Palmerston declared that he hoped Sardinia was not serious about going to war; for her to do so would be 'extreme folly'.[35] The renewal of hostilities in Italy 'might lead to the conquest of Sardinian territory by Austria, but would certainly not lead to the reoccupation of Lombardy by the Sardinians'.[36] Bastide, for his part, admonished Sain de Boislecomte to remind Charles Albert that if he went to war he would certainly face defeat by Austria and deposition by his own subjects.[37] When this seemed to have little effect upon Sardinia, Bastide instructed Sain de Boislecomte to be straightforward in informing Turin:

... that France will go to war, when she deems it necessary, at her time and hour, when she finds it suitable, but she will not be drawn into war against her wishes no matter what is done. If Austria crosses the Tessin and attacks Sardinia, we will defend Sardinia. ... But if Sardinia takes the offensive in the hope of obliging us to make war, well then, it will be at her own risk and peril that she commits this folly. ... Whichever of the two belligerent parties breaks the mediation will have us for an enemy, be it Austria or Sardinia. We will not allow ourselves to be coerced.

Bastide made it quite clear that if Austrian troops crossed the Tessin River, France would defend 'the Tessin as if it were the Var' (the border between France and Sardinia at this time), but that if Sardinia attacked Austria she would have to suffer the consequences of her rash move.[38] Bastide repeated this warning to Turin ten days later. Finally, when he was informed that certain factions within Tuscany were also clamoring for war, he reiterated his statement that France would 'remain a spectator'

---

[35] *Parliamentary Papers*, lviii. 472, 525 (9, 25 Oct., Palmerston to Abercrombie).

[36] Britain, PRO, F.O. 27/813 (28 Sept., Normanby to Palmerston); F.O. 27/800 (3 Oct., Palmerston to Normanby).

[37] FAAE, Corr. pol., Turin 322 (30 Sept., Bastide to Sain de Boislecomte).

[38] Ibid. (10 Oct., Bastide to Sain de Boislecomte).

if Italy took the offensive against Austria.[39] Bastide had made it clear to Turin that the Cavaignac government would not allow the Republic to be drawn into 'a European war' because of an Italian whim.

Despite Bastide's admonitions, ever-increasing pressure within the Sardinian Chambers obliged the Sardinian government to consider going to war. On 15 October the Sardinian foreign minister, Perrone, informed France that his government might have to renounce the armistice of 9 August and reminded the Cavaignac government of its commitment to assist Italy militarily if the mediation were to fail. At the same time he urged Brignole to insist that the French government 'agree with us as soon as possible and in a definitive manner upon the conditions which, were we to have recourse to it, would regulate the sending of an auxiliary corps of French troops'. Three days later Perrone ordered Ricci to remind the Republic of its promise 'to defend the Tessin as she would defend the Var' and to suggest that France send 'an auxiliary army' at the very 'beginning of hostilities'.[40]

Throughout the late summer and autumn the Sardinian government had been trying to conclude a military convention with France to regulate the terms of eventual Franco-Sardinian military 'co-operation' in Northern Italy. Moreover, Turin also hoped to obtain the services of a noted French general to command the Sardinian army. In late August, before Austria had accepted the mediation and when it seemed that the armistice might be of short duration, the Sardinian foreign minister informed his ambassador in Paris that a certain Colonel de la Marmora, a friend of the French general Bugeaud, was being sent to the French capital to request permission for Bugeaud to head the Sardinian army. Upon Marmora's arrival in Paris, however, Cavaignac informed the Sardinian officer that the French government would not allow Bugeaud to accept such a position because of Bugeaud's monarchist tendencies.[41]

With their attempt to acquire Bugeaud's services blocked, the

---

[39] FAAE, Corr. pol., Turin 322 (19 Oct., Bastide to Sain de Boislecomte); Corr. pol., Toscane 192 (23 Oct., Bastide to Benoît-Champy).

[40] Sardinia, AST, Lettere Ministri Francia (15 Oct., Perrone to Brignole; 18 Oct., Perrone to Ricci).

[41] Ibid. (23 Aug., Perrone to Brignole; 26 Aug., Brignole to Perrone); Curato, *Le relazioni diplomatiche fra la Gran Bretagna e il Regno di Sardegna*, i. 329–30 (26 Aug., Abercrombie to Palmerston, from Palmerston's private papers).

Sardinians turned their efforts to the drawing up of a military convention with the Cavaignac government, a convention similar to the one which Brignole had put forth on 7 August.[42] Accordingly, in early August General Joseph Ricci had been sent to Grenoble to confer with General Oudinot of the French Army of the Alps and to lay the groundwork for a military understanding between the two Powers.[43] Then, at the end of August Brignole formally proposed that a military agreement, outlining the 'conditions of friendly co-operation' which would be implemented if France were to intervene in the war against Austria, be established between the two Powers.[44] Sardinia, it seems, now hoped to obtain the services of a French army of 80,000 men—instead of the 40,000–50,000 which she had been prepared to request in early August—which Sardinia would pay and supply once it entered Sardinian territory. And, as part of any agreement, Charles Albert's government expressed its willingness to allow French troops to garrison certain mountain fortresses in Sardinian territory, although not in Savoy.[45]

The French government showed little interest in committing itself to assist Sardinia militarily by drawing up such a convention. Cavaignac categorically refused to allow a French army to assume an auxiliary status. That is, the French government insisted on retaining complete command over any army which it might dispatch to Italy. Bastide and Cavaignac ended up by arguing that it was unnecessary to draw up any convention at the moment; it would be best not to agree to anything in advance, for it would only take 'an hour' to establish such an agreement when the time came to do so.[46] When word that Austria had accepted the joint mediation reached Paris in early September, Cavaignac and Bastide further postponed the signing of any military convention, arguing that it was no longer necessary to anticipate armed action now that a peaceful settlement to the Italian question seemed to be imminent.[47] In early October, as

[42] See above, pp. 153–4.

[43] Sardinia, AST, Lettere Ministri Francia (9 Aug., Pareto to Albert Ricci); Missioni diplomatiche speciali e temporanee (22 Aug., Joseph Ricci to Sardinian foreign minister).

[44] Bianchi, v. 498–9 (31 Aug., Brignole to Perrone).

[45] Sardinia, AST, Lettere Ministri Francia (3 Sept., Perrone to Brignole).

[46] Bianchi, v. 498–9 (31 Aug., Brignole to Perrone).

[47] Sardinia, AST, Lettere Ministri Francia (8 Sept., Brignole to Perrone).

pressure to renew hostilities increased in Sardinia, Perrone sent another military officer, Count Martini, to France, ordering him to concert his efforts with those of Brignole and Albert Ricci in trying to persuade the Republic to send a general other than Bugeaud to command the Sardinian army.[48] Then on 15 October Perrone suggested that Sardinia might renew hostilities and requested France once again to establish a military convention with Italy.

In late October the Cavaignac government had categorically refused to assist Sardinia if she denounced the armistice and resorted to force. The French government was equally categorical in rejecting Sardinia's request for a military agreement of any kind. Bastide sent Thiers to inform Ricci that France 'would never consent to give [Sardinia] a general', for that would 'amount to committing [France] to war, and [France] wants peace'.[49] Thiers did suggest that the French government might permit a French general other than Bugeaud to join the Sardinian ranks if he would first sever all ties with the French army; but Turin showed little interest in a general who would serve simply as an individual and not as a representative of the French armed forces.[50] Then, in mid November Cavaignac acted to quash Sardinia's hopes for any kind of Franco-Sardinian military co-operation. Angered by the fact that a Sardinian dispatch alluding to the use of a French auxiliary army had been made public, Cavaignac publicly humiliated Ricci at a diplomatic reception on 13 November by scornfully inquiring 'whether the Sardinian government had meant to treat the French army merely like Swiss mercenaries'.[51]

When Cavaignac was rebuked by Normanby and other members of the diplomatic corps for his harsh, unconventional treatment of Ricci, he sought to make amends for his action the following day by assuring Ricci of France's 'support' for Sardinia and by promising to use stern language in Vienna to oblige the Austrians to begin negotiations.[52] Cavaignac's conciliatory language seems to have encouraged the Sardinian government to sound out France once again about defending Sardinia's

---

[48] Sardinia, AST, Lettere Ministri Francia (4 Oct., Perrone to Martini; 9 Oct., Perrone to Brignole).

[49] Ibid. (24 Oct., Ricci to Perrone).   [50] Ibid. (3 Nov., Perrone to Martini).

[51] Britain, PRO, F.O. 27/815 (15 Nov., Normanby to Palmerston).

[52] Sardinia, AST, Lettere Ministri Francia (15 Nov., Ricci to Perrone).

borders if Sardinia were to launch an attack against Austrian positions.[53] Charles Albert's government was deceived, however, in its hopes that Cavaignac's apparent modification in tone on 14 November meant a change in France's attitude about going to war for Sardinia. Bastide's reply to Sardinia's inquiry was firm and resolute. The French foreign minister 'once again' informed Turin 'that if it provokes a resumption of hostilities [Sardinia] will not be able to count upon our assistance, even in the case where, after a defeat, its own territory is invaded'.[54] The Cavaignac government remained adamant in its refusal to be drawn into war against its wishes.

While extremely concerned about Sardinia's proclivities for making war in the autumn of 1848, the Republic continued to be equally apprehensive about Austria's intentions *vis-à-vis* Venice. Though France's remonstrances had brought the Austrian government to commit itself in late September not to attack Venice, during October Austrian ships continued to sail off Venice, attempting to blockade the city and adopting a generally hostile attitude toward it. Bastide had doubted all along whether Austria would really desist from attacking Venice.[55] His doubts seemed to be confirmed in late October when Thom once again alluded to Austria's right to 'pacify' Venice.[56] This again led Bastide to protest that French public opinion would not countenance an overt Austrian attack upon Venice, that such an attack would precipitate the 'instantaneous' downfall of the Cavaignac government.[57] Moreover, by the end of October Bastide was also perturbed by Austria's tactic of delaying the opening of the peace negotiations by postponing her appointment of a delegate and refusing to agree upon a mediation site. Austria's attitude toward both Venice and the negotiations seems to have determined the French foreign minister to apply pressure upon an Austrian government which was already hard-pressed by the October uprising in Vienna. Bastide had no illusions about the October revolt in Vienna profoundly weakening Austria.[58] Still, he seems to have felt that Anglo-French pressure

[53] Ibid. (24 Nov., Perrone to Ricci).
[54] FAAE, Corr. pol., Turin 322 (6 Dec., Bastide to Sain de Boislecomte).
[55] Ibid., Corr. pol. des consuls, Autriche 9, Venise (4 Oct., Bastide to Vasseur).
[56] Austria, HHS, Frankreich Korr. Kart. 337 (21 Oct., Thom to Wessenberg).
[57] Ibid. (21 Oct., 4, 5 Nov., Thom to Wessenberg).
[58] FAAE, Corr. pol., Toscane 182 (23 Oct., Bastide to Benoît-Champy).

applied at this propitious moment might make the Imperial Government more amenable to the mediating Powers' aims. Bastide proposed in effect that London should participate in dispatching an Anglo-French–Sardinian fleet into the Adriatic to 'impose more moderation on Austria's actions in the Adriatic' and 'to make the mediation more respected'.[59]

The dispatch of the fleet that Bastide now proposed to send into the Adriatic would not necessarily have constituted a hostile act. It would have had the dual effect of preserving the city from an eventual Austrian attack, while also displaying French sympathy for the Venetian cause. As a matter of fact, a few French ships had been present in the Adriatic since August and the Sardinian fleet returned to that sea in late October. In explaining to Palmerston France's aims in dispatching a tri-national fleet into the Adriatic, the French minister in London said that it would serve the cause of peace by obliging Austria to extend the cease fire to Venice, thus precluding the possibility of an eventual French intervention. The dispatch of such a fleet would thus act to secure Venice from Austrian attack and to placate French and Sardinian public opinion. Furthermore, Beaumont intimated that the mediating Powers might be able to alter the bases of mediation in favour of Venice.[60] The French government was still inclined to assist Venice diplomatically if Great Britain were willing to concur in this action.

Palmerston's reply to Beaumont's proposition was disappointing to the French. Britain would refuse to take part in any naval expedition, even if such a move did have peaceful connotations. As far as the mediation was concerned, the British Foreign Secretary held that it was not in good faith for the mediating Powers to propose a change in the terms of negotiation. This led Beaumont to write in a tone of utter desperation that all Britain desired was 'peace, peace, always peace'. Beaumont came to the same conclusion that he had come to in August: that Britain would never support French attempts to improve the Italians' plight unless Palmerston were convinced that France was ready to resort to arms to attain her goals.[61]

Voicing his agreement with this analysis, Bastide accordingly

---

[59] FAAE, Corr. pol., Angleterre 671 (21 Oct., Beaumont to Bastide).
[60] Ibid. 672 (23 Oct., Beaumont to Bastide).
[61] Ibid.

ordered Beaumont to inform Palmerston that henceforth French ships in the Adriatic would receive the order to oppose an Austrian blockade by force if necessary.[62] In effect, though, there was little possibility of a naval confrontation between Austria and France in the Adriatic. Both sides wished to avoid any incident which might compromise the peace. In fact, there was some indication that the Austrian blockade was being lifted and that the small French squadron would never have to use force to keep the port of Venice open.[63] The French would continue their effort to persuade Britain that they might resort to the use of force in Italy, although their desire to avoid military involvement in the Peninsula was manifest. Bastide remarked to Sain de Boislecomte in early November that the situation in the Adriatic had explosive possibilities; he hoped that negotiations would open as soon as possible so that no 'new incident' would occur which might compromise the peace.[64]

French diplomats flattered themselves by asserting that pressure from Paris and the presence of French naval units had prevented an all-out attack on Venice and that Venice, or at least a part of Northern Italy, would still eventually be liberated from Austria.[65] Bastide, for his part, even gallantly wrote to Manin that France would never abandon Venice to Austria as Britain had done, that as long as he was in office France 'would never accept another Campo Formio'.[66] However, in spite of this official optimism France had actually been able to do very little for Venice. She had committed herself by her proposal of joint mediation to work for a settlement in which Venice would be surrendered to Austria; and by the end of 1848 it was obvious that the French Republic was willing to accept Austrian assurances of constitutionalism and autonomy for Venice, even though a French diplomat had remarked as early as September that Austrian promises of liberal institutions constituted no real

---

[62] Ibid. (24 Oct., Bastide to Beaumont).
[63] Ibid., Corr. pol., Turin 322 (18 Oct., Bastide to Sain de Boislecomte).
[64] Ibid. (7 Nov., Bastide to Sain de Boislecomte).
[65] Ibid., Corr. pol., Angleterre 672 (28 Oct., Beaumont to Bastide).
[66] Ibid., Corr. pol. des consuls, Autriche 9, Venise (17 Nov., Bastide to Manin). Perhaps Bastide was speaking tongue in cheek when he wrote this to Manin, for by mid November it was already quite probable that Louis Napoleon Bonaparte would replace Cavaignac as chief executive and that Bastide's tenure as foreign minister would end shortly after the elections of 10 Dec.

concession on Austria's part.[67] The Cavaignac government was prepared to settle for 'liberal institutions' for Northern Italy, because the only way that area could actually have been 'liberated' from Austria, as the French Constituent Assembly had prescribed, was by the use of arms. And this would have meant the end of the British *entente* and war, a consequence which the French government was determined to avoid at any price. In fact, France had thrown herself into mediation and linked herself by an *entente* with Great Britain in order to preclude the possibility of armed intervention in the Peninsula.

To be sure, France did not subject her entire foreign policy to the dictates of the English *entente*. The French government was openly opposed to attempts by Sir Edward Lyons, the British ambassador in Athens, to exert English influence on the government of King Otto I of Greece.[68] Moreover, the Second Republic in 1848 supported Spain against British efforts to intimidate that country. At one point the Spanish expressed apprehension at the possibility of Britain seizing a Spanish colony as security for the huge debt Spain owed Britain. Bastide assured the Spanish that 'France could not remain indifferent to such projects, if they did in fact exist, and if necessary, especially in the case of the Balearics, we would help Spain to maintain her rights over these important possessions, as much as possible, and in a complete spirit of disinterestedness'.[69] Meanwhile, Bastide had informed the United States that Britain might attempt to seize Cuba so that Washington could take necessary measures to discourage such an action.[70] France could and did show some independence from Great Britain in foreign policy matters of rather minor importance.

Still, once a policy of joint mediation in the Italian question had been conceived of by the Cavaignac government, France tried to correlate her foreign policy in every way possible with that of Great Britain. The French government sought to concert its actions with those of the British government in diplomatically protesting against Russia's occupation of the Danubian Principalities, and by August was making a conscious attempt to co-

---

[67] FAAE, Corr. pol., Angleterre 671 (15 Sept., Beaumont to Bastide).
[68] Ibid., Corr. pol., Grèce 50 (2 June, Bastide to Thouvenel).
[69] Ibid., Corr. pol., Angleterre 670 (19 June, Bastide to Tallenay).
[70] Ibid., Corr. pol., États-Unis 104 (6 July, Bastide to Bourboulon).

operate with Britain in seeking a joint settlement to the Sicilian question.[71] Bastide informed Normanby concerning Sicily that his government 'wished in this as in every other part of the Italian question to be able to follow precisely the same course as that of Her Majesty's Government'.[72] Similarly, Bastide expressed the desire to co-operate with Britain in mediating the Schleswig-Holstein problem 'just as' the two Powers 'were joined in negotiating the Italian question'.[73] As far as the joint mediation itself was concerned, the French had obviously been willing to go to any extremes to preserve the *entente* with Britain and the peace of Europe. The Cavaignac government considered mediation with Great Britain as a means of simulating support for Italy without resorting to arms. There was obviously some validity in the allegations made by the French radicals that the Republic was following the policy of Guizot in regards to Italy. Guizot, they believed, had turned his back on the Peninsula after 1846 because of his desire for an Austrian alliance and the preservation of the peace of Europe. Cavaignac and Bastide courted British support because they had no intention of assisting the Italians by the use of force, firmly believing that it was not in France's national interest to do so.

By November diplomatic activity had slowed down to a virtual standstill. The political instability which reigned in Austria as a result of the Viennese insurrection of October made it impossible to carry on meaningful mediation with Vienna during most of October and the early part of November.[74] In late November France's diplomatic representations did seem to have the effect of deciding Austria to accept Brussels as a mediation site, but this was a meagre concession by Vienna and the mediation as a whole continued to languish.[75] Then, too, the Powers seemed to prefer to wait until the results of the December French presidential elections were known before committing themselves to serious

[71] Ibid., Corr. pol., Naples 174 (13 June, Baudin to Bastide); Corr. pol., Naples 176 (14 Aug., Bastide to Reyneval).

[72] Britain, PRO, F.O. 27/812 (14 Aug., Normanby to Palmerston).

[73] FAAE, Corr. pol., Danemark 211 (24 Aug., Bastide to Dotézac); Corr. pol.. Angleterre 671 (24 Aug., Bastide to Beaumont).

[74] *Parliamentary Papers*, lviii. 538 (31 Oct., Palmerston to Abercrombie); Denmark, Rigsarkivet, Frankrig II (3 Nov., E. C. L. Moltke to Knuth).

[75] FAAE, Corr. pol., Autriche 437 (23 Nov., Delacour to Bastide); Austria, HHS, Frankreich Korr. Kart. 337 (27 Nov., Schwarzenberg to Thom).

negotiations with the Republic.[76] The Sardinian envoy in Paris, for one, was convinced that France could not really diplomatically exercise 'all the influence to which her power and her geographic position give her the right to aspire' to until after the presidential elections.[77] Cavaignac himself felt convinced that 'nothing serious' could be accomplished diplomatically before the French presidential elections, a sentiment which he expressed even to foreign diplomats residing in Paris.[78] At a diplomatic reception on 13 November the General inadvertently blurted out his conviction that the French government, busily preparing for the elections, would have 'no time' to devote to the mediation problem 'for six weeks'.[79] As a result, the important diplomatic questions facing Europe remained in a state of suspension while France and the other Powers awaited the outcome of the all-absorbing internal developments preoccupying the French Republic.

When it had become quite apparent in late autumn that France had no intention of flying to the aid of Italy and launching a European-wide war, the French radicals moved in to the attack, levelling bitter invective at their government for its foreign policy failures. On the floor of the National Assembly Ledru-Rollin rose up to criticize the Cavaignac government's inclination to accept 'a bastard independence' for Italy. He admonished his government to demand the complete liberation of the Peninsula and to resort to arms if necessary to achieve this end.[80] Another Montagnard, Francisque Bouvet, asserted that he personally 'blushed in shame for his country', that 'the abandonment of Italy by France would be more than a weakness, it would be an act of cowardice'.[81]

The leftist press was even more vitriolic in its criticism. *L'Atelier* declared that it was either out of weakness or stupidity that France had joined England in mediation, for England did not want the liberation of Italy. France should have entered Italy when the Italians made their first call, for it was better to choose war than to go against one's principles. The day when

[76] Britain, PRO, F.O. 27/815 (11 Nov., Normanby to Palmerston).

[77] Sardinia, AST, Legazione in Parigi (14 Nov., Ricci to Perrone).

[78] De Tocqueville, *Œuvres complètes*, vol. viii, part 2, p. 100 (14 Nov., Tocqueville to Beaumont).

[79] Britain, PRO, F.O. 27/815 (15 Nov., Normanby to Palmerston).

[80] *Le Moniteur universel*, 3 Oct.   [81] Ibid., 8 Nov.

France refused to draw the sword would bring the death of the Republic.[82] *La Réforme* agreed with *L'Atelier* that 'our foreign policy will ruin us in the near future, after having dishonoured us'; for 'while Italy is falling in a pool of her blood, we are entering into discussions with her assassins [Austria]'. *La Réforme* bitterly remarked: 'As it was under Louis Philippe, the shameful maxim of "peace at all costs" seems to be the motto of the present ministers of the Republic.'[83] Proudhon's *Le Peuple* joined in the chorus of discontent, exclaiming:

No, the French Republic does not want to reconstitute the nations of Europe. . . . What does she care about oppressed nations? France, enslaved by the bourgeoisie, is afraid of liberty. What does she care about the victories of despots, the defeat of republicans?

France, corrupted by the capitalists, wants to preserve privileges at all costs. She applauds the martyrdom of peoples, the carnage of proletarians! . . .

France has 500,000 men under arms. But the soldiers do not aim their guns against the Cossacks. . . . The soldiers aim their guns against the proletariat. The army menaces the populous *faubourgs* of the main cities of France.

Finally, *Le Peuple* summed up radical criticism of the government in a poignant article entitled 'Intervention in Italy'. It asserted that

The revolution has been done away with in official circles. The Cavaignac ministry and their allies treat peoples as M. Guizot did; the words of Lamartine were only words, but at least they were worthy of France. Today the honour of the nation, the independence of our allies, the cause of freedom, all is forgotten and disdained. . . .

Patriots, our brothers, you who have succumbed at Vienna for the sovereignty of your Diet, for the independence of peoples and for the social revolution, France denies you through the mouth of the man who aspires to govern her.[84]

The French radicals were calling Cavaignac to task for his foreign policy and at the same time reminding him that their votes would count in the forthcoming presidential elections.

Indictments which contained many elements of truth must have been the source of much dismay for the troubled Cavaignac

[82] *L'Atelier*, 4 Sept.
[83] *La Réforme*, 18 Sept., 2 Oct.
[84] *Le Peuple*, 24, 30 Nov.

government. The presidential elections were to be held on 10 December and Cavaignac's prospects were not promising. The General had alienated the radicals by his conservative internal and foreign policy. By the end of the autumn he had also lost the support of the monarchists and 'the party of order', who were convinced that his policies were not reactionary enough. At the same time Louis Napoleon's campaign for the presidency was gaining momentum. Already on 31 October a Russian agent in Paris could report back to the Tsar that Napoleon's victory was a certainty.[85] It seems that by late October and early November even the members of the French government whose fate depended upon the outcome of the elections seem to have come to the same conclusion. Bastide admitted to the Austrian chargé d'affaires in Paris that Louis Napoleon's election to the presidency seemed to be 'nearly inevitable'.[86] Cavaignac too made it clear in a conversation with the Danish minister to Paris that he had little hope of being elected.[87] With Louis Napoleon's star on the rise the Cavaignac government seems to have become convinced that a forceful move of some kind was needed to win over public opinion. It decided to make a desperate bid for the votes of Catholic and patriotic France by announcing that the French Republic was about to save the Pope from the popular disorders which threatened him in Rome.[88]

As far back as August the Pope had intimated that he might need the protection of French troops, troops that probably would have been used against the Roman radicals rather than against the Austrians.[89] As the autumn wore on Pius IX became increasingly alienated from the Roman populace, because, among other things, of his refusal to support the Italian cause against the arch enemy Austria.[90] Trouble flared up in Rome in the middle of November. On 15 November the Pope's prime

[85] Pokrovski, pp. 75–6.

[86] Austria, HHS, Frankreich Korr. Kart. 337 (25 Oct., Thom to Wessenberg).

[87] Denmark, Rigsarkivet, Farnkrig II (9 Nov., E. C. L. Moltke to Knuth).

[88] The diplomatic community in Paris was convinced that France's espousal of the Roman issue was inspired by electoral motives. Bastide himself admitted as much in the book which he later wrote on Italy (Bastide, p. 199; Normanby, *A Year of Revolution*, ii. 357; Britain, PRO, F.O. 27/815, 28 Nov., Normanby to Palmerston; Sardinia, AST, Legazioni in Parigi, 30 Nov., Ricci to Perrone).

[89] See above, p. 176.

[90] Gilbert de Chambrun, 'Un projet de séjour en France du Pape Pie IX', *Revue d'histoire diplomatique*, l (1936), 323–4.

minister, Rossi, was assassinated and riots which posed a threat to the Pope's safety broke out in Rome. Two days later the French ambassador in Rome, Harcourt, wrote that the Pope felt that he would have to flee the Holy City; there was the possibility that he might come to Marseilles.[91] On 24 November the Pope finally left Rome, intimating that he might go to France.

In the meantime the Papal nuncio in Paris had asked Cavaignac if France would provide a haven for Pius IX.[92] Cavaignac immediately telegraphed orders to Toulon and Marseilles to assemble 3,500 French troops and a squadron of four ships. As soon as Bastide had heard of Rossi's assassination he had sent a special envoy, Corcelle, to Rome with the power to debark the French troops and use them if necessary to provide for 'the personal security of His Holiness'.[93] Bastide also instructed Harcourt to invite the Pope formally to seek exile in France, 'that nation which would always remain the eldest daughter of the Church'.[94] The French felt certain that the Pope would come to France. Bastide sent orders to the Prefect in Marseilles, instructing him to receive Pius IX with all the solemnity due to 'a sovereign'.[95] Cavaignac's government, seeking votes in the forthcoming elections, announced with great pride to the French nation that the Pope was on his way to France.

The Pope, it seems, had assured Harcourt that he wanted to seek exile in France.[96] Accordingly, Harcourt travelled to Civitavecchia with the Pope's luggage to place it in a French ship stationed in the harbour, while the Pope sought immediate safety in the city of Gaeta. Harcourt, supposedly, would board the ship, call for the Pontiff in Gaeta, and then proceed with him to Marseilles. However, when the Pope arrived in Gaeta, which was in Neapolitan territory, he was met by the King of Naples himself. After an extremely friendly reception by King Ferdinand the Pope's enthusiasm for journeying to France waned, and by 30 November he was suggesting to Harcourt that he would prefer to seek exile not far from Rome.[97] While expressing

[91] FAAE, Corr. pol., Rome 988 (17 Nov., Harcourt to Bastide).
[92] Ibos, p. 213.
[93] FAAE, Corr. pol., Rome 988 (17 Nov., Bastide to Harcourt).
[94] Ibid. (26 Nov., Bastide to Harcourt).
[95] Ibid. (2 Dec., Bastide to Prefect of Bouches-du-Rhône).
[96] Chambrun, *Revue d'histoire diplomatique*, l. 338.
[97] FAAE, Corr. pol., Rome 988 (30 Nov., Harcourt to Bastide).

confidence in Cavaignac, the Pope now seemed concerned about taking refuge in a country which might soon be governed by a Bonaparte.[98] The Pope proclaimed his desire to 'visit France' and he 'announced his formal intention to go to France, as soon as circumstances permitted'.[99] He reiterated these intentions in a personal letter to General Cavaignac, dated 10 December.[100] Nevertheless, by mid December the Pope was speaking about 'only making a short visit' to France while *en route* to Majorca, where he now envisaged establishing himslf until conditions permitted him to return to Rome.[101]

As late as 23 December the Pope repeated that he would like to visit France some day, 'but without fixing the date'.[102] It was quite evident by this time, though, that he preferred the hospitality of the notoriously reactionary 'King Bomba', whom he saw as being 'eminently religious', to a refuge in unsettled, republican France.[103] Cavaignac's scheme to gain votes had miscarried. Normanby remarked that any beneficial effect which the Republic's Roman policy might have had upon the presidential election was undone when the Pope failed to arrive in France and the government's motives became known. The original public enthusiasm, according to the British ambassador, gave way to 'disappointment founded on deceit', a 'most dangerous feeling on the eve of an election'.[104] The Austrian chargé d'affaires agreed with Normanby's belief that the Pope's failure to come to France had definitely hurt Cavaignac in the election.[105] In the election Louis Napoleon Bonaparte received 5,534,520 votes while Cavaignac received 1,448,302.

The Pope never came to France. But the significance of the entire incident lies in the fact that France in late 1848 had been ready to intervene in Rome to guarantee 'the personal security

[98] Jean Leflon, 'La mission de Claude de Corcelle auprès de Pie IX après le meurtre du ministre Rossi', *Archivum historiae pontificiae*, i (1966), 397.

[99] FAAE, Corr. pol., Rome 988 (9 Dec., Corcelle to Bastide).

[100] AD Sarthe, Documents des archives privées de M. Eugène Cavaignac, reel 26.

[101] Ferdinand Boyer, 'Pie IX à Gaète et l'amiral Baudin', *Istituto per la Storia del Risorgimento Italiano, Messina, 1954*, pp. 59–60.

[102] FAAE, Corr. pol., Rome 988 (23 Dec., Harcourt to Drouyn de Lhuys).

[103] Chambrun, *Revue d'histoire diplomatique*, l. 350.

[104] Britain, PRO, F.O. 27/816 (10 Dec., Normanby to Palmerston).

[105] Austria, HHS, Politisches Archiv IX, Frankreich Kart. 29 (17 Dec., Thom to Schwarzenberg).

of His Holiness'. It is true that Bastide always defended the Corcelle mission by arguing that French troops had specific orders not to become involved in Roman internal affairs. And a study of Bastide's instructions to Corcelle does show that the special envoy was instructed 'to intervene in no way in the dissension which today separates the Pope from the people whom he governs'. Nevertheless, Corcelle was empowered to use troops against the Roman populace if need be to protect the Pope or 'to guarantee the success' of his mission.[106] There was a definite possibility that the Roman populace would have opposed with force the landing of French troops—as they did in 1849—and that as a result republican troops would have fired upon the Roman populace.[107] Moreover, there is some evidence to suggest that the Cavaignac government had actually considered using force to re-establish the Pope in the Holy City. It seems that the Papal nuncio in Paris had been prepared to request 'the intervention of the French government to re-establish the authority of His Holiness' in Rome.[108] Furthermore, the Pope had originally requested from Harcourt either refuge in France 'or at any rate such assistance as should enable him to restore order among his subjects'. Normanby recounted to Palmerston that 'M. Bastide said he did not know how it was possible to refuse such a request, and that I might inform your Lordship that if such a step were to be taken, such was the whole object of the expedition, and that the Pope's authority restored, the troops would be immediately withdrawn'.[109] Finally, Harcourt had seemingly assured the Pope that if he came to France French troops would guarantee his re-establishment in Rome.[110]

The Cavaignac government, it seems, was prepared if need be to intervene in Rome against the Roman people, as Louis Napoleon's troops would do some six months later. Palmerston perceived this when he accused the French of being prepared to intervene in the Roman States in the same way as the Russians had marched into the Danubian Provinces, of contemplating acting in a manner contradictory to their self-proclaimed principle

[106] *Parliamentary Papers*, lviii. 626–7 (27 Nov., Bastide to Corcelle).
[107] FAAE, Corr. pol., Rome 988 (7 Dec., Harcourt to Bastide).
[108] Sardinia, AST, Legazione in Parigi (27 Nov., Ricci to Perrone).
[109] Britain, PRO, F.O. 27/815 (27 Nov., Normanby to Palmerston).
[110] FAAE, Corr. pol., Rome 988 (30 Nov., Harcourt to Bastide).

of non-interference in the internal affairs of other countries.[111] *Le Peuple* remarked that France 'had not intervened in Italy to chase out the Austrians', but she was now prepared 'to intervene to subdue the Romans'.[112] All in all, the question of French intervention in Rome in late 1848 was an unfortunate prologue to the young Republic's diplomatic efforts, for if such an intervention had occurred it might very well have been directed against rather than in favour of a subjected people. By December the Revolutions of 1848 were ended or expiring and anti-republican forces were about to emerge victorious from the French presidential elections. Instead of acting to aid the European revolutionary movement, the Republic of 1848 was now seemingly prepared only to act to preserve order in Italy. It seems that there was more continuity between the policies of the defunct July Monarchy and the foreign policy of the Second Republic than the republicans of 1848 liked to admit.

[111] Britain, PRO, F.O. 27/801 (2 Dec., Palmerston to Normanby).
[112] *Le Peuple*, 3 Dec.

CONCLUSION

THE Roman crisis provided an appropriate conclusion to the foreign policy endeavours of the 1848 French republican governments. On the one hand the Cavaignac administration's reaction to this series of events foreshadowed the policy which Louis Napoleon's regime would pursue toward the Roman Republic in the spring of 1849. On the other hand, France's diplomatic stance during this crisis in November–December 1848 served to re-emphasize several of the major themes which had dominated French diplomacy since the February Revolution. The Roman question brought out once again the basic conservatism and traditionalism of French foreign policy in 1848, its anti-revolutionary nature, and its dependence upon French internal developments. The Roman crisis also served to stress the basic duality in the Second Republic's attitude toward the use of force, the dichotomy between its apparently menacing attitude and its profound reluctance to become militarily involved even in the Italian Peninsula.

That France would pursue a cautious, basically conservative foreign policy in 1848 seems to have been partially determined almost from the outset of the republican regime, when a moderate republican faction, hard pressed by Jacobin elements which favoured an adventuresome foreign policy, assumed the leadership of the newborn Second French Republic. The internal instability which plagued the Republic throughout 1848, and especially in the spring when the basic lines of French diplomacy were being drawn up, also was a cardinal factor in discouraging the governments of the Second Republic from adopting a more active foreign policy similar to that of the First Republic. The republican tradition, the need to break with the diplomacy of the July Monarchy, and the constant pressure exerted by radical elements combined in obliging the Provisional Government in the spring of 1848 to make diplomatic pronouncements which committed the Republic to assisting oppressed peoples liberate themselves. Still, the moderate-dominated French governments of 1848 had little desire to adopt an aggressive policy which might have had the effect of bringing on a European-wide conflict and strengthening the leftists—as in 1792–3—within France. In 1848 the different French governments may have issued bellicose sounding statements in favour of the fraternity of peoples and the liberation of subjected nationalities, but their true position is evidenced by their espousal of an English *entente* designed to end French isolation and enhance the Republic's diplomatic stature. As the year wore on and a combination of European and internal developments made French military involvement in Europe increasingly distasteful to the French government, the Republic continued to press for an English alliance which would serve to preserve the peace and obviate the need for France to intervene even in Italy.

During the year of European revolution France pursued a cautious, traditionalist oriented foreign policy. Following the February Revolution French republican diplomats demonstrated an acute awareness of the legacy imposed upon France's diplomacy by the revolutionary, Napoleonic, restoration, and Orleanist periods. The French republicans in 1848 felt constrained to honour the revolutionary tradition by calling for the emancipation of peoples and to deny the humiliating defeat countenanced during the Restoration by denouncing the detested 1815 settlement. In a similar manner, the Second Republic's policy toward nations such as Britain, Italy, Austria, Switzerland, and Spain was deeply influenced by a desire to reverse the diplomatic failures of the July Monarchy. Throughout 1848 the formulators of French foreign policy, Lamartine, Bastide, and Cavaignac, showed themselves to be fully aware of France's traditional, historic diplomatic interests. Even Lamartine's willingness to intervene on a limited scale in Italy in the spring of 1848 was largely determined by a desire to further France's traditional, strategic interests.

The French government in 1848 also demonstrated its profound concern for France's strategic interests by the attitude which it adopted toward the emerging force of nationalism. By early summer French statesmen had become fully disenchanted with nationalism and its concomitant movement in favour of national unification, clearly foreseeing the dire consequences which these movements could have for France in the not too distant future. The realization that the unification of Germany

and Italy was not in France's interest resolved the French government in the summer of 1848 to abstain from militarily assisting
Italy and to follow France's traditional policy of discouraging
German unity. At a time when the revolutions of 1848 had
temporarily disrupted the established European diplomatic order
and plunged the continent into a state of diplomatic flux, the
cautious, traditionalist outlook of France's statesmen was a
primary factor in determining France's republican government
to follow unswervingly the path of peace.

BIBLIOGRAPHY

I. UNPUBLISHED DIPLOMATIC DOCUMENTS

AUSTRIA, Haus-, Hof-, und Staatsarchiv:
>   Frankreich Korrespondenz Karton 337.
>   Frankreich Korrespondenz Karton 338.
>   Politisches Archiv IX, Frankreich Karton 29.

DENMARK, Rigsarkivet, Udenrigsministeriet:
>   Frankrig I.
>   Frankrig II.

FRANCE, Archives des Affaires Étrangères:

Correspondance politique:
>   Allemagne 805–6.
>   Angleterre 670–2.
>   Autriche 435–7.
>   Bade 34.
>   Bavière 224.
>   Belgique 30.
>   Danemark 211–12.
>   Espagne 834.
>   États-Unis 104.
>   Grèce 50.
>   Hambourg 149.
>   Hanovre 68.
>   Hesse-Cassel 34.
>   Mayence 22.
>   Naples 174–6.
>   Pays-Bas 650.
>   Prusse 302–3.
>   Rome 988.
>   Russie 202
>   Sardaigne 321–2.
>   Saxe 108–9.
>   Suède 324.
>   Suisse 562.
>   Toscane 182.
>   Wurtemberg 72.

Correspondance politique des consuls:
>   Autriche 8–9, Venise.
>   Autriche 10B, Milan.

Autriche 14, Trieste.
Espagne 48, Barcelone . . . Valence.
Mayence-Hess-Darmstadt 1, Mayence.
Naples 1–2, Palerme, Messine.
Prusse 1, Dantzig, Stettin.
Rome 3, Ancône.
Russie–Varsovie 6, Varsovie.
Sardaigne 5, Gênes.
Sardaigne 7, Nice.
Saxe 1, Leipzig.
Suède et Norvège 2, Christiania.

Mémoires et documents:
Allemagne 129, 162–3, 171
Angleterre 127.
Autriche 52, 71.
Belgique 9.
France 740, 2118.
Italie 35–6.
Naples 14.
Rome 121.
Russie 43.

GREAT BRITAIN, Public Record Office:

General Correspondence, France:
F.O. 27/797–F.O. 27/816.
F.O. 27/824–F.O. 27/826.

SARDINIA, Archivio di Stato, Turin. Archivio del Ministero per gli Affari Esteri:

Lettere Ministri Francia.
Legazione in Parigi.
Missioni diplomatiche speciali e temporanee.

II. OTHER UNPUBLISHED PRIMARY SOURCES

France, Archives départementales de la Sarthe. Documents des archives privées de M. Eugène Cavaignac. Reels 24–6.
France, Archives nationales, BB¹⁸, 1467A, pièce 6307. Ministère de Justice. Proceedings against the press.
France, Archives nationales. C 926, 3. Assemblée nationale constituante. Procès-verbaux du comité des affaires étrangères.
France, Bibliothèque nationale. Various posters, handbills, and pamphlets concerning French foreign affairs in the series Lb⁵³. 1151–60, Lb⁵⁴. 125–2042, Ye 40704–55471.

III. PUBLISHED DOCUMENTS AND SOURCES

Comité national du Centenaire de 1848. *Documents diplomatiques du*

Gouvernement provisoire et de la Commission du Pouvoir exécutif. Charles Pouthas, ed. 2 vols. Paris: Imprimerie nationale, 1953–4.

Comité national du Centenaire de 1848. *Procès-verbaux du Gouvernement provisoire et de la Commission du Pouvoir exécutif (24 février– 22 juin 1848).* Introduction by Charles Pouthas. Paris: Imprimerie nationale, 1950.

Curato, Federico, ed. *Le relazioni diplomatiche fra il Regno di Sardegna e la Gran Bretagna.* 3rd series. Vol. i (3 gennaio–31 dicembre 1848). Documenti per la storia delle relazioni diplomatiche fra gli stati italiani e le grandi potenze europee, 1814–1860. Part 1. Documenti italiani. Fonti per la storia d'Italia. Rome: Istituto Storico Italiano per l'Età Moderna e Contemporanea, 1961.

—— ed. *Le relazioni diplomatiche fra la Gran Bretagna e il Regno di Sardegna.* 3rd series. Vol. i (4 gennaio–31 dicembre 1848). Documenti per la storia delle relazioni diplomatiche fra le grandi potenze europee e gli stati italiani, 1814–1860. Part 2. Documenti esteri. Fonti per la storia d'Italia. Rome: Istituto Storico Italiano per l'Età Moderna e Contemporanea, 1961.

Great Britain. *Parliamentary Papers.* Vols. lvi–lix: *Correspondence Respecting the Affairs of Italy, 1846–1849.*

Kretzschmar, Hellmut, and Schlechte, Horst, eds. *Französiche und sächsische Gesandschaftsberichte aus Dresden und Berlin.* Berlin: Rütten und Loening, 1956.

Marchetti, Leopoldo, ed. *1848: Il carteggio diplomatico del governo provvisorio della Lombardia.* Part 1: *Le relazioni del governo provvisorio della Lombardia con gli stati italiani.* Museo del Risorgimento e Raccolte Storiche del Comune di Milano. Milan: Antonio Cordani, 1955.

Planat de la Faye, F., ed. *Documents et pièces authentiques laissés par Daniel Manin.* 2 vols. Paris: Furne et Cie., 1860.

Ridder, Alfred de. *La Crise de la neutralité belge en 1848: le dossier diplomatique.* 2 vols. Brussels: Weissenbruch, 1928.

Saitta, Armando, ed. *Le relazioni diplomatiche fra la Francia e il Granducato di Toscana.* 3rd series. Vol. i (7 marzo 1848–29 dicembre 1850). Documenti per la storia delle relazioni diplomatiche fra le grandi potenze europee, 1814–1860. Part 2. Documenti esteri. Fonti per la storia d'Italia. Rome: Istituto Storico Italiano per l'Età Moderna e Contemporanea, 1959.

IV. NEWSPAPERS

Unless otherwise indicated, all of the following newspapers were published in Paris

L'Alliance des peuples, L'Ami du peuple, L'Assemblée nationale, L'Atelier, Le Bien public, Le Bon Conseil, La Commune de Paris, Le Constitutionnel, Le Courrier français, La Démocratie pacifique, L'Événement, La Gazette de France, La Gazette du Midi (Marseilles), *Le Journal des débats, Le Lampion, La Liberté, Le Moniteur universel, La Montagne de la fraternité, Le National, L'Opinion publique, La Patrie, Le Père Duchêne, ancien fabricant, Le Père Duchêne, gazette de la révolution, Le Peuple, Le Peuple constituant, La Presse, La Propagande républicaine, La Réforme, Le Représentant du peuple, La République française, Le Sémaphore de Marseille* (Marseilles), *La Sentinelle du peuple. Le Siècle, Le Tribun du peuple, La Voix des clubs, La Vraie République.*

V. WORKS PUBLISHED BY CONTEMPORARIES

Apponyi, Rudolphe, *Vingt-cinq ans à Paris, 1826–1852: journal du comte Rudolphe Apponyi, attaché de l'ambassade d'Autriche à Paris.* 4 vols. Paris: Plon, Nourrit et Cie., 1913–26.

Baubaud-Laribière, François-Saturnin-Léonide. *Histoire de l'Assemblée nationale constituante.* 2 vols. Paris: Michel Lévy Frères, 1850.

Barrot, Odilon. *Mémoires posthumes.* 4 vols. Paris: Charpentier, 1875.

Bastide, Jules. *La République française et l'Italie en 1848: récits, notes et documents diplomatiques.* Leipzig: Alphonse Dürr, 1858.

Blanc, Louis. *Histoire de la révolution de 1848.* 2 vols. Paris: Librairie Internationale, 1870.

Castille, Hippolyte. *Histoire de la Seconde République française.* 4 vols. Paris: Lecou, 1854–6.

Chenu, Adolphe. *Les Conspirateurs: les sociétés secrètes, la préfecture de police sous Caussidière, les corps-francs.* Paris: Garnier Frères, 1850.

Circourt, Adolphe de. *Souvenirs d'une mission à Berlin en 1848.* Georges Bourgin, ed. 2 vols. Paris: Alphonse Picard et Fils, 1908.

Gallois, Léonard. *Histoire de la révolution de 1848.* 8 vols. Paris: Pagnerre, 1849–51.

Garnier-Pagès, Louis-Antoine. *Histoire de la révolution de 1848.* 10 vols. Paris: Pagnerre, 1861–72.

Lamartine, Alphonse de. *Correspondance de Lamartine.* 6 vols. Paris: Hachette, Furne, Jolivet et Cie, 1873–5.

—— *La France parlementaire (1834–1851): œuvres, oratoires et écrits politiques.* 6 vols. Paris: Librairie Internationale, 1864–5.

—— *Histoire de la révolution de 1848.* 2 vols. Paris: Perrotin, 1849.

—— *Lettre aux dix départements.* Paris: Lévy Frères, 1848.

—— *Œuvres complètes.* 41 vols. Vol. xxxix: *Mémoires politiques.* Paris: Chez l'Auteur, 1860–6.

—— *Le Passé, le Présent et l'Avenir de la république.* Brussels: Muquardt, 1850.

—— *Le Piémont et la France en 1848: lettre de M. de Lamartine à M. Sinéo, député piémontais.* Paris: Imprimerie de Cosson, 1859.

—— 'La question d'Orient, la guerre, le ministère', *Vues, Discours et Articles sur la question d'Orient.* Brussels: Hauman et Cie., 1841.

—— *Trois Mois au Pouvoir.* Paris Lévy Frères, 1848.

Ledru-Rollin, A.-A. *Discours politiques et Écrits divers.* 2 vols. Paris: Librairie Germer Baillière, 1879.

Lesseps, Ferdinand de. *Recollections of Forty Years.* 2 vols. New York: Appleton and Co., 1888.

Longepied and Laugier. *Comité révolutionnaire, Club des Clubs et la Commission*. Paris: Garnier Frères, 1850.

Lucas, Alphonse. *Les Clubs et les clubistes*. Paris: E. Dentu, 1851.

Metternich, Fürst Clemens Lothar Wenzel von. *Mémoires, Documents et Écrits divers laissés par le prince de Metternich, chancelier de cour et d'état*. 8 vols. Paris: Plon et Cie., 1880–4.

Montanelli, Joseph. *Mémoires sur l'Italie*. 2 vols. Paris: F. Chamerot, 1856.

Nesselrode, Karl Robert, comte de. *Lettres et Papiers du chancelier comte de Nesselrode*. 11 vols. Paris: A. Lahure, 1904–12.

Normanby, Constantine Henry Phipps, Lord. *A Year of Revolution; from a Journal Kept in Paris in 1848*. 2 vols. London: Longmans, 1857.

—— *Une Année de révolution, d'après un journal tenu à Paris en 1848, par le marquis de Normanby*. 2 vols. Paris: H. Plon, 1858.

Ollivier, Émile. *L'Empire libéral: études, récits, souvenirs*. 16 vols. Paris: Garnier Frères, 1895–1912.

Pepe, général Guglielmo. *Histoire des révolutions et des guerres d'Italie en 1847, 1848 et 1849*. Paris: Pagnerre, 1850.

Regnault, Élias. *Histoire du Gouvernement provisoire*. Paris: Lecou, 1850.

Reiset, Gustave-Armand-Henri, comte de. *Mes Souvenirs*. 3 vols. Paris: Plon, Nourrit et Cie., 1901–2.

Robin, Charles. *Histoire de la révolution française de 1848*. 2 vols. Paris: Penaud Frères, 1849–50.

Russell, Lord John. *The Later Correspondence of Lord John Russell, 1840–1878*. Edited by G. P. Gooch. 2 vols. London: Longmans, Green and Co., 1925.

Sand, George. *Souvenirs de 1848*. Paris: Calmann Lévy, 1880.

Senior, Nassau William. *Journals Kept in France and Italy from 1848 to 1852*. 2 vols. London: Henry S. King and Co., 1871.

Stern, Daniel (pseud. for Comtesse d'Agoult). *Histoire de la révolution de 1848*. 2 vols. Paris: Charpentier, 1862.

Tocqueville, Alexis de. *Œuvres complètes*. Vol. viii, part 2: *Correspondance d'Alexis de Tocqueville et de Gustave de Beaumont*. Edited by J.-P. Mayer. Paris: Gallimard, 1967.

—— *The Recollections of Alexis de Tocqueville*. New York: Columbia University Press, 1949.

VI. SECONDARY WORKS

Almanach national annuaire de la République française pour 1848–1849–1850: présenté au Président de la République. Paris: Chez A. Guyot et Scribe, 1850.

Antony, Alfred. *La Politique financière du Gouvernement provisoire, février–mai 1848*. Paris: Rousseau, 1910.

Ashley, Evelyn. *The Life of Henry John Temple, Lord Palmerston: 1846–1865. With Selections from his Speeches and Correspondence*. 2 vols. London: Richard Bentley and Sons, 1876.

Bapst, Edmond. *L'Empereur Nicolas 1er et la Deuxième République française*. Paris: Imprimerie Générale Lahure, 1898.
—— *Les Origines de la guerre de Crimée: la France et la Russie de 1848 à 1854*. Paris: Delagrave, 1912.
Bell, Herbert C. F. *Lord Palmerston*. 2 vols. London: Longmans, Green and Co., 1936.
Benson, Arthur Christopher and Esther, Viscount, eds. *The Letters of Queen Victoria. A Selection from Her Majesty's Correspondence between the Years 1837 and 1861*. 3 vols. London: J. Murray, 1907.
Bessler, Hans. *La France et la Suisse de 1848 à 1852*. Paris: V. Attinger, 1930.
Bianchi, Nicomede. *Storia documentata della diplomazia in Italia dall'anno 1814 all'anno 1861*. 8 vols. Torino: Società l'Unione Tipografico-Editrice, 1865–72.
Blaison, colonel Louis. *Un Passage de vive force du Rhin français en 1848*. Paris: Éditions Berger-Levrault, 1933.
Bouniols, Gaston. *Histoire de la révolution de 1848*. Paris: Delagrave, 1918.
Bouteiller, Paul. *La Révolution française de 1848 vue par les Hongrois*. Paris: Presses Universitaires de France, 1949.
Boyer, Ferdinand. *La Seconde République, Charles-Albert et l'Italie du Nord en 1848*. Paris: Pédone, 1967.
Buchner, Rudolf. *Die deutsch-französische Tragödie, 1848–1864*. Würzburg: Holzner-Verlag, 1965.
Calman, Alvin. *Ledru-Rollin and the Second French Republic*. New York: Columbia University Press, 1922.
Chérest, Aimé. *La Vie et les Œuvres de A.-T. Marie*. Paris: A. Durand et Pédone-Lauriel, 1873.
Costa de Beauregard, Charles-Albert, *Les Dernières Années de Charles-Albert*. Paris: Plon, Nourrit et Cie, 1890.
De Luna, Frederick A. *The French Republic under Cavaignac, 1848*. Princeton: Princeton University Press, 1969.
Dessal, Marcel. *Un Révolutionnaire jacobin, Charles Delescluze, 1809–1871*. Paris: Marcel Rivière, 1952.
Doumic, René. *Lamartine*. Paris: Librairie Hachette, 1912.
Eichthal, Eugène de. *Alexis de Tocqueville et la démocratie libérale: étude suivie de fragments des entretiens de Tocqueville avec Nassau William Senior (1848–1858)*. Paris: Calmann-Lévy, 1897.
Eyck, Frank. *The Frankfurt Parliament, 1848–1849*. London: Macmillan, 1968.
Fejto, François, ed. *The Opening of an Era, 1848: An Historical Symposium*. London: Wingate, 1948.
Girard, Louis. *La IIe République*. Paris: Calmann-Lévy, 1968.
Godart, Justin. *A Lyon en 1848, 'les Voraces'*. Paris: Presses Universitaires de France, 1948.
Gooch, Brison D. *Belgium and the February Revolution*. The Hague: Martinus Nijhoff, 1963.
Greer, Donald M. *L'Angleterre, la France et la révolution de 1848: le*

troisième ministère de Lord Palmerston au Foreign Office (1846–1851). Paris: Rieder et Cie., 1925.

Guichen, Eugène, le vicomte de. *Les Grandes Questions européennes et la diplomatie des puissances sous la Seconde République française*. 2 vols. Paris: V. Attinger, 1925–7.

Henry, Paul. *La France devant le monde, de 1789 à 1939*. Paris: Aubier, 1945.

Ibos, Général Pierre-Émile-Marius. *Le Général Cavaignac: un dictateur républicain*. Paris: Hachette, 1930.

La Gorce, Pierre de. *Histoire de la Seconde République française*. 2 vols. Paris: Plon, 1914.

Loubère, Leo A. *Louis Blanc: His Life and his Contribution to the Rise of French Jacobin-Socialism*. Evanston: Northwestern University Press, 1961.

McKay, Donald Cope. *The National Workshops: A Study in the French Revolution of 1848*. Cambridge: Harvard University Press, 1933.

Maes, Léon. *L'Affaire de Risquons-Tout*. Mouscron: Imprimerie d'Averbode, 1935.

Malo, Henri. *Thiers, 1797–1877*. Paris: Payot, 1932.

Moscati, Ruggero. *La diplomazia europea e il problema italiano nel 1848*. Florence: Sansoni, 1943.

Mosse, Werner. *The European Powers and the German Question, 1848–1871*. Cambridge: Cambridge University Press, 1958.

Moulin, Charles. *1848: le livre du centenaire*. Paris: Éditions Atlas, 1948.

Namier, Lewis B. *1848: The Revolution of the Intellectuals*. New York: Anchor, 1964.

Parménie, A. and Bonnier de la Chapelle, C. *Histoire d'un éditeur et de ses auteurs, J.-P. Hetzel*. Paris: Albin Michel, 1953.

Pokrovski, M. N. *Pages d'histoire: la méthode du matérialisme historique appliquée à quelques problèmes historiques concrets*. Paris: Éditions Sociales Internationales, 1929.

Pouthas, Charles. 'La politique étrangère de la France sous la Seconde République et le Second Empire'. ('Les Cours de Sorbonne'.) Paris: Centre de Documentation Universitaire, 1949.

—— 'La révolution de 1848 en France et la Seconde République'. ('Les Cours de Sorbonne'.) Paris: Centre de Documentation Universitaire, 1952.

Quentin-Bauchart, Pierre. *Lamartine, homme politique: la politique intérieure*. Paris: Plon, 1903.

—— *Lamartine et la politique étrangère de la révolution de février, 24 janvier–24 juin 1848*. Paris: Librairie Félix Juven, 1907.

Scharff, Alexander. *Die europäischen Grossmächte und die deutsche Revolution, deutsche Einheit und europäische Ordnung, 1848–1851*. Leipzig: Koehler und Amelang, 1942.

Schmidt, Charles. *Des Ateliers nationaux aux barricades de juin*. Paris: Presses Universitaires de France, 1948.

—— *Les Journées de juin 1848*. Paris: Hachette, 1926.

Seignobos, Charles. *La Révolution de 1848: le Second Empire.* Edited by Ernest Lavisse. (*Histoire de la France contemporaine depuis la Révolution jusqu'à la paix de 1919,* vol. vi.) Paris: Hachette, 1921.

Taylor, Alan John Percival. *The Italian Problem in European Diplomacy, 1847–1849.* Manchester: Manchester University Press, 1934.

Tersen, Émile. *Le Gouvernement provisoire et l'Europe: 25 février– 12 mai 1848.* Paris: Presses Universitaires de France, 1948.

Walpole, Spencer. *The Life of Lord John Russell.* 2 vols. London: Longmans, Green and Co., 1889.

Wassermann, Suzanne. *Les Clubs de Barbès et de Blanqui en 1848.* Paris: Édouard Cornely et Cie., 1913.

VII. ARTICLES

Adami, Vittorio. 'Dell'intervento francese in Italia nel 1848', *Nuova Rivista storica,* xii (1928), 136–68.

Amann, Peter. 'A "Journée" in the Making: May 15, 1848', *The Journal of Modern History,* xxxxii (1970), 42–70.

—— 'Writings on the Second French Republic', ibid. xxxiv (1962), 409–29.

Andics, Elizabeth. 'La France, l'Angleterre et la révolution hongroise de 1848', *Actes du congrès historique du centenaire de la révolution de 1848,* pp. 219–27. Paris: Presses Universitaires de France, 1948.

Barbieri, V. 'I tentativi di mediazione anglo-francese durante la guerra del 48', *Rassegna storica del Risorgimento,* xxvi (1939), 683–726.

Bourgin, Georges. 'La marina francese in soccorso della Repubblica di Venezia nel 1848 e 1849', *Istituto per la Storia del Risorgimento italiano, atti e memorie del XXVIII congresso, comitato di Milano, 1948,* pp. 107–9.

Boyer, Ferdinand. 'L'Armée des Alpes en 1848', *Revue historique,* ccxxxiii (1965), 71–100.

—— 'Charles-Albert et la Seconde République, de juin à août 1848', *Rassegna storica del Risorgimento,* l (1963), 463–512.

—— 'Comment la France arma le Piémont en 1848', ibid. xxxix (1962), 485–90.

—— 'Écrits et paroles à l'adresse du gouvernement français, 1848 (Chialiva, Frapolli, Lizabe Ruffoni, Gioberti)', ibid. liv (1967), 48–56.

—— 'Les entretiens franco-autrichiens de juin 1848', *Revue des travaux de l'Académie des Sciences morales et politiques* (1953), 15–24.

—— 'Les fournitures d'armes faites par le gouvernement français aux patriotes italiens en 1848 et 1849', *Rassegna storica del Risorgimento,* xxxvii (1950), 95–102.

—— 'Lamartine et le Piémont', *Revue d'histoire diplomatique,* lxiv (1950), 37–57.

—— 'La marine de la Seconde République et la révolution sicilienne de février à juillet 1848', *Études d'histoire moderne et contemporaine,* ii (1948), 184–203.

Boyer, Ferdinand. 'Pie IX à Gaète et l'amiral Baudin', *Istituto per la Storia del Risorgimento Italiano, atti del XXXIII congresso di storia del Risorgimento italiano*, Messina, 1954, i. 56–63.

——— 'Les premiers contacts entre Lamartine et Brignole Sale, ambassadeur de Sardaigne à Paris, 24 février–20 mars 1848', *Revue d'histoire diplomatique*, lxxix (1965), 22–35.

——— 'Le problème de l'Italie du Nord dans les relations entre la France et l'Autriche, février–juillet 1848', *Rassegna storica del Risorgimento*, xxxxii (1955), 206–17.

——— 'Les rapports entre la France et le Piémont sous le ministère de Jules Bastide, 11 mai–juin 1848', *Revue d'histoire moderne et contemporaine*, v (1958), 129–36.

——— 'Le roi de Deux-Siciles, Ferdinand II, d'après un diplomate français (André de Bois-le-Comte)', *Archivio storico messinese*, lxvi–lxv (1964–5), 13–27.

——— 'Le vice-amiral Baudin, chef des forces navales françaises en Méditerranée et la révolution sicilienne en 1848–1849', *Istituto per la Storia del Risorgimento italiano, atti e memorie del XXVII congresso, comitato di Milano, 1948*, pp. 111–24.

Broglie, Albert de. 'De la politique étrangère de la France depuis la révolution de février', *Revue des deux mondes*, xxxiii (1848), 293–321.

Bullen, Roger. 'Guizot and the "Sonderbund" crisis, 1846–1848', *The English Historical Review*, lxxxvi (1971), 497–526.

Calman, Alvin. 'Delescluze, Ledru-Rollin et l'échauffourée de Risquons-Tout', *La Révolution de 1848*, xvi (1920–1), 45–50.

Chaboseau, A. 'Les constituants de 1848', ibid. vii (1910), 287–305, 413–25, viii (1911), 67–80.

Chalmin, Pierre. 'La crise morale de l'armée française', *L'Armée et la Seconde République* ('Bibliothèque de la révolution de 1848', vol. xviii, 1955), pp. 28–76.

Chambrun, Gilbert de. 'Un projet de séjour en France du Pape Pie IX', *Revue d'histoire diplomatique*, l (1936), 322–64, 481–508.

Coquerelle, Suzanne. 'L'armée et la répression dans les campagnes', *L'Armée et la Seconde République* ('Bibliothèque de la révolution de 1848', vol. xviii, 1955), pp. 121–59.

Curato, Federico. 'La Toscana et la mediazione anglo-francese', *Archivio storico italiano*, cvi (1948), 96–183.

Dessal, Marcel. 'Les incidents franco-belges en 1848', *Actes du congrès historique du centenaire de la révolution de 1848*, pp. 107–13. Paris: Presses Universitaires de France, 1948.

Duveau, Georges. 'Les relations internationales dans la pensée ouvrière (1840–1865)', ibid. pp. 277–83. Paris: Presses Universitaires de France, 1948.

Fasel, George W. 'The French Election of April 23, 1848: Suggestions for a Revision', *French Historical Studies*, v (1968), 285–98.

Gossez, Rémi. 'Notes sur la composition et l'attitude politique de la troupe', *L'Armée et la Seconde République* ('Bibliothèque de la révolution de 1848, vol. xviii, 1955), pp. 77–110.

Guichonnet, Paul. 'L'affaire des "voraces" en avril 1848', *Istituto per la Storia del Risorgimento italiano, comitato di Torino*, 1st series, no. 4, 1949, pp. 1–52.

Guyard, Marius-François. 'Les idées politiques de Lamartine', *Revue des travaux de l'Académie des Sciences morales et politiques*, 1966, 2ᵉ sémestre, pp. 1–16.

Henry, Paul. 'La France et les nationalités en 1848, d'après des correspondances diplomatiques', *Revue historique*, clxxxvi (1939), 48–77; clxxxviii (1940), 234–58.

Henry, Paul. 'Le Gouvernement Provisoire et la question polonaise en 1848', ibid. clxxviii (1936), 198–240.

Jennings, Lawrence C. 'French Diplomacy and the First Schleswig-Holstein Crisis', *French Historical Studies*, vii (1971), 204–25.

—— 'Lamartine's Italian Policy in 1848: A Reexamination', *The Journal of Modern History*, xxxxii (1970), 331–41.

Knight, Jean. 'La politique de Lamartine', *Revue d'histoire diplomatique*, xx (1906), 260–84.

Lefèvre, André. 'La reconnaissance de la Seconde République par l'Angleterre', ibid. lxxxii (1968), 213–31.

Leflon, Jean. 'La mission de Claude de Corcelle auprès de Pie IX après le meurtre du ministre Rossi', *Archivum historiae pontificiae*, i (1966), 356–402.

Loubère, Leo A. 'Les idées de Louis Blanc sur le nationalisme, le colonialisme et la guerre', *Revue d'histoire moderne et contemporaine*, iv (1957), 33–63.

Manzone, B. 'L'intervento francese in Italia nel 1848', *Rivista storica del Risorgimento*, ii (1897), 553–8.

Mollat, Guillaume. 'La fuite de Pie IX à Gaëte (24 novembre 1848)', *Revue d'histoire ecclesiastique*, xxxv (1939), 266–82.

Morelli, Emilia. 'Mazzini et la révolution de 1848 en France', *Actes du congrès historique du centenaire de la Révolution de 1848*, pp. 285–93. Paris: Presses Universitaires de France, 1948.

Paul, Pierre. '1848: la révolution française et l'Europe', *Revue historique del l'Armée*, iv (1948), 25–32.

Renouvin, Pierre. 'L'idée d'États-Unis d'Europe pendant la crise de 1848', *Actes du congrès historique du centenaire de la révolution de 1848*, pp. 31–45. Paris: Presses Universitaires de France, 1948.

Ridder, Alfred de. 'La Belgique et la reconnaissance de la Deuxième République française', *Université de Louvain, Recueil de travaux publiés par les membres des conférences d'histoire et de philologie*, xxxxi (1914), 579–93.

Spellanzon, Cesare. 'Francia e Gran Bretagna in Sicilia nel 1848 e elezione del nuovo sovrano', *Rassegna storica del Risorgimento*, xxxvii (1950), 465–80.

Valsecchi, Franco. 'L'intervention française et la solidarité révolutionnaire internationale dans la pensée des démocrates lombards en 1848', *Actes du congrès historique du centenaire de la révolution de 1848*, pp. 165–76. Paris: Presses Universitaires de France, 1948.

S

Vermeersch, Arthur J. 'L'opinion belge devant la révolution française de 1848', *Revue du Nord*, xlix (1967), 483–508.

Vidal, César. 'La France et la question italienne en 1848', *Études d'histoire moderne et contemporaine*, ii (1948), 162–83.

—— 'La Toscane et la France au lendemain de la chute de Louis-Philippe, mars–septembre 1848', *Bullettino senese di storia patria* (1951–2), pp. 19–27.

Wright, Gordon. 'A Poet in Politics: Lamartine and the Revolution of 1848', *History Today*, viii (1958), 616–27.

Zaniewicki, Witold. 'l'armée au lendemain de la révolution de 1848', *Cahiers d'histoire (Clermont — Grenoble)*, xiv (1969), 393–419.

VIII. UNPUBLISHED DISSERTATIONS AND THESES

Bernstein, Paul. 'The Rhine Problem during the Second Republic and Second Empire.' Ph.D. dissertation, University of Pennsylvania, 1955.

Chastain, James Garvin. 'French "Kleindeutsch" Policy in 1848.' Ph.D. dissertation, University of Oklahoma, 1967.

De Luna, Frederick A. 'The Republic of Cavaignac.' Ph.D. dissertation, State University of Iowa, 1962.

Gallaher, John G. 'An Evaluation of the Revolution of 1848 by American Diplomats.' Ph.D. dissertation, Saint Louis University, 1961.

Hahn, Robert John. 'The Attitude of the French Revolutionary Government toward German Unification in 1848.' Ph.D. dissertation, Ohio State University, 1955.

Jennings, Lawrence C. 'The Conduct of French Foreign Affairs in 1848: The Diplomacy of a Republic Divided within Itself.' Ph.D. dissertation, Wayne State University, 1967.

Martin, Kenneth Robert. 'British and French Diplomacy and the Sardinian War, 1848–1849.' Ph.D. dissertation, University of Pennsylvania, 1965.

Pincetl, Stanley. 'Republics in Conflict: Episodes in Franco-American Relations, 1848–1851.' Ph.D. dissertation, University of California, Berkeley, 1954.

Williams, Harvey R. 'British Policy and Attitudes toward France, February 22 to June 23, 1848.' Ph.D. dissertation, University of Chicago, 1962.

Wilson, Prince E. 'Anglo-French Diplomatic Relations, 1848–1851.' Ph.D. dissertation, University of Chicago, 1954.

Zaniewicki, Witold. 'L'armée française en 1848, introduction à une étude militaire de la Deuxième République (22 février–20 décembre 1848).' 2 vols. *Thèse de 3e cycle*, Université de Paris, 1966.

INDEX

Abeille du Nord, L' (St. Petersburg newspaper), 29
Abercrombie, Lord (British diplomat in Turin), 153
Adige, river, 145, 146
Adriatic Sea, 231, 240
Albert, Prince (consort of Queen Victoria), 118
Albert, Alexander Martin, 21, 66
Algeria, 65 *bis*
Alps, the, 30, 32, 40, 41, 114, 204; French Army of, *see* Army of the Alps
Alsace-Lorraine, 93 *bis*, 129 *bis*, 208, 209–10
Ami du peuple, L' (Raspail's radical newspaper), 81, 94
Ancona, 18
Anglo-French *entente*, 7, 8, 15 *bis*, 20, 49, 50, 87, 137, 139, 242, 243, 252
Anglo-French mediation (limiting) agreement, 35
Anglophobia in France, 49
Annuaire historique, 131
Apponyi, Rudolphe (Austrian ambassador in Paris), 1, 18, 25, 28, 60, 63, 76, 107 *bis*, 108
Arago, Emmanuel (French commissary in Lyons and later minister in Berlin), 51, 52, 96, 103, 129, 131–3 *passim*, 196, 208, 210–11, 214, 220, 225
Arago, François, 21, 51, 65 *bis*, 96, 103
Army of the Alps, French, 40, 41, 42, 53, 63, 64, 65, 83, 95, 99 *bis*, 101–2, 103 *bis*, 107, 119, 151, 167, 184, 192
Arnim, Baron von (Prussian foreign minister), 72 *bis*, 132 *bis*, 160
Assemblée nationale, L' (French monarchist paper), 17, 79
Atelier, L' (French leftist paper), 94, 244–5
Austria, Empire of: and February Revolution, *q.v.*, 4; and her provinces in Northern Italy, 29, 36, 72 (*see also* relations with France and Sardinia); and war with Sardinia, 39, 107–10, 137 (*see also* Austro-

Sardinia war); Palmerston's terms, 109–10; Bastide's terms, 110; and a new offensive in Italy, 113; and Lombardy, Parma, and Venice, 113; and armistice with Sardinia (9 Aug.), 158; would call for German support, 160, 161; and France, after June Days, 168; and mediation terms (158 n), 174; entry into Papal Legations and advance on Bologna, 175, 176, 189; intransigent, 177–8, 183–4, 186; responds to French intimidation, 189; will evacuate Legations, grant Lombardy and Venice liberal institutions, and accept joint mediation (but not on proposed bases), 189–90; and uprising in Vienna, 205 (*see also* Vienna); will not give up North Italy voluntarily, 228; wants *status quo ante bellum*, 228; and Venice, *q.v.*, 228–33; Emperor's Manifesto to Lombardy–Venetia, 232; intends to retain her possessions in North Italy, 234; no longer afraid of French, 234
Austria (*foreign relations*): Belgium, 4; France, 15, 18, 25, 27–33 *passim*, 36, 60, 63 *bis*, 72 *bis*, 76, 100–1, 106–7, 108, 112, 118, 120, 133, 141, 144 *bis*, 145, 157, 174–90 *passim*, 218–19; Germany, 101; Great Britain, 3, 18, 87, 101, 106–10 *passim*, 111, 135, 137; Italian States, 3, 4, 15, 28–9, 38–9, 43, 72, 75, 83, 99, 134–46; Prussia, 3; Russia, 3 *bis*, 14, 221–2; Sardinia, 4, 5, 35, 39–40, 43 *bis*, 75, 83, 85–8 *passim* (*see also* Austro-Sardinian war); Switzerland, 34, 35
Austro-Sardinian war, 39, 43 *bis*, 75, 83, 85, 86, 87, 106, 107, 114, 134–6 *passim*, 145, 147

Baden, 67–9 *passim*, 160, 202, 209
Bakunin, Michael, 36
Balearic Islands (Spanish), 242
Balkans, the, 218–20 *passim*

Belgium: and February Revolution, 2, 3, 4; independence and neutrality of, 4, 5, 8, 27; establishment of, 14; Lamartine's special agents in, 25; its Paris embassy and Belgian 'legions', 59

Belgium (*foreign relations*): Austria, 4; France, 25, 27, 30, 53, 58, 59, 63, 168; Great Britain, 4, 5, 53; Prussia, 4

Benoît-Champy, Adrien-Théodore (French chargé d'affaires and minister in Florence), 191

Berlin: Assembly, 220; Cabinet (Prussian), 45; March revolution in, 34, 36, 44

Bern, 31, 33-4, 35, 163

Bien Public, Le (Lamartine's paper), 115

Bismark, Otto von, 161

Bixio (French envoy and minister in Turin), 25, 39, 42, 83-7 *passim*, 102, 103, 135, 163; warns Lamartine against intervention in Italy, 83-7 *passim*; changes tune, 88-9; reports that Sardinia fears France as much as she does Austria, 103

Blanc, Louis, 1, 14, 21, 64, 66, 78, 96, 121, 201

Blanqui's Club (Paris), 80

Bohemia, 36

Bologna, 175, 177

Bon Conseil, Le (French radical paper), 80, 81

Bonapartism in France (*see also* La Liberté *and* Louis Napoleon), 170, 202

Bourgoing, Paul (French diplomat), 162, 169

Bouvet, Françisque (Montagnard deputy), 244

Boyer, Ferdinand, 82-3, 85-6

Brignole (Sardinian ambassador in Paris), 17, 40, 76, 83, 84, 86, 101-2, 117, 223, 236, 238, 244; reassured by Lamartine and National Assembly, 105; and Recurt's speech in Assembly, and Bastide's reassurances, but doubtful about Savoy, 115-16; and joint mediation in Italy, 149; and Cavaignac, 151, 223; and French intervention, 151-2, 153-4; and French desire for peace, 196; con-

siders France unable to make war, 202; and Lombardy and Sardinia, 223, 226; and a military convention with France, 237 *bis*

British government, *see* Great Britain

Broglie, Albert de, 208

Brussels as possible mediation site, 243

Bucharest, 218

Bugeaud, General, 236 *bis*

Bunsen, Baron von (Prussian minister in London), 9

Campo Formio, Treaty of (1797), 111, 241

Carbonari, 163

Castellane, General, 62

Castres, 65

Caussidière, Marc (Paris Prefect of Police), 54, 121, 201

Cavaignac, General Eugène (French Minister of War, and afterwards head of government), 119, 120-1, 124-5, 124 n, 148; and Bastide, *q.v.*, 124-5, 151, 156 *bis*; and Normanby, *q.v.*, 148, 152, 156 *bis*, 175; unwilling to intervene in Italy, 148; and Ricci, *q.v.*, 150-1, 152; and Brignole and Guerrieri, 151; and Austria, Sardinia, and Anglo-French mediation in Italy, 155, 158, 172-3, 177, 184, 185, 190, 200, 201, 243; dislikes Charles Albert, 156; and Lombardy, 157 *bis*; and state of siege in Paris, 167; and internal security and foreign adventure, 168-9, 169-70; and Austria's advance on Bologna, 175; his argument to Britain, 193-4; and French public opinion, 194; defends his policy, 198-9, 199; and German unification, and Frankfurt, 207 *bis*, 211; and de Tocqueville, 211; and Russia, 216, 220; and Kisselef, 217; and the German menace, 217; and Poland, 220; and Nice and Savoy, 223; refuses to lend General Bugeaud and French troops to Sardinia, 236, 237; humiliates Ricci and Sardinia, but offers amends, 238-9; says mediation must await French presidential elections, 244; attacked by radicals, 244-6; and Louis Napoleon as President of